Metabase Up and Running

Introduce business intelligence and analytics to your company and make better business decisions

Tim Abraham

Packt

BIRMINGHAM—MUMBAI

Metabase Up and Running

Copyright © 2020 Packt Publishing

All rights reserved. No part of this book may be reproduced, stored in a retrieval system, or transmitted in any form or by any means, without the prior written permission of the publisher, except in the case of brief quotations embedded in critical articles or reviews.

Every effort has been made in the preparation of this book to ensure the accuracy of the information presented. However, the information contained in this book is sold without warranty, either express or implied. Neither the author, nor Packt Publishing or its dealers and distributors, will be held liable for any damages caused or alleged to have been caused directly or indirectly by this book.

Packt Publishing has endeavored to provide trademark information about all of the companies and products mentioned in this book by the appropriate use of capitals. However, Packt Publishing cannot guarantee the accuracy of this information.

Commissioning Editor: Sunith Shetty
Acquisition Editor: Ali Abidi
Senior Editor: David Sugarman
Content Development Editor: Sean Lobo
Technical Editor: Manikandan Kurup
Copy Editor: Safis Editing
Project Coordinator: Aishwarya Mohan
Proofreader: Safis Editing
Indexer: Pratik Shirodkar
Production Designer: Nilesh Mohite

First published: September, 2020
Production reference: 1290920

Published by Packt Publishing Ltd.
Livery Place
35 Livery Street
Birmingham
B3 2PB, UK.

ISBN 978-1-80020-231-3

`www.packt.com`

Packt.com

Subscribe to our online digital library for full access to over 7,000 books and videos, as well as industry leading tools to help you plan your personal development and advance your career. For more information, please visit our website.

Why subscribe?

- Spend less time learning and more time coding with practical eBooks and Videos from over 4,000 industry professionals
- Improve your learning with Skill Plans built especially for you
- Get a free eBook or video every month
- Fully searchable for easy access to vital information
- Copy and paste, print, and bookmark content

Did you know that Packt offers eBook versions of every book published, with PDF and ePub files available? You can upgrade to the eBook version at packt.com and as a print book customer, you are entitled to a discount on the eBook copy. Get in touch with us at customercare@packtpub.com for more details.

At www.packt.com, you can also read a collection of free technical articles, sign up for a range of free newsletters, and receive exclusive discounts and offers on Packt books and eBooks.

Contributors

About the author

Tim Abraham is originally from Oakland, California, and currently lives in the San Francisco Bay Area. He has been working in data science for 10 years, spending his time working at consumer technology companies including StumbleUpon, Twitter, and Airbnb, and advising a few others. He also spent time as a data scientist in residence at Expa, the start-up studio that Metabase came out of, which is where he got to know the product and the founding team. Find him on Twitter at `@timabe`.

About the reviewer

Jeff Bruemmer is a senior technical writer at Metabase. He earned his MFA in writing as a Michener Fellow at the University of Texas at Austin, and holds a bachelor's degree in English from the University of Wisconsin-Madison.

Packt is searching for authors like you

If you're interested in becoming an author for Packt, please visit `authors.packtpub.com` and apply today. We have worked with thousands of developers and tech professionals, just like you, to help them share their insight with the global tech community. You can make a general application, apply for a specific hot topic that we are recruiting an author for, or submit your own idea.

Table of Contents

2

Deploying Metabase with AWS

Section 2: Setting Up Your Instance and Asking Questions of Your Data

3

Setting Up Metabase

4
Connecting to Databases

5
Building Your Data Model

6

Creating Questions

7

Creating Visualizations

8
Creating Dashboards, Pulses, and Collections

9
Using the SQL Console

Section 3: Advanced Functionality and Paid Features

10
Advanced Features, Getting Help, and Contributing

Other Books You May Enjoy

Index

Preface

Metabase is a piece of analytics software that enables your entire organization to derive insights from your data. While analytics software has been around for some time, the offerings have tended to be quite expensive. Metabase, on the other hand, is open source and free. Because the free offering comes with no dedicated engineering support, non-technical users might struggle with getting everything up and running. That's why this book was written. No matter your technical background, this book will gently guide you through the process of hosting, running, setting up, and building out a robust analytics platform using Metabase.

You'll learn how to configure an environment on **Amazon Web Services** (**AWS**) that you can use to host a scalable and customizable instance of Metabase. Once it's deployed, you'll learn how to use your own subdomain for Metabase and set up an email server or use Google Sign-in to invite other users. You'll learn the best practices for connecting to databases, and even build your own database using some sample data specific to this book. You'll get to know Metabase through and through, learning how to curate your data model, create powerful charts, build beautiful dashboards, leverage your SQL skills, and schedule reports to go out via email or Slack.

Who this book is for

This book is for anyone interested in analytics and analytics software. Although it touches upon a wide range of technical subjects, from AWS and software deployment to database technologies and SQL, it is written for a beginner audience. People in analytics come from all backgrounds, and this book embraces that.

What this book covers

Chapter 1, Overview of Metabase, provides an introduction to Metabase, its origin story, and how to install it locally or via Heroku.

Chapter 2, Hosting Metabase on AWS, takes a deep dive into AWS and teaches you the best practices on how to host Metabase on AWS using their Elastic Beanstalk service.

Chapter 3, Setting Up Metabase, shows the reader how to set up a subdomain, host Metabase over HTTPS, allow Metabase to send emails over an SMTP server, set up Google Sign-in, and connect Metabase to Slack.

Chapter 4, Connecting to Databases, explains all the major databases that Metabase works with, and shows the reader how to set up a PostgreSQL database on AWS with sample data.

Chapter 5, Building Your Data Model, showcases Metabase's powerful admin tools that allow you to curate layers of useful metadata on top of the data in your database.

Chapter 6, Creating Questions, shows the reader how to explore data in Metabase and answer questions with or without SQL.

Chapter 7, Creating Visualizations, teaches the reader about every kind of data visualization that can be made in Metabase.

Chapter 8, Building Dashboards, Pulses, and Collections, shows the reader how to create attractive dashboards and reports, while also learning how to keep everything in Metabase well organized.

Chapter 9, Using the SQL Console, gives opinionated advice on when and how to use SQL in Metabase such that it will benefit other non-technical users.

Chapter 10, Advanced Features, Getting Help, and Contributing, showcases some of Metabase's special features and introduces the reader to the Metabase community.

To get the most out of this book

You will need to sign up for a free AWS account to run Metabase. Many of the examples in this book also assume you own a web domain and can manage its DNS service.

Software/hardware covered in the book	OS requirements
Metabase	Windows, Mac OS X, and Linux (Any)
Git/GitHub	
AWS	
PostgreSQL	

If you are using the digital version of this book, we advise you to type the code yourself or access the code via the GitHub repository (link available in the next section). Doing so will help you avoid any potential errors related to the copying and pasting of code.

Also, Metabase is a constantly evolving project, while this book is not. You may see features and designs in the most recent version of Metabase that don't match what you see in this book, which was finished in September 2020.

Download the example code files

You can download the example code files for this book from your account at `www.packt.com`. If you purchased this book elsewhere, you can visit `www.packtpub.com/support` and register to have the files emailed directly to you.

You can download the code files by following these steps:

1. Log in or register at `www.packt.com`.
2. Select the **Support** tab.
3. Click on **Code Downloads**.
4. Enter the name of the book in the **Search** box and follow the onscreen instructions.

Once the file is downloaded, please make sure that you unzip or extract the folder using the latest version of:

- WinRAR/7-Zip for Windows
- Zipeg/iZip/UnRarX for Mac
- 7-Zip/PeaZip for Linux

The code bundle for the book is also hosted on GitHub at `https://github.com/PacktPublishing/Metabase-Up-and-Running`. In case there's an update to the code, it will be updated on the existing GitHub repository.

We also have other code bundles from our rich catalog of books and videos available at `https://github.com/PacktPublishing/`. Check them out!

Download the color images

We also provide a PDF file that has color images of the screenshots/diagrams used in this book. You can download it here: `https://static.packt-cdn.com/downloads/9781800202313_ColorImages.pdf`

Conventions used

There are a number of text conventions used throughout this book.

`Code in text`: Indicates code words in text, database table names, folder names, filenames, file extensions, pathnames, dummy URLs, user input, and Twitter handles. Here is an example: "The database username will be `postgres`."

A block of code is set as follows:

```
SELECT
id_order
, single_item_orders->>'id_menu' as id_menu
, single_item_orders->>'count' as item_count
FROM
(
    SELECT
    id_order
    , json_array_elements(order_description) as
single_item_orders
    FROM
        orders
) each_order
```

Bold: Indicates a new term, an important word, or words that you see onscreen. For example, words in menus or dialog boxes appear in the text like this. Here is an example: "The dataset is based on a fictional e-commerce business called **Pickles and Pies**."

> **Tips or important notes**
> Appear like this.

Get in touch

Feedback from our readers is always welcome.

General feedback: If you have questions about any aspect of this book, mention the book title in the subject of your message and email us at `customercare@packtpub.com`.

Errata: Although we have taken every care to ensure the accuracy of our content, mistakes do happen. If you have found a mistake in this book, we would be grateful if you would report this to us. Please visit `www.packtpub.com/support/errata`, selecting your book, clicking on the Errata Submission Form link, and entering the details.

Piracy: If you come across any illegal copies of our works in any form on the Internet, we would be grateful if you would provide us with the location address or website name. Please contact us at `copyright@packt.com` with a link to the material.

If you are interested in becoming an author: If there is a topic that you have expertise in and you are interested in either writing or contributing to a book, please visit `authors.packtpub.com`.

Reviews

Please leave a review. Once you have read and used this book, why not leave a review on the site that you purchased it from? Potential readers can then see and use your unbiased opinion to make purchase decisions, we at Packt can understand what you think about our products, and our authors can see your feedback on their book. Thank you!

For more information about Packt, please visit `packt.com`.

Section 1: Installing and Deploying Metabase

In this section, you will learn what Metabase is and why it was created as an open source business intelligence tool. You'll install a local version of Metabase and learn why hosted versions are necessary for use in an organization. Then, you'll learn how to deploy hosted versions using popular methods.

This section contains the following chapters:

1
Overview of Metabase

Metabase is a free and open source **analytics** software that allows you and everyone in your organization to ask questions of your data, create visualizations and dashboards, send out daily reporting, and much more.

Traditionally, organizations with good analytics either had to pay for expensive enterprise software, employ a cadre of data scientists and data engineers, or both. The value of analytics was high but the barrier to entry was even higher. Today, the value of analytics continues to grow, but the introduction of software such as Metabase has lowered the barrier to entry. This book will teach you, regardless of your background in analytics and engineering, how to create a robust and scalable analytics environment for your organization using Metabase.

This chapter will be a gentle introduction to Metabase, where we'll learn what it is and how to install it. We will then learn about more powerful, cloud-based installation methods that allow for collaboration. By the end of the chapter, you will learn how to deploy your own instance of Metabase to the cloud.

In this chapter, we are going to cover the following main topics:

- Introducing Metabase
- Metabase's origins
- Why open source?
- Installing Metabase locally
- Installing and deploying Metabase via the cloud

Technical requirements

To follow along, you'll just need a computer: macOS, Windows, or Linux are all adequate operating systems. You'll also want to create a **Heroku** account. Heroku is a cloud application platform we'll use to deploy Metabase at the end of the chapter. You can sign up for an account at `https://www.heroku.com/`.

Throughout this book, we'll be using a program called **Git**. Git is a **version control** system that helps track code changes in a project. Git has a high learning curve for beginners, and while we will not be covering any Git tutorials in this book, I intend to make the examples easy to follow. No prior knowledge of Git is required.

Often in this book, we'll use **GitHub** (`https://github.com/`) in conjunction with Git. GitHub is a code-hosting platform that relies heavily on the Git program. While Git helps you track changes to your code base, GitHub allows you to host that code online, so that others can access, edit, or contribute to it. The Metabase project lives on GitHub. That means that if you wanted to, you could contribute to the building of Metabase. Later in this book, we'll learn how you can get involved in that, even if you don't know how to program.

There is a GitHub repository for this book, too, at `https://github.com/PacktPublishing/Metabase-Up-and-Running`. I'll use this repository to share code examples and data useful to you as you work through the examples in the book.

Introducing Metabase

Before we get started, let's learn about what Metabase is and how it came to be. Metabase is software for **analytics**. Traditionally, we might refer to it as software for **Business Intelligence**, or **BI**. BI generally refers to software that aids in transforming data into actionable insights and visualizations. BI software has been around for a long time; Tableau and MicroStrategy are traditional examples. Today, many people in the industry, myself included, prefer the term *analytics software* over BI. I will be using that term going forward.

Finding answers in your database

Today, all organizations rely on analytics to stay competitive. As a famous saying goes, *"you can't manage what you can't measure."* Imagine you are a company selling products online and want to measure the number of products you have sold. While that seems like a simple question, many would have no idea of how to actually arrive at a number. Would you manually count the number of units leaving your warehouse? Sure, you could, but it seems like there should be an easier way – and there is. Most organizations rely on **databases** to store their transactions, so getting your transaction data from your database is generally the easiest and most accurate way to measure your sales.

The downside to databases is that they can be intimidating to work with. Connecting to them is often challenging due to security and technical reasons. Plus, once you connect to them you need to know how to query them. Most databases can be queried with **Structured Query Language**, or **SQL**, but not everyone knows (or should know) SQL. Once you get your query to work, turning the raw data from the query results into something interpretable, such as a chart, is something that databases are no good for – you need additional software to visualize your data.

So, while viewing the number of sales in your organization seems simple, it's actually far from that. This is where Metabase helps.

Metabase was made to connect to all of today's most popular databases. While users with more of a technical background can use SQL with Metabase, it also has a well-designed query builder so that knowledge of SQL is not required. Furthermore, Metabase has a terrific visualization library. Going from query to visualization is often as simple as the click of a button. Metabase makes it easy and intuitive to go from a question in your head, such as the number of sales over time, to a visualization of the answer such as that shown in *Figure 1.1*:

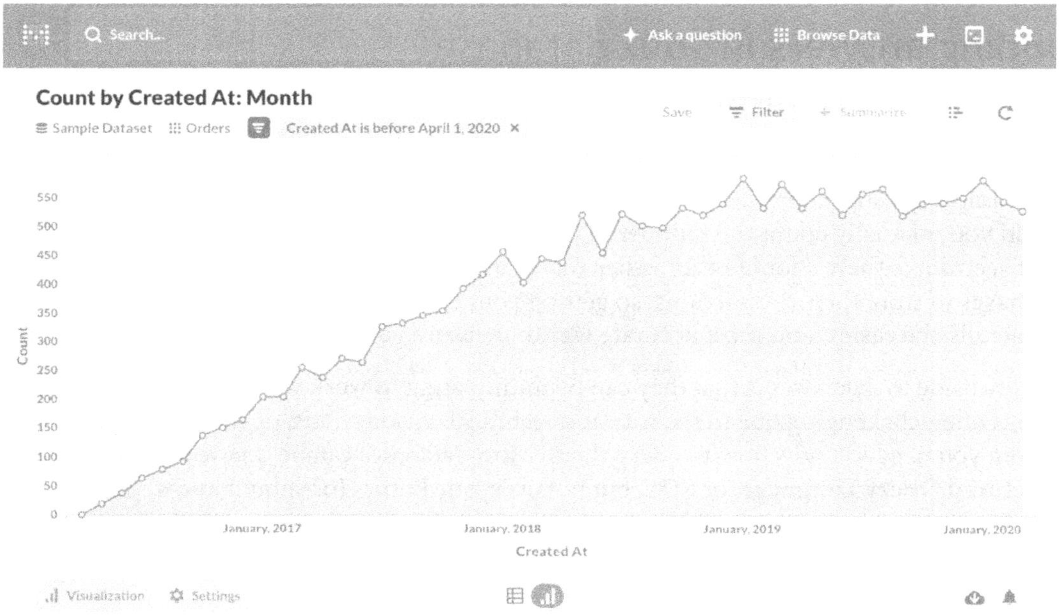

Figure 1.1 – Counting transactions with Metabase's sample dataset

Now that we've learned what Metabase is, let's learn about who it was built for.

Who should use Metabase?

Metabase is designed for all roles in an organization, not just data scientists, analysts, or engineers. You don't need to be highly technical or highly analytical to find value in Metabase. From what I've witnessed, there are four types of Metabase users. I have represented them in *Figure 1.2*, a two-by-two matrix with shading as a third dimension:

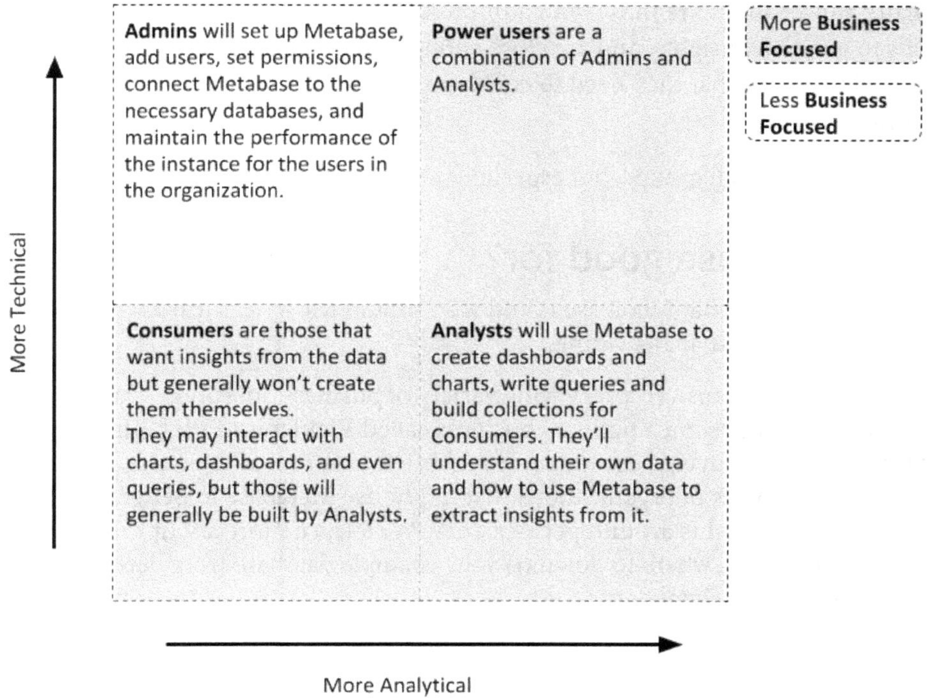

Figure 1.2 – The four types of Metabase users

Going back to our example question of sales over time, let's see the roles these four types of users might play:

1. **Admins** make sure Metabase is up to date and running smoothly. They are the ones who install Metabase and give everyone a login. It is the admins' responsibility to make sure that other users can view the sales numbers, but they will probably not have to pay attention to the numbers themselves.
2. **Consumers** are people whose jobs are closely tied to the sales numbers, but may not be technical enough to produce a chart on their own. While they don't normally make the charts themselves, they are able to easily click around and edit a chart for their specific use case. For example, a consumer who is responsible for business in California is able to filter the chart to show only sales in California.
3. **Analysts** are those who have a deep understanding of data, including metrics, statistics, and databases. They are close to the business but perhaps not as close as some consumers, who they consider their stakeholders. Analysts make all the critical charts and metrics in Metabase to ensure data accuracy. They are thought of as the curators of Metabase and the people to whom the consumers often go to for help.

4. Finally, **power users** are those with admin skills to set up Metabase, analyst skills to generate insights, and are close enough to the day-to-day operations of the business such that they need to consume the results to make sound business recommendations.

This book is written for all groups, but especially with power users in mind.

What is Metabase good for?

Now that we've learned what Metabase is and who should use it, let's learn what kind of questions Metabase is best at answering.

Metabase can be used to answer a very wide variety of business questions. Throughout this book, we'll be focusing on a fictional business called **Pickles and Pies**. This business, which is modeled after a hybrid e-commerce and brick-and-mortar business, is representative of the types of organizations that might use Metabase to better understand trends, patterns, and insights around performance. We'll learn more about this fictional business, including about where to download the example database from, later on in *Chapter 4, Connecting to Databases*.

Some of the questions that Metabase can help us answer about this business are as follows:

- How many orders have been placed?
- What types of users are placing orders?
- What are the most popular items on our menu?
- What parts of our business are growing the fastest or slowest?

These are just a few simple examples. Today, analytics is far-reaching and can get very sophisticated. With that said, Metabase is generally not the preferred tool to perform certain analytical functions, such as the following:

- Advanced statistical modeling
- Statistical inference
- Machine learning and artificial intelligence

Now that we know what kind of questions Metabase will help us answer, let's learn what kind of data we can connect to it.

What kind of data does Metabase accept?

Data comes in many formats, from spreadsheets and CSVs to large distributed databases. Let's learn which of these formats are particularly well suited for Metabase.

Simply put, Metabase is a tool to help us understand data in **databases**. If your organization keeps data in a SQL or **NoSQL** database, Metabase will almost certainly be able to connect to it.

If your organization generally works with CSV exports or reports from external websites, Metabase is likely not the best tool for you. However, you should make sure that there isn't already some database upstream from these CSVs and reports that you can connect to. Often, there will be!

If you have really **big data** and are looking to do some **ETL** (**Extract, Transform, Load**) operations to create smaller, pre-aggregated tables, you should still use Metabase on your tables post-ETL. However, Metabase is not the right tool to perform the actual ETL operations.

We will now learn about how Metabase came to be.

Metabase's origins

Metabase began as an internal tool at Expa (`https://www.expa.com`), a start-up studio in San Francisco run by Garrett Camp, the co-founder of Uber. His CTO, Sameer Al-Sakran, had been working on simple ways to serve actionable data to CEOs and investors of companies in the Expa portfolio.

These start-ups needed an easy, low-cost, and low-friction way to understand their product data and measure things such as growth and engagement. It didn't take them long to realize that if the tools they were building were helpful for Expa's start-ups, they would probably be helpful to other start-ups, technology companies, and other organizations. They decided to turn this internal project into a company. Soon after, they put the source code for their project on **GitHub**, a website for collaborative software development that we'll rely on throughout this book. It became available for everyone to use, and Metabase was born.

On October 21, 2015, Metabase debuted to the public via the popular product discovery website **Product Hunt** (`https://www.producthunt.com/`).

Interestingly enough, I had joined Expa as a data scientist in residence just 9 days prior to Metabase's public launch on Product Hunt. I was coming from Twitter, where we had struggled to keep an internal analytics tool called BirdBrain both usable and free of bugs. I immediately saw the value of an open source project designed to give companies easy access to insights around their data. I quickly became a Metabase fan.

Why open source?

One of the unique things about Metabase that sets it apart from other analytics software is that it is **open source**. That means the source code for Metabase is freely available to be downloaded, redistributed, and modified. All the code for Metabase is hosted on the project's GitHub repository at `https://github.com/metabase/metabase`. So why is open source a big deal and how might it benefit you, the user?

It's free

Analytics software can be pricey. The goal of Metabase is to offer the same (or better) quality for free, so you can get the most value from your data without paying a third party. Metabase's open source software is and always will be 100% free to use. You may be wondering: how does Metabase make money? Recently, they've come out with an Enterprise version and a cloud hosting solution, both of which they charge for. The Enterprise version has some powerful features, some of which might make sense for certain organizations. In this book, we'll focus on the open source product.

You are in control of your data

Another downside to paying for an analytics software solution, aside from the cost, is an intrinsic lack of control. In most cases, this means that your data either sits on or is connected to a third party's servers. For organizations with privacy concerns, this can be a deal breaker. In my career, I've seen many companies balk at purchasing analytics software when they learn that their data will be ingested by a third party. In today's world, data can be too valuable or sensitive to take that risk.

However, because Metabase is open source, you get full control. This means that instead of paying for a license to access software on a third party's server that connects to or ingests your data, you install Metabase on your own server. You connect your data to your own server. Everything stays within your organization's network environment.

It is also more robust than most enterprise software because the code will always be available to run. Even if Metabase should one day go out of business, you will still have access to the source code and can continue to run it. This would not be necessarily true for an enterprise analytics software product.

What's the catch?

If Metabase is free, safer, and the more robust option, then what is the catch? Third-party software providers will often offer lots of support (at a price, of course) to make setting up and using their software as easy as possible. With Metabase, you are more or less on your own. While Metabase has an Enterprise version you can pay for, and recently released a cloud hosting service, this book will focus on teaching you how to master the free offering. The Metabase team has plenty of documentation meant to help, and any gap there will be filled in with this book so that installing, using, and collaborating with Metabase is super simple. By following along with all the examples and tutorials in the book, it'll be as if you have your own dedicated support team!

Now that we have a good background on Metabase, let's go ahead and learn how to install it.

Installing Metabase locally

By far the easiest way to try out Metabase is to install it locally. Installing Metabase locally means that you are running the program from your own computer, rather than off some external server (for those unfamiliar with servers, you can think of them as computers that are always running and accessible via the internet). While running Metabase locally is not the ideal way to run Metabase, it was created to be perfect for beginners who just want to kick the tires, try it out, and gain familiarity with the product. I'll go into detail about its limitations later in this chapter, but for now, let's go ahead and install it.

Installing on Mac

To familiarize yourself with Metabase's website, head to `https://www.metabase.com`. There you'll see a **Get Started** button. Click that and you'll be taken to a page with all the various installation options, with their Metabase Cloud hosted version highlighted by default. Click the **Host it myself** button, and from there click **Get started** on the **Open Source** option.

On the next page, scroll down to the bottom until you see the link to download the Mac App. Click that link to download it. Alternatively, you download directly by going to the URL `https://www.metabase.com/start/oss/mac.html`.

Once downloaded, open the .dmg file. After it installs, drag the Metabase icon into your Applications folder to complete the install. Now you can find Metabase in your Applications folder, or via macOS's Spotlight feature, and run it, just as you would any other program.

Installing on Windows or Linux

Running Metabase locally on a PC with Windows or Linux installed requires Java and a terminal instance.

> **Important Note**
>
> This installation requires Java 8 or higher. If you don't already have Java installed or don't have a recent version, you can download it at `https://www.java.com/en/download/`.

The simplest way to open a terminal instance on Windows is to type `Command Prompt` in the search bar under the Start menu. We will be using the terminal a lot over the course of this book, so if you're unfamiliar with using it, don't worry – I plan to make it as straightforward as possible.

Download the `.jar` file from `https://www.metabase.com/start/oss/`. Next, open up your terminal and run the following command to complete the installation. It will take a few minutes for the installation to complete:

```
java -jar metabase.jar
```

Make sure to run this command from the directory that contains the `metabase.jar` file. If you downloaded it into your **Downloads** directory, for example, change directories there first before running the following command:

```
cd ~/Downloads
```

Once this command is done running, Metabase will open in a browser window, running on port `3000`. If this doesn't happen automatically, simply open a browser up and type `http://localhost:3000/`. You should see the Metabase logo and **Welcome to Metabase**, just like in the following screenshot:

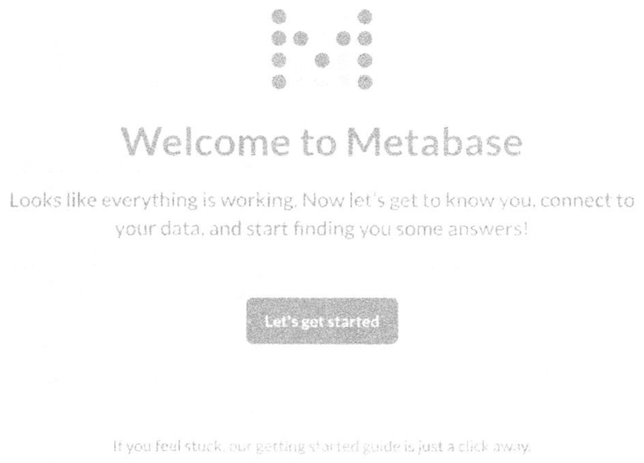

Figure 1.3 – Metabase's welcome screen

Congratulations, you have installed Metabase! At this point, you can sign up and start connecting to your data. If you want to dive right into the features and capabilities of Metabase, feel free to skip ahead to *Chapter 4, Connecting to Databases*. However, I encourage you to read this section first, where you'll learn what limitations you face with the local install.

Limitations of installing locally

Running Metabase locally means that once you close your laptop, the program is no longer running. Even though the Java-based installation runs Metabase in your web browser, you can't share the link, `http://localhost:3000/`, with anyone else and have them see what you are seeing. Everything is confined to your local computer. Even if your co-worker installs Metabase on their computer, your Metabase and theirs will be different.

While this is great if you are a one-person team or are just looking do some analysis on your own, the true power of Metabase is revealed when it can be used *collaboratively* with others in your organization. When multiple users can use the same installation of Metabase, everyone gets to access the same metrics, and can share links with each other and view the same dashboards. Having Metabase always running also means it can do tasks such as email reports to your inbox every morning, allow anyone to connect at any time, and even power dashboards and visualizations on external websites.

You can imagine how important this might all be in a data-driven organization. So, while the local install is simple and great for familiarizing yourself with Metabase, installing it so that multiple users can use it at the same time, over the web, is far more powerful. The way we do that is by installing and deploying Metabase to a cloud-hosted server. Let's learn how.

Installing and deploying Metabase via the cloud

In the last section, we learned how to install Metabase locally on our computers. We also learned the limitations of running it locally. By installing and deploying to the cloud, we unlock Metabase's true power. Let's get started.

Running software in the cloud

The good news is that it is not too much more complicated to get Metabase running on a web server. Practically, this means that when you run Metabase on a web server and close up your laptop, Metabase will stay up and running (unlike a locally installed version).

While you could go out and buy a web server and plug it in at home, today that is rarely done. Running a server in your home or office is referred to as **on-premises**, or on-prem. Some organizations may have their own servers on-prem for security reasons but nowadays most servers are run in the **cloud**. Today you can pay companies including Amazon, Microsoft, and Google a very small amount of money and they will run and maintain a virtual server that you can have access to. This is how most companies today prefer to run their software, and many of the web pages you frequent are hosted on servers in the cloud like this. Running Metabase on a cloud-based server is by far the most recommended way to go.

The Metabase team recommends using **Amazon Web Services**, or **AWS**, and we will dedicate all of the next chapter to this topic. For now, I'd like to show you the absolute simplest way to run Metabase in the cloud.

Heroku – an easy platform for cloud-based applications

Heroku is a cloud platform as a service. It helps developers in building, running, and scaling their services. Instead of setting up a web server ourselves, Heroku's platform will take care of all of that. They'll provision the web server and all the other services and processes we need to run Metabase. This includes a unique URL, which they will generate for us, that we can use to interact with our **instance** of Metabase. Going forward, I'll be referring to a single copy of Metabase running as an instance.

The great thing about Heroku is that they make it easy to deploy software. In fact, Metabase's Heroku deployment pipeline has been made so simple that all we really need to do is click a single button! Let's get started.

Signing up for a Heroku account

The following steps will take you through the Heroku sign-up process:

1. Visit `www.heroku.com` in a web browser.
2. At the top right you'll see a **Sign up** button – click it.
3. Fill out the fields on the sign-up page, noting that the account is free. Heroku's Free Tier covers more than enough for us to get Metabase up and running and connect a few users to it.

4. After you sign up for a Heroku account, you'll receive a confirmation email. You will need to confirm your account before proceeding.
5. After clicking the confirmation email, choose a strong password and proceed onward to the welcome page:

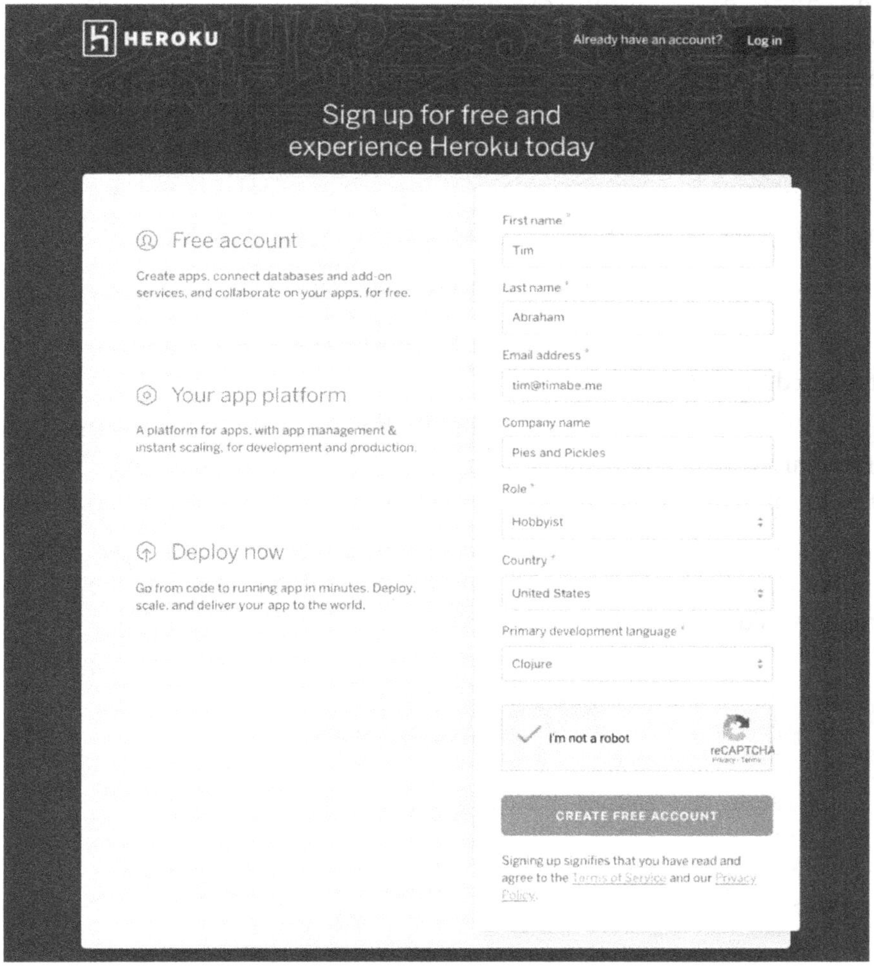

Figure 1.4 – Example of how you might sign up for Heroku

> **Important Note**
>
> You may have noticed that in the sign-up flow, I selected **Clojure** as my primary development language. Clojure is actually a relatively obscure programming language, ranked the second *least* popular language among respondents in Stack Overflow's 2019 developer survey (`https://insights.stackoverflow.com/survey/2019#technology`).
>
> Despite its lack of popularity, or perhaps because of it, Clojure garners a lot respect in the developer community. Clojure programmers are an elite group, and Metabase is primarily written in Clojure, making it one of the more famous Clojure projects being developed today.

Deploy Metabase to Heroku with one click

Now that we have signed up for a Heroku account, we can deploy Metabase:

1. Go to `https://www.metabase.com/start/oss/` and click the **Get Started** button.
2. Scroll to the very bottom of the page and click to **Read about how to run Metabase on Heroku**. Alternatively you can visit `https://www.metabase.com/docs/latest/operations-guide/running-metabase-on-heroku.html`.
3. Find the small purple button that reads **Deploy to Heroku**, as in *Figure 1.5*. Go ahead and click it. Clicking this button will redirect you back to the Heroku website:

Figure 1.5 – The one-click option to deploy Metabase on Heroku

You'll see a form similar to *Figure 1.6*. All you will be required to input is a name for your app. *Metabase* might seem like a good name, but unfortunately, this name has to be unique, so put something meaningful to you in the field. A common convention is to use the name of your organization along with the word Metabase, all in lowercase and strung together with dashes. Since in this book we'll be working with a fictional dataset around a company that makes pies and pickles, I've chosen `pickles-and-pies-metabase`:

Figure 1.6 – Heroku's app configuration page

Once you've settled on an available name, you can click the **Deploy app** button at the bottom of the form. This will trigger the deployment pipeline. One by one, you should see green checkmarks appear next to the deployment steps. Once the final checkmark turns green, it will display a message saying **Your app was successfully deployed**, as in *Figure 1.7*. Click the **View** button below this to open your newly created app in a new window:

> **Important Note**
>
> You may notice there is an add-on called Heroku Postgres. If you are already familiar with databases, you likely know of **Postgres**. Postgres is a popular, open source, and widely used relational database. When we deploy Metabase, we will also get a free, Hobby-Tier version of Postgres deployed in parallel. You may think that this is to store the data we will eventually analyze with Metabase, but it is not. Rather, it is our application database, which stores things such as user information, passwords, saved definitions for charts, collections, and queries. Think of it as Metabase's database. Very meta, right?

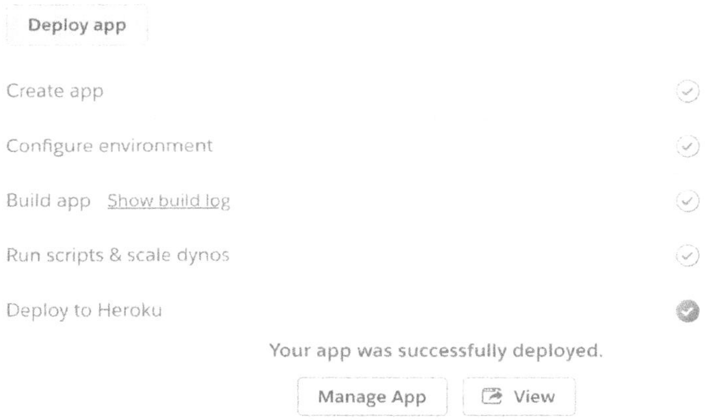

Figure 1.7 – Confirmation in Heroku that the deployment of Metabase was successful

You'll notice that the URL for your Heroku Metabase instance will look like `<your_application_name>.herokuapp.com`.

It may take a few seconds or even up to a minute the first time you visit your application, but soon enough you should see the welcome screen. It should look just like the welcome screen on the Mac and Java apps, which we saw in *Figure 1.3*.

Sign up before proceeding

And just like that, you've successfully deployed Metabase with Heroku. Note that anyone can visit this URL. If you like, test it out by having a friend open the link or try it in a private browsing session. The app is available to what we refer to as the **public internet**, which means that anyone with an internet connection can send a request to the server and get a response.

It's unlikely that someone you do not know will visit your uniquely created URL (how would they guess the URL?), but either way, it's smart to go through the sign-up flow to create your account immediately. This secures your instance and prevents any other visitors to the URL from signing up before you. Should this unlikely event happen, no problem – go to the next section where I explain how to manage your Heroku app, including instructions on how to delete it.

For now, though, let's sign up. Enter your name and email, choose a strong password, and enter a name for your organization. I've done my own, as shown in the following screenshot:

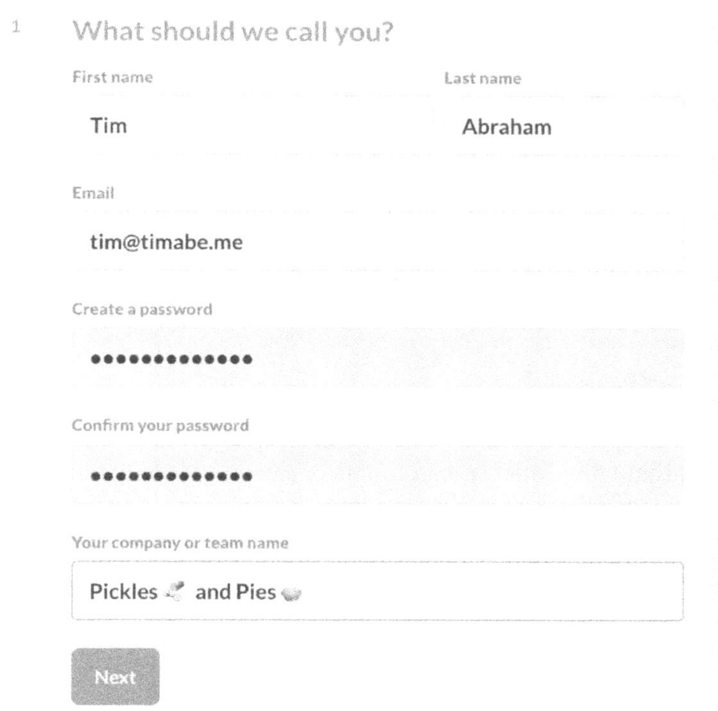

Figure 1.8 – Metabase's signup flow. Throughout this book we'll be using data from a fictional pickle and pie-selling business

Next, you'll be asked to add your data. This is where we would add our database credentials. We're going to skip this step for now, as I'll be dedicating much more space for this topic later in the book in *Chapter 4, Connecting to Databases*. Instead, click **I'll add my data later**.

You will be asked whether you want to allow Metabase to collect some data. This is entirely up to you; rest assured that if you say yes, Metabase will only collect high-level information and everything will be anonymized. If you want to know exactly what they collect, you can read their documentation at `https://www.metabase.com/docs/latest/information-collection.html`.

The last step will give you an option to subscribe to email updates. After that, you're done. Click **Take me to Metabase** to conclude the sign-up flow. Next, we'll learn about some of the features and limitations that come with Heroku.

Limitations of Heroku's Free Tier

Although incredibly easy to deploy, relying on your free Heroku account to provision Metabase to many users across your organization may not be wise, as the Free Tier may not be powerful enough. In this section, we'll learn about some of the limitations you may run into.

Heroku Metabase is in beta

According to the official Metabase documentation, as of the time of writing, the ability to run Metabase on Heroku is in beta. Personally, I've seen many small start-ups run Metabase on Heroku and have no issues, but the path recommended by the Metabase team is to use AWS.

Going to sleep

Apps deployed under Heroku's Free Tier will go to sleep after 30 minutes of inactivity. In a small organization, that will probably lead to lots of sleeping. It only takes about a minute for Metabase to wake up, which doesn't seem long, but imagine if a web page you visited took a minute to load – you would probably get a little frustrated, right? So, this is one limitation to bear in mind.

Metabase also has some useful features that send out reports via email or to Slack on a scheduled basis. Most users like to schedule these so that they hit their inbox in the morning, just as they get into work or are sipping their morning coffee. If your Metabase instance is constantly going to sleep after 30 minutes of inactivity, you can expect these scheduling features not to function smoothly.

The easiest way to get around this is to upgrade to the Hobby Tier, which as of the time of writing is $7 per month.

Memory issues

Another issue you may run into, aside from your app going to sleep, is memory usage. The Free Tier gives you 512 MB of memory. That should be fine for you and perhaps a few other users. If you find that you are running out of memory and you want to stick with Heroku, upgrade to the Standard 2x tier. All tiers between Free and Standard 2x provide 512 MB of memory. You can see all the tiers at `https://www.heroku.com/dynos`.

SSL

SSL, or **Secure Sockets Layer**, is a security layer that ensures data passed between the server and client (that is, the web browser) is encrypted. You may have noticed that some websites begin with `https`, while others begin with `http`. The ones that begin with `https` have SSL. Most websites nowadays have SSL, including the instance of Metabase you just deployed. However, maybe one day you want to stop using the URL provided by Heroku (the one we made was `https://pickles-and-pies-metabase.herokuapp.com/`), and instead create a subdomain under your own website. In that case, you'd need to upgrade to the Hobby Tier to use SSL.

Upgrading and deleting your Heroku app

Let's move on. In this section, you will learn how to upgrade or delete your Heroku app. When you log into your Heroku account going forward, you'll see your Metabase app in the list of running apps and pipelines. Clicking on your app will take you to an interface with seven tabs, as in *Figure 1.9*, all of which allow you to configure or view your app under different conditions. There is also an activity feed on the right side of the page:

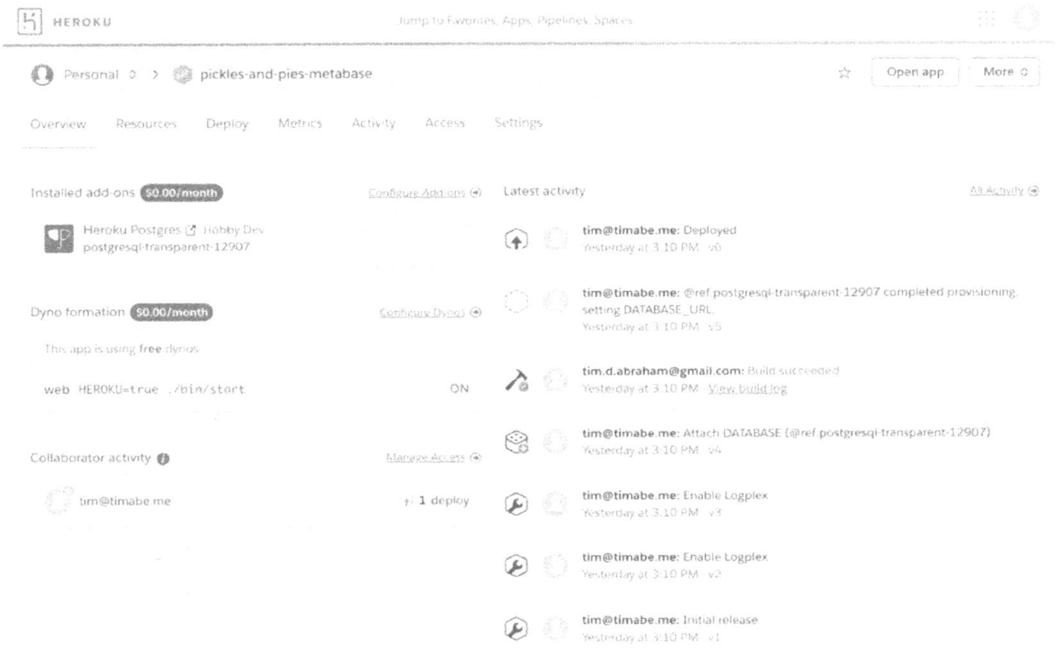

Figure 1.9 – The app status page on Heroku

We do not need to know what is under all seven of these tabs. The most common actions you will likely make using this view are upgrading and terminating your app, so we will focus on those.

Upgrading Heroku Metabase

Metabase is under active development and the product is constantly getting new features, performance enhancements, and design updates. Just like you would update your browser or smartphone software to take advantage of new features, the same goes for Metabase. Now I am going to take you through the steps of upgrading Metabase.

Determining your Metabase version

Before you attempt to upgrade, make sure you are not on the latest version already. If you just installed Metabase, chances are that there is not a new version quite yet!

To find out which version you are using, follow these steps:

1. Go to your instance and click the **Settings** gear in the upper-right corner.
2. Click the option that reads **About Metabase**. A modal like that shown in *Figure 1.10* will pop up displaying, among other things, the version number. Take note of it:

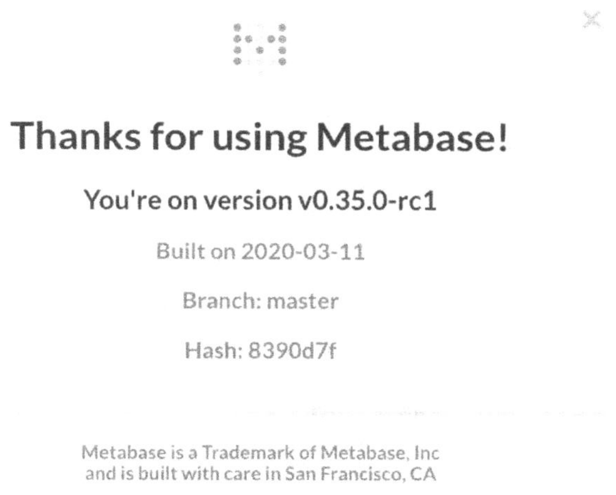

Thanks for using Metabase!
You're on version v0.35.0-rc1
Built on 2020-03-11
Branch: master
Hash: 8390d7f
Metabase is a Trademark of Metabase, Inc
and is built with care in San Francisco, CA

Figure 1.10 – Identifying the version of Metabase you are using

3. Metabase posts all their releases in reverse chronological order at `https://github.com/metabase/metabase/releases`. Visit this URL and compare the latest version number with your version. If the version at the top of this page doesn't match your version, then it's time to upgrade.

Note that even if you are on the latest version, you can still go through the next few steps for learning purposes.

Installing the command-line interface for Heroku

To upgrade an instance of Metabase on Heroku, the first thing you need to do is install Heroku's **Command-Line Interface**, abbreviated as **CLI**:

1. On the **Deploy** tab, you will find a link to **Download and Install the Heroku CLI**. Click that link or visit the page directly at `https://devcenter.heroku.com/articles/heroku-command-line`.

2. Here you will find downloads for macOS, Windows, and Linux. Note in the instructions that one prerequisite is to have `git` installed. This is a good time to install `git` if you haven't already. You can find the download links and installation instructions for `git` at `https://git-scm.com/book/en/v2/Getting-Started-Installing-Git`. Many computers have `git` preinstalled, too, so downloading it may not be necessary. To check whether you have it installed, run the following command in a terminal session:

```
which git
```

3. If you see no response, it means you do not have `git` installed. If you see something like `/usr/local/bin/git`, it means you do.
4. Once you've installed the Heroku CLI and optionally, `git`, you can open up a terminal instance and run the following command:

```
heroku login
```

5. You'll be prompted to enter any key, which will open a browser window allowing you to continue the login process. Then return to your terminal. If it worked, you will see a line in your terminal that reads as follows:

```
Logged in as <your_email_address>
```

Cloning Metabase's metabase-deploy Git repository

Next, you want to clone one of Metabase's Git repositories, or **repos**, as they are commonly referred to. *Cloning* means simply copying the source code maintained by the Metabase team to your computer. Let's see how it's done:

1. Using the same terminal instance from the last step, run the following command:

```
git clone https://github.com/metabase/metabase-deploy.git
```

2. This will create a directory called `metabase-deploy` in your computer's filesystem. Move into that directory with `cd`, the change-directory command.

```
cd metabase-deploy
```

3. Then run the following line, replacing `pickles-and-pies-metabase` with the name of your Heroku Metabase app:

```
git remote add heroku https://git.heroku.com/pickles-and-
pies-metabase.git
```

4. You can find the full URL in the **Settings** tab on your app's configuration page in Heroku, as shown in the following screenshot:

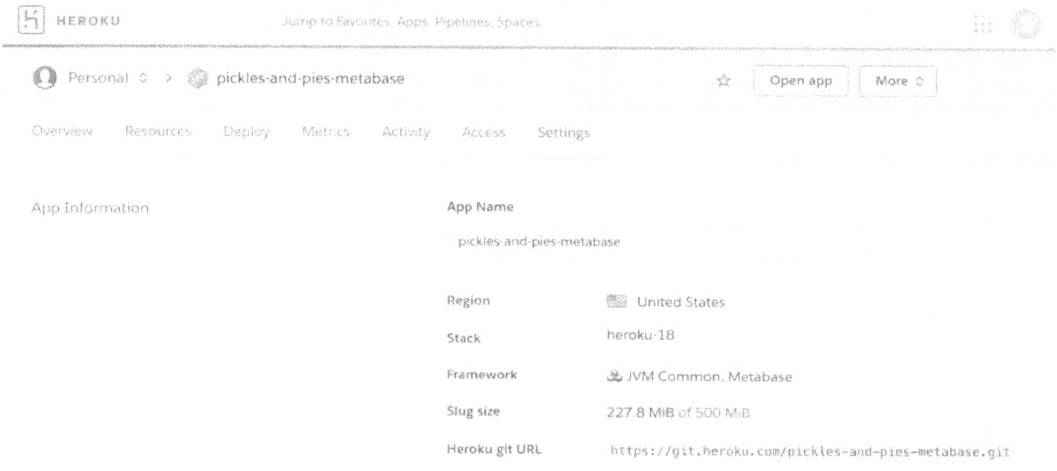

Figure 1.11 – Should you need to find your app's URL, it is on this page

5. Finally, run the following command to deploy any updates:

```
git push -f heroku master
```

Now let's cover some different ways to take down our application.

Deleting your Metabase instance on Heroku

To take your app offline, there are two options: putting it in **maintenance mode** and **full deletion**:

- Turning maintenance mode on will take your app offline. All the configuration in Heroku will still exist, but the URL will return a Heroku-specific page reading **Offline for Maintenance**. You'll find this option under the **Settings** tab (`https://dashboard.heroku.com/apps/pickles-and-pies-metabase/settings`), toward the bottom of the page.
- Also, at the bottom of the **Settings** tab, you will find a red button to delete your app. This will remove the app entirely. It will also remove the Postgres application database.

Summary

At this point, we have learned what Metabase is, what it is used for, and who should use it. We've outlined the four types of Metabase users: admins, consumers, analysts, and power users – the latter of which you will be by the end of this book!

We have installed Metabase locally, and in the cloud, using Heroku. We have an instance of Metabase running and have signed up for an account. We're all but ready to add other users and start analyzing our data.

At the same time, we now understand the limitations of using Heroku's Free Tier to administrate our Metabase instance. As mentioned throughout the chapter, the recommended way to run Metabase is with AWS. Doing so is a much more involved process than the one-click method Heroku offers, but a necessary step for those who want more control and oversight.

In *Chapter 2, Hosting Metabase on AWS*, we will take a detailed look at running Metabase with AWS.

2
Deploying Metabase with AWS

Now that we have learned the simple way to deploy Metabase to the cloud, this chapter will focus on the official paved path for users who want to self-host. This path involves using **Amazon Web Services**, or **AWS** as I'll be referring to it going forward. For software, AWS can do just about everything – it is massively complex, and explaining it thoroughly would fill entire libraries. A full explanation of all AWS can offer is far beyond the scope of this book, and as such, this chapter's goal is to explain only the relevant parts of AWS in a gentle but thorough manner.

Readers with backgrounds in technical operations or experience with AWS may skip some of the sections in this chapter. However, many people interested in using Metabase have backgrounds in analytics but know very little about software development operations. For users such as these, this chapter will be extremely useful as I will gently but comprehensively explain the services and terminology to run Metabase on AWS in a scalable way using best practices.

In this chapter, we're going to cover the following main topics:

- Introduction to Amazon Web Services
- Signing up for a free trial of AWS
- Metabase on Elastic Beanstalk
- Using best practices for Metabase on AWS
- Creating an IAM user
- Creating a Virtual Private Cloud
- Creating the Metabase application
- Monitoring costs on AWS

Technical requirements

You will need to sign up for an AWS account. The account offers free access to many services for one year but does require you to enter a credit card. The services we will be using throughout this book can all be used cost-free, provided you complete everything within one year of signing up. I also highly recommend having some password management software, as we'll be creating many different login credentials and you will be glad to have them organized.

Introduction to Amazon Web Services

While most of us think of Amazon as a retailer, their web services actually account for the bulk of the tech giant's profits. Many internet services we use daily are being run on Amazon's various data centers around the world. Today, AWS is the most broadly adopted cloud platform in the world.

AWS is made up of various **services**. A service can be vaguely thought of as a cloud-based solution to some technical problems, such as database management, machine learning, or computation. As of this writing, AWS has over 175 unique services, but luckily for us, we will only need to use a few.

Rather than explain upfront what all these services are and do, let's start instead by signing up for an AWS account and learn as we go.

Signing up for a free trial of AWS

The first thing we will need to do is sign up for an AWS account. To get started, visit `https://aws.amazon.com/` in your browser. Note the yellow button in the middle of the page reading **Create a Free Account**. Click that button to begin the signup process.

You can learn about what the Free Tier actually offers by clicking the link underneath the **Sign Up** button. The relevant parts of the free tier for our purposes are the following:

- 12 full months of selected free services, starting at the time you create an account.
- 750 hours per month of compute and database services. A 31-day month has 744 hours in it, so 750 hours is enough to let them run all month without worry.
- 5 GB of storage. We will use their storage service, **S3**, to keep log files and things of that nature, so 5 GB is plenty.

After clicking the **Sign Up** button, you may create your account:

1. Enter your email, a strong password, and a username.
2. On the next screen, fill in your contact information.
3. Next, add your credit card information. Note that you will not be charged anything if you follow the guidelines in this book. Should your free trial end, the services we will use here won't cost more than a couple of dollars a month anyway.

4. After entering your credit card details, you will need to verify your account by either having an SMS or voice call sent to your phone and solving a CAPTCHA.
5. Once your account has been verified, you will be asked which tier you want to sign up for. Choose the **Free Basic Plan**:

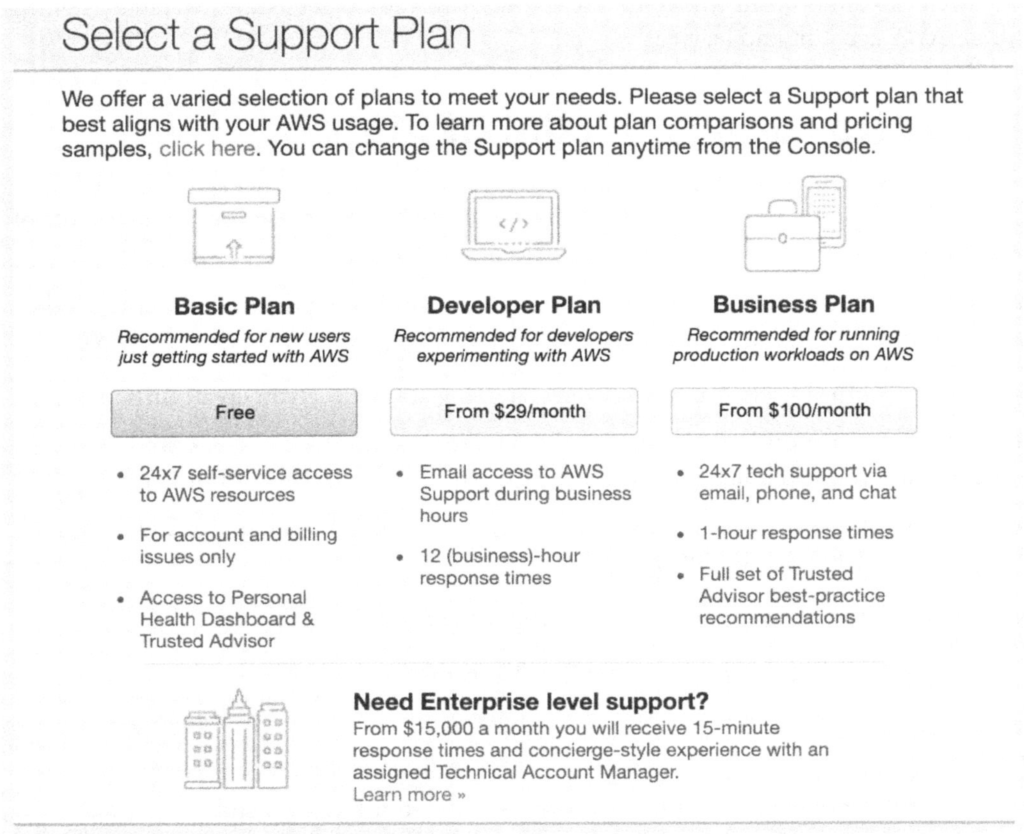

Figure 2.1 – The three tiers of support on AWS. We will use the Free tier

Signing in as the root user

At this point, you have successfully signed up for an account. You will need to sign back in to get started:

1. Click the **Sign In to the Console** button.
2. You'll be asked if you want to sign in as the **Root user** or an **IAM user**. As of now, you have only created credentials for a **root** user, so choose that option.
3. Sign in with the credentials you just created as the **Root user**.

The root user can be thought of as the administrator of AWS – they can access any of the services, create other users, view billing information, and even delete the account. In other words, the root user has a lot of power. You can imagine how in a larger organization it would not be smart to freely hand out the root user credentials. To address that risk, AWS has a service called **Identity and Access Management**, or IAM. This service allows the creation of other AWS accounts with narrower permissions. For example, a root user may want to create their own IAM user account that only allows them to use the services related to their Metabase instance. We will do so later in the chapter. For now, sign in with the credentials you just created as the root user.

The sign-in process will take you to the **Amazon Management Console**, or what I'll refer to as the AWS console. In the upper right-hand corner of the page, you will see your username and a location. This location refers to the physical **data center** AWS is using for the services launched by your account. AWS has data centers all over the world and they are massive. When we deploy Metabase, we'll find it's easiest to use the **Northern Virginia** region.

> **Important note**
>
> Not all AWS services are available in every single region. Also, the look and design of the AWS Management Console in one region may differ from another. Thirdly, AWS is constantly making UI changes to improve its design. This is all to say that you should not be surprised if what you see in your AWS console doesn't perfectly line up with the screenshots or descriptions in this book. To have the most consistent experience, I recommend setting your region to **Northern Virginia**.

Now that we've signed up and logged into our AWS account, we can move on and learn how to deploy Metabase using a service on AWS called **Elastic Beanstalk**.

Metabase on Elastic Beanstalk

One of the most popular services AWS offers is called **EC2**, and stands for **Elastic Cloud Compute**. You can think of these EC2 instances as virtualized servers, and they are building blocks for many of the other services offered. We will be running Metabase on one or more of these EC2 instances and connecting it to a Postgres application database.

While we could deploy these services individually and connect them up, doing so is not easy. This is where the Elastic Beanstalk service comes in handy, and that is what we will use to deploy our Metabase application. The Elastic Beanstalk service abstracts away a lot of the challenges in software deployment, like installing the software, provisioning the database, monitoring the service, and handling spikes in traffic. In that sense, Elastic Beanstalk is similar to Heroku.

Specifically, when we use Elastic Beanstalk to deploy Metabase, it will automatically do the following with just a little bit of configuration:

- Create one EC2 instance to run Metabase on. As more users start using your Metabase instance, more EC2 instances may be created to handle the increased traffic.
- Create another EC2 instance, called a **Load Balancer**. This will help route traffic evenly across the EC2 instances running Metabase.
- Create a Postgres application database.
- Optionally, keep log files in the AWS **S3** storage service.
- Monitor the health of your Metabase instance and alert you when things need attention.

Now that we know a little about what Elastic Beanstalk is, in the next section, we'll learn the quick way to launch Metabase using it. I include this "quick launch" method for readers who want to get Metabase running quickly, and a "best practices" method for readers who want something more suitable for running in a real, functioning, organization. You may choose to do one or both.

Quick launch on Elastic Beanstalk

Let's learn how to quickly launch Metabase on Elastic Beanstalk. These are the absolute minimum number of steps needed:

1. After you sign in to the AWS Management Console as the root user, open a new browser tab, and visit `https://www.metabase.com/docs/latest/operations-guide/running-metabase-on-elastic-beanstalk.html`.
2. Halfway down the page, you will find a link in purple font reading **Launch Metabase on Elastic Beanstalk**. Click this link.

3. Your browser will redirect you to the AWS console with a prompt to **Create a Web App**. Note that if you were in any other region than Northern Virginia up to this point, clicking this link will change your default region to Northern Virginia.

Many of the fields in the **Create a web app** form will be pre-populated:

1. The **Application Name** field should be populated with `Metabase`.
2. The **Environment Name** field should read `Metabase-env`.
3. The **Platform** section as of this writing will have the platform set as **Docker**, the **Platform Branch** set as **Docker running on 64bit Amazon Linux 2**, and the **Platform version** set as **3.1.0.**. These could change in the future, but whatever is defaulted to here is what you should go with.
4. In the **Application Code** section, click the radio button next to **Upload your code**. Doing so should reveal a URL under the **Public S3 URL** radio button. The URL should be from `https://downloads.metabase.com.s3.amazonaws.com` with a path to the current version's zip file, as in Figure 2.2:

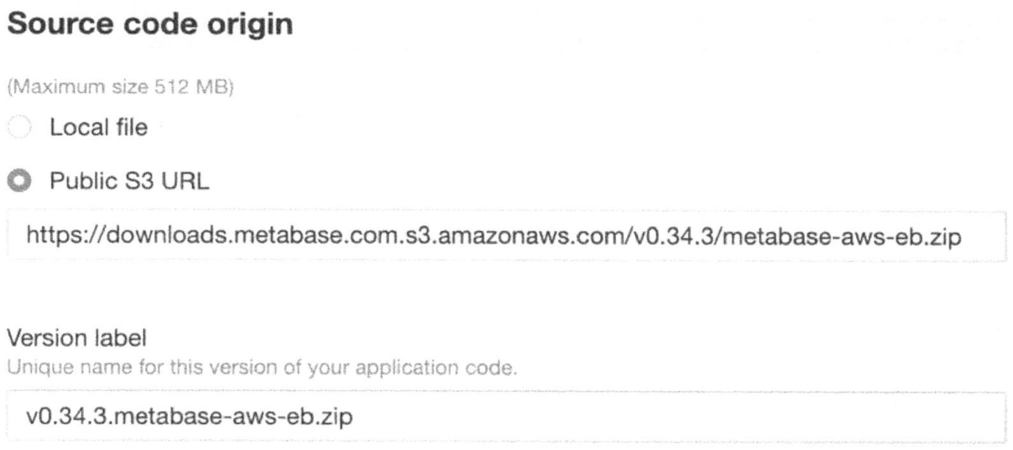

Figure 2.2 – Specifying the source code origin

5. Once you've done that, you may click the **Review and launch** button at the bottom of the page.

Now we will learn how to configure our app's environment using the minimum number of steps.

Configuring your application for quick launch

After clicking **Review and launch**, you will be taken to the configuration page. Here, you will see 12 different cards laid out in a 4x3 grid. The only cards that will need attention are the **Capacity**, **Network**, and **Database** ones:

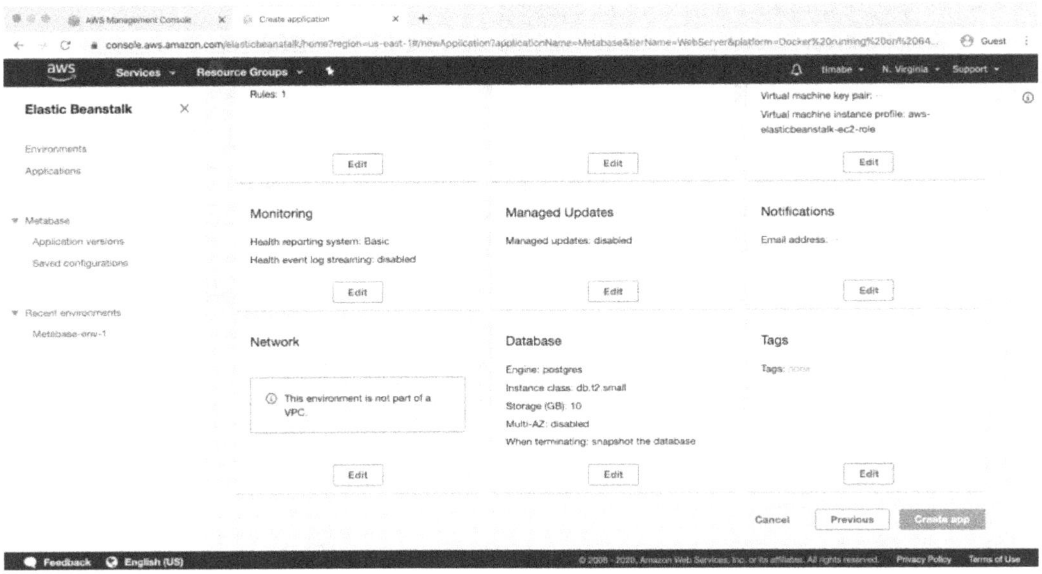

Figure 2.3 – The environment configuration page. We need to configure Capacity, Network, and Database

Let's learn how to configure our **Capacity** environment for our app.

Capacity

In the **Capacity** card, scroll down to **Instance type**. The default value should be `t2.small`. This is the recommended EC2 instance size for Metabase. However, it is not available on the AWS Free tier, so to keep things free, change it to `t2.micro`.

Click **Save** at the bottom of the form to return to the configuration page. Next, we'll configure the **Network** card.

Network

In the **Network** card, notice the information prompt reading *This environment is not part of a VPC*. **VPC** stands for **Virtual Private Cloud** and can be thought of as a virtual network, created and maintained by AWS, to simulate a traditional network. A VPC helps you limit traffic to internal resources for security purposes. Later on in the chapter, we'll create our own VPC, but for now, this is all you need to know about them. To fill out this card, we will do the following:

1. Click **Edit** on the Network card to reach the **Modify Network** page.
2. In the **Virtual Private Cloud** section, there will be a dropdown with your default VPC populating it. When you create an account with AWS, it automatically sets up a VPC for you in each region.

> **Important note**
>
> If, by chance, you see a message reading **Your account doesn't have a default VPC for this region**, click the link to create a default VPC.

Since this section is the quick launch one, I will not go into detail about what anything on this page means. All will be explained in the next section. For now, all you need to do is the following:

1. Set **Load Balancer Visibility** to **Public**.
2. Check all boxes to **On** next to the availability zones in the **Load Balancer** settings.
3. Check the box next to **Public IP Address** in **Instance Settings** to **On**.
4. Check all the boxes to **On** next to availability zones in **Instances Settings** and **Databases**.

Our network configuration is now done, and we can proceed to set up our application database.

Database

The next card that requires attention is the **Database** card. Recall that when we deployed Metabase with Heroku in *Chapter 1, Overview of Metabase*, the deployment process created a Postgres database to serve as the application database. This step accomplishes that same task. Here is what we need to do:

1. Click the **Edit** button in the **Database** card to open up the page. You'll be taken to another form to fill out, with two red callouts, as shown in *figure 2.4*:

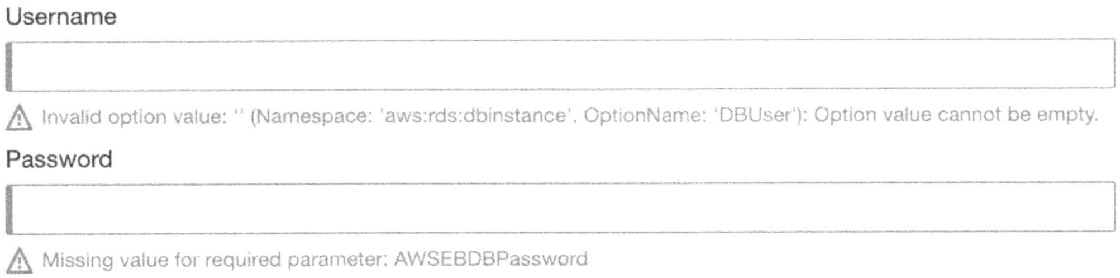

Figure 2.4 – Form with two red callouts

2. Choose a username, for example, `mbAppDB`.
3. Choose a password. I recommend keeping all your credentials organized since we'll be creating quite a few throughout this book.
4. To keep AWS costs at zero, change **Instance class** to `db.t2.micro`. Keeping it at the default value of `db.t2.small` will cause you to incur charges.
5. Click **Save**.

> **Important Note:**
> Recently a bug in AWS was introduced that may cause the Database card section to malfunction. If you are unable to select values in the Database card form, please visit `https://github.com/PacktPublishing/Metabase-Up-and-Running/tree/master/chapter2` for alternative instructions that will unblock you.

You'll be taken back to the page with the 12 cards. At this point, you've done all the configuration needed and you may click **Create app**. This will trigger the creation of your app's environment, after which you will have successfully deployed Metabase.

Now that we've learned the simple and quick way to deploy, next we will learn how to deploy using best practices. We will also go into greater detail with explanations so that you can understand exactly what each step is accomplishing.

Using best practices for Metabase on AWS

In the last section, we deployed Metabase with Elastic Beanstalk using the minimum number of steps to configure and secure the application. In this section, we trade speed for best practices. By following best practices, we can have more control over our application, make it more scalable and robust, and monitor its performance. If you are going to be administering Metabase within your organization, you will want to follow this guide.

The first thing we want to do is stop using our root credentials. As mentioned previously, using root credentials to build in AWS is not recommended, as it is too easy to make a critical error. The recommended path is to create individual accounts with limited permissions, and that's exactly what we will do in the next section.

Creating an IAM user

When we deployed Metabase in the last section, we did so as the **Root User**. I mentioned that the root user has all the power and permissions, including deleting all your services and even your AWS account.

If you are working in an organization that already uses AWS today, don't expect to be given Root user access. The standard practice is to create accounts within AWS that let the user do only what they need to do. In this section, we'll learn how to create an account with the IAM service to use going forward for all things related to Metabase:

1. In the AWS Management Console, click **Services** in the upper left-hand corner.
2. A dropdown showing the 175+ services will appear. Rather than finding IAM manually, just type it in the search bar and select it, as in *Figure 2.5*:

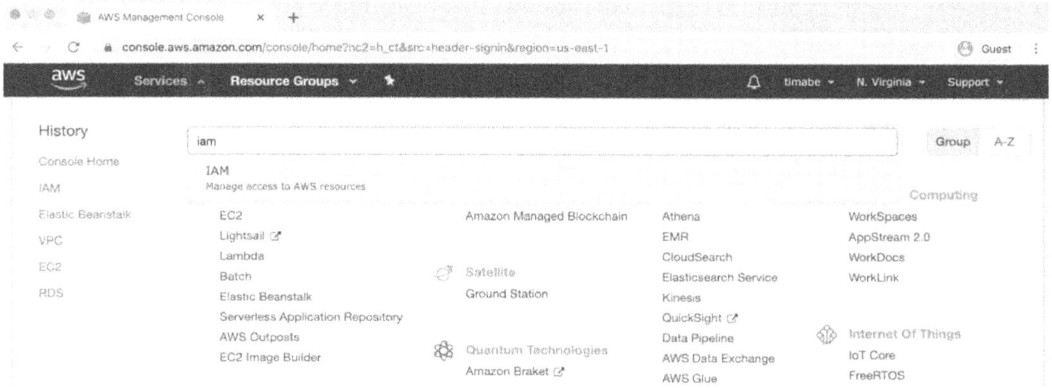

Figure 2.5 – Searching for the IAM service in the AWS console

3. Within the IAM service, we will expand the **Create individual IAM users** dropdown and click **Manage Users** as in *Figure 2.6*:

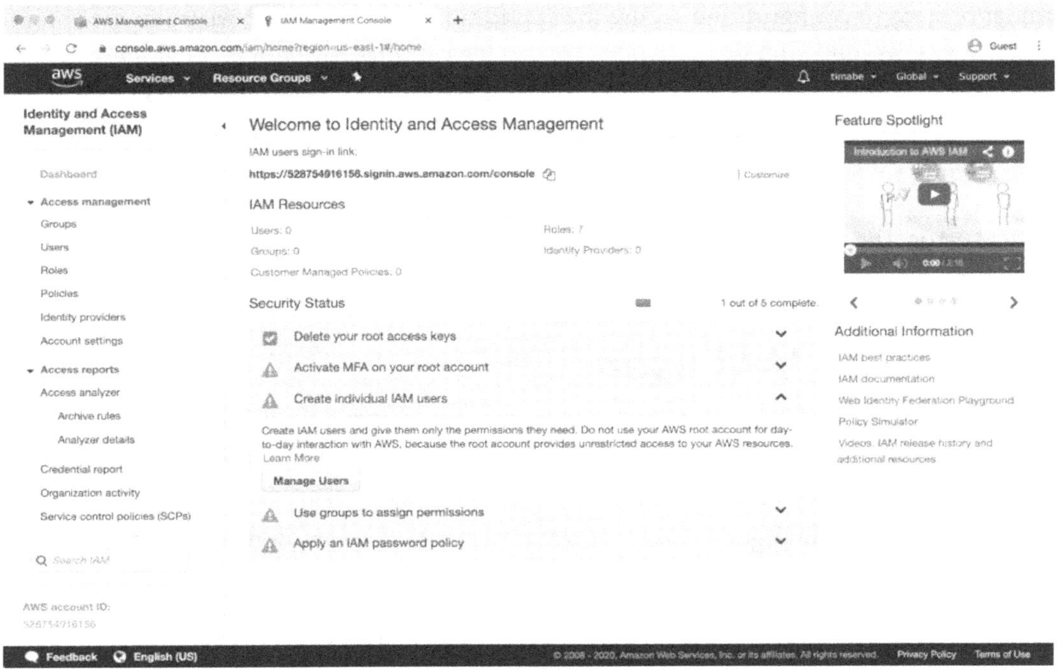

Figure 2.6 – The IAM service

4. On the next screen, click the **Add User** button.
5. On the **Add User** form, create a username (I chose `metabase-admin`).
6. Under **Access Types**, there are two options: **Programmatic access** and **AWS Management console access**. For this user, we only need **Management console** access, so check the latter.
7. The **Autogenerated Password** radio button should be on by default. If not, click it.
8. The **Require Password Reset** radio button should also be on by default; click it if not.
9. Click **Next: Permissions**.

Here, we will create a **Group** with the permissions necessary to properly administer Metabase in the context of this book:

1. Create a group called `Metabase-group` with the following policies:

   a. AmazonEC2FullAccess

   b. AWSElasticBeanstalkFullAccess

   c. AmazonVPCFullAccess

   d. AmazonRDSFullAccess

2. Click **Next: Tags**, but we will not add any tags in this step.
3. Click **Next: Review**.
4. Click **Create user**.

> **Important note**
>
> Before clicking the newly created URL, download the user credentials CSV. This is the only time you will be able to download this file and it contains the temporary password to sign in to the newly created user account. If you accidentally skip this step, you have to sign back in as the Root User and delete the newly created user and then recreate it.

Once the user has been created, you'll see a new URL that users with AWS Management Console access can sign in at. It will look something like `https://12345678.signin.aws.amazon.com/console`, with a string of 12 random digits instead of `12345678`. That 12-digit number is your account ID. Make note of the URL as this will be the URL to use to sign in as your IAM user going forward. At some point, you'll want to use the root credentials again, perhaps to adjust your account at the end of the 1-year trial period, but for now, we can use this URL. Do not click it until you've downloaded the credentials file.

Once you've downloaded the `credentials.csv` file, you may click the URL. You'll see the login page looks different; your account ID will be populated. Sign in using the newly created `metabase-admin` username, or whatever username you chose. You can find the password in the `credentials.csv` file. The file is comma-separated with two rows. The second value in the second row is the password – it should be 12 characters long. Once you sign in, you'll be asked to change your password. Change it to something longer. Take note of everything – the sign-in URL, the username, and the password.

After signing in, you'll see the same view of the Management Console but your username will be different.

> **Important note**
>
> **Multi-Factor Authentication** (**MFA**) is highly recommended if you are going to be using AWS for anything serious (such as running your organization's website). I recommend installing an authenticator app, such as Google Authenticator, on your mobile phone. At the minimum, you should protect your root account with MFA but it's probably smart to protect all AWS accounts.

Now that we have our IAM user created, we will be using it for the remainder of the chapter. In the next section, we will learn how to create a **Virtual Private Cloud** (**VPC**).

Creating a Virtual Private Cloud

As mentioned earlier, AWS configures a default VPC for you in each region when you create your account. You can also create your own VPC, which is exactly what we will learn to do in this section. Even if your organization already has an AWS account with a VPC configured, going through this section will still be a valuable learning experience. It will also help you understand what configuration changes may be necessary for your existing VPC to launch Metabase.

In this section, we'll learn how to create a VPC configured with the required network infrastructure for Metabase. Specifically, that means creating a VPC with two public subnets in two different availability zones, both with internet gateways in their routing table. We'll also learn what all this means, and why it's important. To get started, search for the VPC service in the AWS Management Console, just as we did with the IAM service. This will take you to the VPC Management Console:

1. At the top of this page, you will click a blue button reading **Launch VPC Wizard**. This is the easiest way to create the kind of VPC we'll need, and although it abstracts away some of the finer points on configuring a VPC, that is fine for our purposes.
2. On the next page, you'll be presented with four different VPC configurations, as in *Figure 2.7*. Choose the first one, **VPC with a Single Public Subnet**. We actually will need two public subnets in our VPC, but since that is not an option in the wizard, we'll go with this one and create another subnet in the next section:

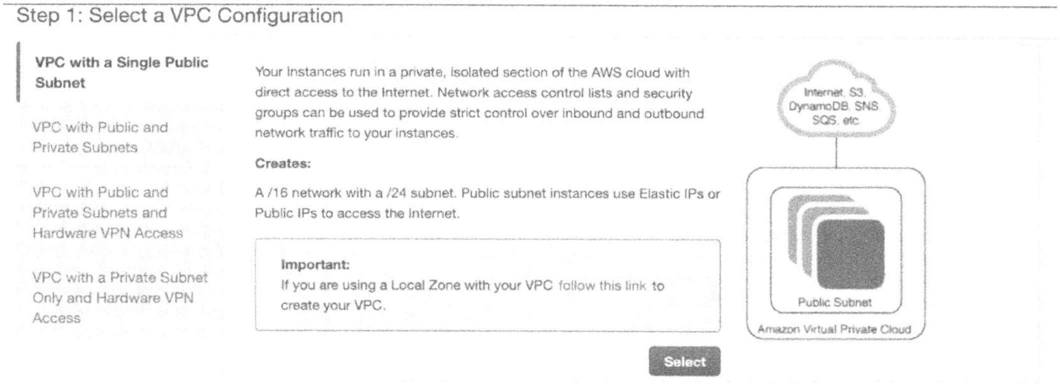

Figure 2.7 – The 4 VPC configurations. You want to choose the highlighted VPC with a single public subnet

3. On the next page, **Step 2: VPC with a Single Public Subnet**, enter a name in the **VPC name** field, for example, `vpc-metabase`.
4. Pick an Availability Zone for the public subnet, for example, `us-east-1a`. Make a note of the availability zone you pick.
5. You may leave the subnet's IPv4 CIDR address defaulted to `10.0.0.0/24`. Make a note of this address.
6. Click **Create VPC**.

Since those steps were quite technical, let's summarize what we just did.

First, we created a VPC, which can just be thought of as a range of IP addresses that we can use to have resources communicate with one another.

Next, we created a subnet, which is a subset of the IP addresses in our VPC.

Our subnet is a public subnet, which just means that in addition to being able to communicate with other resources in our VPC, it can also receive requests from the public internet.

Lastly, we specified that all resources in our VPC will be launched in the `us-east-1a` Availability Zone, which is a physical region in the Northern Virginia data center.

Now that we've created our VPC with a single public subnet, the next thing we need to do is add another public subnet in a different availability zone. It turns out that this is a requirement for running Metabase. Let's get started by navigating to the VPC dashboard page, which you should be redirected to anyway after creating your VPC:

1. On the left rail, find and click the **Subnets** option.
2. At the top of the screen, click the blue **Create Subnet** button.
3. On the next page, enter the following:

   a. **Name tag**: Put anything you like here, for example, `Subnet 2`.

   b. **VPC**: Pick `vpc-metabase`, which we just created.

   c. **Availability zone**: Pick any zone except the zone you already created the public subnet in. If you chose `us-east-1a` for the first one, you could pick `us-east-1b` here.

   d. **IPv4 CIDR block**: If you used `10.0.0.0/24` in the first step, you can use `10.0.2.0/24` in this step. Understanding CIDR blocks is beyond the scope of the tutorial, although if you want to learn more, the official documentation can be found at `https://tools.ietf.org/html/rfc4632`.

You have just created your second subnet in your VPC. To make this a public subnet we need to allow it to receive traffic outside of our VPC. We will do this by adding an internet gateway to our subnet's routing table. An internet gateway was already created when we made our first subnet, so we will just reuse it again here.

Let's learn how to make our subnet a public one:

1. From the VPC dashboard, select **Subnets** again.
2. Click on the button next to **Subnet 2**, the subnet you just created.
3. Scroll down to the bottom of the page. You will see a tab called **Route Table**.
4. The **Route Table** should have a single row in it, with a **Destination** of `10.0.0.0/16` and a **Target** of `local`. Click the blue button titled **Edit route table association**.

5. On the **Edit route table association page**, go to the dropdown. Your route table ID will be in there by default. Click the dropdown. There will only be one option to choose from in the dropdown. The option is for a route table associated with our first public subnet and is what we want to use for our second public subnet as well. Select it from the dropdown. Because this route table has an internet gateway associated with it, it will allow resources in your subnet to communicate with the public internet.
6. To confirm you associated the route table correctly, your route table should now show two rows. The second row will have a **Destination** of `0.0.0.0/0` and a link to the internet gateway in the **Target** column, similar to *Figure 2.8*, but of course with different IDs. Click **Save**:

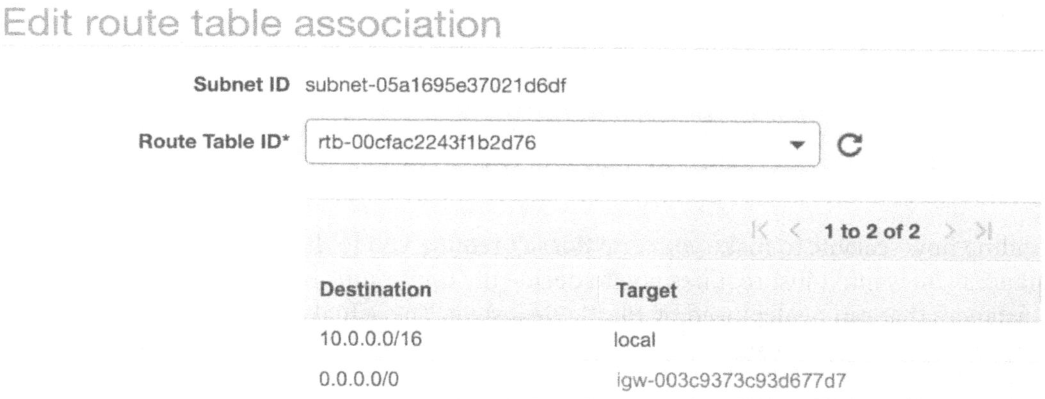

Figure 2.8 – Route table associations

Congratulations, your VPC is now properly configured with the required network infrastructure for Metabase, which is two subnets with internet gateways in their routing tables in two different availability zones.

> **Important note**
>
> If your organization is already using AWS, you will want to work with the IT or operations team to make sure your VPC has what is needed, which is at least two public subnets in two different availability zones.

Now that we have our user account and VPC set up, we are all but ready to deploy our application.

Deciding on scalability, availability, and cost

In this section, we will learn about scalability, availability, and financial cost. This will involve weighing how scalable and available our app needs to be against the monetary costs that come with a more resource-intensive deployment.

First, let's learn about **scalability**, or our app's ability to grow or shrink based on how many users are accessing it. If you were wondering why the service we use is called Elastic Beanstalk, you should be able to connect the dots here.

Scalability

Scalability refers to how your app's EC2 instances will grow (or shrink) as more (or fewer) users use it. While the default configuration for your application is to start with a single EC2 instance, a single load balancer, and a single database, it is set up to automatically launch up to three *additional* EC2 instances to handle increased traffic.

Depending on the size of your organization and how many users you expect will be using your Metabase instance at one time, Elastic Beanstalk may add additional instances. You can customize the rules for how you want your app to scale up and down, too, and we will learn how to do that when we configure our app in the next section.

Deciding how scalable to make your app doesn't require you to decide how many compute instances you want; it just requires you to decide the minimum and maximum number of instances that can be deployed by Elastic Beanstalk. The actual deployment of these resources will be handled automatically (or based on rules you decide) to ensure your app is in good health.

Availability

Availability refers to how accessible your app is when things like outages happen. Each AWS data center has a number of Availability Zones in it. From time to time, these Availability Zones can go down. Downtime is infrequent and usually does not last long. Services can avoid the negative consequences of these outages by being available in multiple Availability Zones. That way, if one goes down, all traffic is routed to the other one.

Tolerance for an outage is a complex equation. For example, a service with many users such as Netflix or Facebook may have zero-tolerance – they need their service running 24/7. If you typically have 4 or 5 users per day using your Metabase instance for an average of 30 minutes, you can likely tolerate an outage, although it's up to you to determine your tolerance.

Cost

The more instances you have running your app, the higher your app's cost will be. Recall that on the AWS Free tier, you get 750 hours a month of free compute (EC2, size `t2.micro`) and database service. There are 744 hours in a 31-day month, so you have enough coverage on the Free tier to run one EC2 instance and one database instance all year long. Should you exceed 750 hours per month, know that at the time of this writing, the on-demand `t2.micro` EC2 instance costs $0.0116 per hour and the `t2.small` I recommend for the app costs $0.023 per hour (`https://aws.amazon.com/ec2/pricing/on-demand/`).

I recommend using the following 2x2 matrix framework, as pictured in *Figure 2.9*, to decide on the best solution for you. If you are not sure what is best for you, I recommend the **High Scalability and Low Availability** option. I recommend high scalability because I think for most organizations a single instance will be adequate, but the option to scale it up if needed for a few dollars a month is worth it. I recommend low availability because I think an application like Metabase doesn't need 100% uptime like Netflix or Facebook.

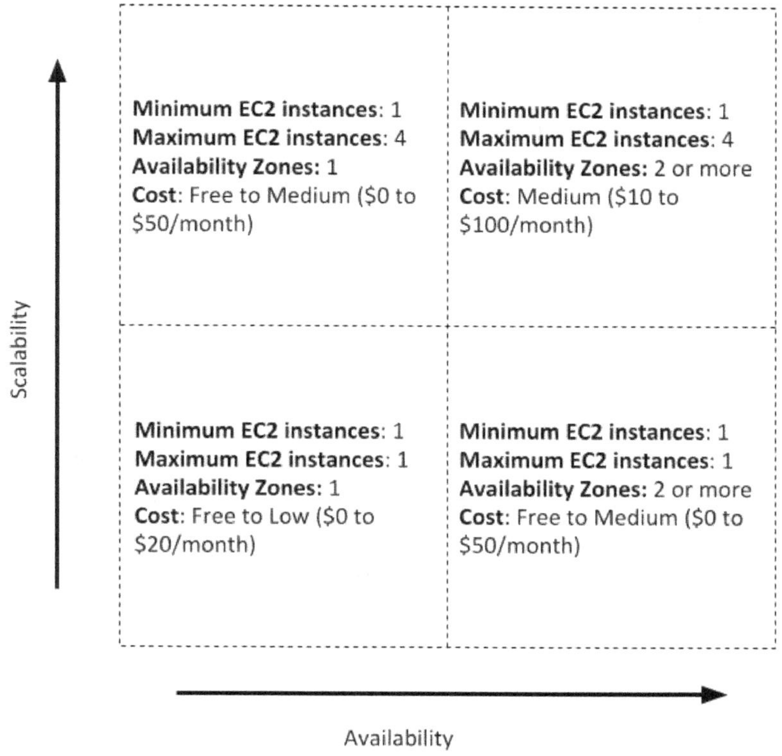

Figure 2.9 – Decision-making framework for scalability, availability, and cost

Creating the Metabase application

With our sizing decisions made, and our IAM user and VPC created, we can now configure and deploy our Metabase instance inside our new VPC. We'll get started by leaving AWS momentarily to visit `https://www.metabase.com/start/oss/`:

1. Scroll down to the bottom of the page, where it reads **Read about how to run Metabase on AWS**, and click the AWS link.
2. From there, click the **Launch Metabase on Elastic Beanstalk** link. You'll be redirected to the AWS console and prompted to create the web app.

Creating a web app in Elastic Beanstalk

Before we continue on the **Create a web app** page, let's get clarity on some confusing AWS terminology.

In Elastic Beanstalk, an **application** is defined as a "logical collection of components, including environments and configurations" and can be thought of as a folder. The actual running instance of Metabase, what we generally think of as "our application," is called an **Environment** in Elastic Beanstalk parlance. An Elastic Beanstalk application can contain multiple environments, meaning we could have several different Metabase instances running. Reasons we might want multiple instances would be having a testing and production environment, or to keep an older and newer version of Metabase running concurrently.

Now that we understand what AWS considers an application versus an environment, let's create both. Follow these steps to fill out the form properly:

1. In the **Application Information** section, you are asked to provide an application name. It can be anything you like, although I think the default of `Metabase` makes the most sense.
2. Next, let's fill out the **Environment Information** section. As mentioned above, the environment refers to this specific instance of Metabase being deployed. In the **Environment name** field, enter a name. This is simply a label and won't appear outside of AWS. I would recommend keeping the default `Metabase-env`. Next, we will add a domain, or URL, for our environment.

Under **Domain**, you will choose a unique domain name for your app, which will be the URL that will take you to your Metabase instance, so make it something memorable. I'm picking the name `pickles-and-pies` to go along with my made-up business from *Chapter 1, Overview of Metabase*, which we'll explore in more detail later. Whatever you pick will be concatenated with `.us-east-1.elasticbeanstalk.com`, so it will not be the most attractive and shareable URL. To remedy that, we'll learn how you can redirect this to your own domain or preferably a subdomain in *Chapter 3, Setting Up Metabase*. Most organizations like to use a format like `www.mb.mydomain.com` or `www.metabase.mydomain.com`.

3. The **Platform** section, as of this writing, will be prefilled with the following values. These will change as new versions are released, so I recommend just using whatever is prefilled:

   a. **Platform**: `Docker`

   b. **Platform branch**: `Docker running on 64bit Amazon Linux 2`

   c. **Platform version**: `3.1.0`

4. The next section is called **Application Code**. Click the radio button next to **Upload your code**. Clicking this button should reveal another section called **Source code origin**.
5. In the **Source code origin** section, a radio button should be next to **Public S3 URL**. There should be a URL prepopulated from `downloads.metabase.com`. There should also be a default value in the **Version label** section.
6. Click **Review and launch** to configure your environment.

> **Important note**
>
> Although the link Metabase provides redirects you to the Northern Virginia region in the AWS console, you are allowed to pick a different region if you like. However, the public S3 URL in *step 6* is specific to Northern Virginia, so you will get an error if your region differs. To fix this, you can visit the Public S3 URL in a browser and download the zip file locally. Then, change the **Source Code Origin** to **Local file** and upload the zip file you just downloaded.

You have now created both an application called `Metabase` and an environment called `Metabase-env`. Next, we will configure this specific environment.

Configuring your environment

The next page presents us with a 4x3 grid of configuration options. This is where we can fine-tune everything about our application. Let's learn what each card is and what we should do with each one.

We'll start with software, which is the option in the upper left-hand corner of the grid. Click **Edit** on the card to get started.

Software

There is not much you need to do in this section. Most of it will just be ensuring that the defaults are properly filled in:

1. In **Container Options**, the proxy server should be `Nginx`.
2. Make sure **AWS X-Ray** is not enabled (unchecked).

The next two sections have to do with storing log files. Your Metabase application has a feature where you can view log files, but if you would also like to store your logs using other AWS services, you may do so (you may incur costs by doing this):

1. If you would like to be able to store logs in Amazon's S3 storage system, click the **Enabled** checkbox in the **S3 log storage section**.
2. You can also stream logs to another AWS service called CloudWatch, which is a service that allows you to monitor the health of your app. To turn this on, click the **Enabled** checkbox under **Log Streaming**. If you do, you can also choose a retention policy for your logs, which will determine how many days the logs are kept. You can also decide whether you want to retain these logs after your environment is terminated or delete them.
3. The final section, **Environment Properties**, allows you to pass environment variables to your application. Since we will never need shell access to instances running our application, we will leave this blank.

At this point, you can click **Save**. Even though there were not any required actions to do in this section, you now know what all the options are for. Next, let's move on to the **Instances** card.

Instances

In this section, you can configure the storage options for your instances. However, unless you have a good reason to change it, I recommend keeping the `Container Default` option.

Leave the **Instance Metadata service** (**IMDS**) section blank. The EC2 security groups should also be blank. We will learn more about security groups later in the chapter. You may click **Save** or **Cancel** since we didn't take any action in this step.

Next, we will configure the **Capacity** card.

Capacity

Earlier in the chapter, we learned about scalability. In this section, we will learn exactly how to configure your app's scalability to meet your needs. Note that you can also skip this section, but if you want to learn what everything means, read on.

The first section is named **Auto Scaling Group**. This is where we specify how many EC2 instances we'd like to be able to scale up and down to:

1. The first section allows us to select our **Environment Type**, which can either be **Load Balanced** or **Single Instance**. Choose **Load Balanced**, which should be the default. Even if you think a single instance is more than adequate for your application, I noticed at the time of this writing that when I try to select **Single Instance**, it just seems to refresh the page.
2. Next, in the **Instances** section, we get to pick the minimum and maximum number of EC2 instances we'd like our environment to scale up and down to. I recommend keeping **Min** at `1` and **Max** at `4`, but you can lower it if you want a low scalability option. Next, we will learn about the **Fleet Composition** section.
3. The **Fleet Composition** section allows you to decide whether you want to use on-demand EC2 instances or a combination of on-demand and something called spot instances. Let's learn quickly what these are:

   a. **On Demand** means you pay the *a la carte* price for your instance.

   b. A **Spot instance** is something you bid for, and if there are resources available at prices under your max bid, you get them.

   Spot instances are an interesting idea, but I recommend keeping it simple and starting with on-demand only. As you learn about your app's needs, you can revisit this section and opt into a mixture of on-demand and spot price instances. There are many options to configure this section and they can get pretty sophisticated.

Next, we will choose our instance type, which determines how powerful we want our compute instances to be.

> **Important note**
>
> The default value in **Instance Type** is `t2.small`, however, this is one size too large for coverage under AWS's free tier. This is the size Metabase recommends, but if you want to avoid incurring costs, use the `t2.micro` version instead.

4. In **Instance type**, change from `t2.small` to `t2.micro`. While this is great for a tutorial, if you end up using it for more data-intensive purposes, I do recommend paying for the `t2.small` instance.
5. The next section is the **AMI ID** section. AMI stands for Amazon Machine Image, and is what contains the information required to launch your instance. There will be a default value here, which you will keep as is.
6. For the **Availability Zones**, choose `Any`. This will not affect the availability of your app, as we will configure that part later.
7. Leave **Placement** blank, since we chose `Any` in the last section.

We have now picked the minimum and maximum number of EC2 instances in our scalability equation. You may be wondering how our application will decide to scale up or down. That is covered in the **Scaling triggers** section, which we'll learn about next. I also recommend keeping the defaults here, but read on if you'd like to understand how it works:

1. The **Metric** option lets you pick a metric to base your scaling decisions on. The default is `NetworkOut`, which measures the amount of outbound traffic. The idea is that if outbound traffic gets high enough, another EC2 instance will be launched and the load balancer will start routing traffic there. In addition to `NetworkOut`, there are about 10 other metrics you can base your scaling decisions on.
2. **Statistic** lets you specify what aggregation of your metric to base your scaling decisions on. The options are **Minimum**, **Maximum**, **Sum**, and **Average**. The default and recommended statistic is **Average**.
3. **Period** is the time grain on which the statistic will be measured. The default is 5 minutes. If you've chosen `NetworkOut` as your metric and **Average** as your statistic, then the scaling decisions will be based on the average `NetworkOut` over 5-minute intervals.

4. **Breach Duration** is the amount of time your metric needs to exceed the threshold before the scaling operation is triggered. The default and recommended value is 5 minutes.
5. Lastly, you will specify the threshold values for your metric. The default upper threshold is 6,000,000 bytes, or 6 MB. That means that once the average network output over a 5-minute interval is above 6 MB, another EC2 instance will be added to handle the increased traffic. Similarly, the lower threshold is 2 MB. When the average network output is under 2 MB, additional EC2 instances will be removed (but won't go to zero).

Now that we know exactly how to set the rules for scaling our environment up and down, you may be wondering what it takes to reach 6 MB of network output. As I write this, I have two users using Metabase. Later in the chapter, we will learn how to monitor various performance-related statistics, but for now, here is a graph of my environment's average network output (*Figure 2.9*), currently showing about 1 MB per user:

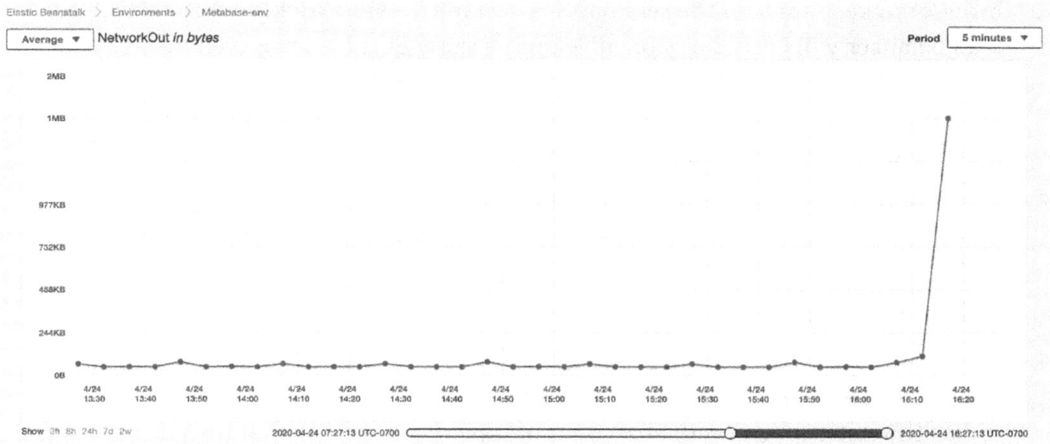

Figure 2.10 – Monitoring Metabase's NetworkOut with two active users

Next, we will configure the **Load Balancer** card.

Load Balancer

Let's learn all the ways we can set up our load balancer. Remember that a load balancer decides which EC2 instance should be used for traffic based on usage, so if you do not believe your app is going to require multiple EC2 instances, you can skip over all these steps:

1. At the top of the page, you'll see three different load balancer options: **Application**, **Classic**, and **Network**. **Classic Load Balancer** should be selected.

   Below the load balancer options is a section named **Listeners**. By default, you will have a listener configured to use **Port 80**, which is the standard port for HTTP traffic. You need not make any changes here for now. In *Chapter 3*, *Setting Up Metabase*, we'll learn how to configure listeners to send traffic over the more secure HTTPS protocol.

2. The next section is named **Sessions**. A session in this context is a web browser connected to your app for some period of time. The app uses a cookie in the browser to keep track of the session. By checking **Session stickiness enabled**, your load balancer will keep a session alive on the same EC2 instance even if there is another instance available with a lower load. You can also configure how long you want that session to persist. My recommendation is to leave this disabled, but based on your specific needs, you might want to try it out.
3. Next, in the **Cross-Zone Load Balancing** section, you can check whether you want your load balancer to span across multiple availability zones. If you have decided to deploy all your resources in the same availability zone, then checking this option will have no effect.
4. In the **Connection Draining** section, checking the **Connection draining enabled** box will cause your load balancer to keep connections alive to instances in unhealthy states for a specified amount of time. I generally do not turn this on, since high availability and functionality usually isn't a requirement.
5. Finally, the last section is **Health Check**. In the **Health Check Path** field, enter `/api/health`. Elastic Beanstalk will send a **GET** request to this path to determine whether your instances are in a good state. You can alter the configuration as you please, knowing that it is defaulted such that:

   a. The GET request will happen every 10 seconds.

   b. It will wait 5 seconds for a response.

    c. Five failures in a row will throw an **Unhealthy** status.
    d. Three successes will flip an **Unhealthy** status back to **healthy**.

6. Click **Save** to move on.

Now that we understand how to configure our load balancer, let's move on to the next section: **Rolling Updates and Deployments**.

Rolling Updates and Deployments

This section allows you to configure your environment so you can update it in a rolling fashion across instances and prevent downtime. That means that when one EC2 instance gets taken offline for a software update, the load balancer will route traffic to another. Since 100% uptime is not a requirement for us, and we will likely just have a single EC2 instance, we will leave this alone.

Security

We will leave the defaults in this section and move on to **Monitoring**.

Monitoring

In this section, we'll learn how to configure various health reporting options for our app:

1. If you skipped the configuration of your load balancer, enter `/api/health` in the **Health Check path** field. This field is only available if you've enabled classic load balancing.
2. Next, in the **Health reporting** section, turn on the **Enhanced** option. This is available on the Free tier and lets you see the health of your instances in Elastic Beanstalk.
3. In **Health monitoring rule customization**, you can choose to exclude ranges of status codes from your health reporting. For our application, I recommend leaving this section unchecked.
4. I recommend keeping **Health event streaming to CloudWatch logs** unchecked. I feel like with the configuration we have now, we have plenty of information to monitor our app.

These steps will allow us to easily monitor the health of our application on the Elastic Beanstalk dashboard. Now let's move on to the next card: **Managed Updates**.

Managed Updates

This section allows you to schedule managed updates at the platform level. This is different from updating Metabase to newer versions, which we'll learn about later in the chapter. I generally leave this off.

Notifications

Moving on to the **Notifications** section, enter your email address in the field to get email notifications about your app. Note that you have to confirm the subscription from your email.

We are almost done with configuration. In the next step, **Network**, we'll configure the environment so that our newly deployed resources live in the VPC we created.

Network

Here is where we will select which subnets in our newly created VPC we want various resources to be launched in. Let's get started:

1. In **Load Balancer Settings**, set **Visibility** to **Public**.
2. For a low-availability deployment, check *only one* of the subnets, such as `us-east-1a`. For high availability, check both. Check that both subnets are in different availability zones.
3. In **Instance Settings**, check the **Public IP Address** option.
4. Again, for a low-availability deployment, check off the same subnet you checked two steps ago. For high availability, check both.
5. Finally, choose *both* subnets for **Database Settings**. It is required to choose two for the app to properly deploy, so there is no single-subnet option here.

Now that we've applied our VPC settings to the environment, the last step we need to do is configure our application database.

Configuring your database

This section is where you will configure your application database:

1. The **Engine** section should default as `postgres`. Although different database engines will work as an application database, PostgreSQL is recommended.
2. To stay on the Free Tier, change the instance class to `db.t2.micro`.
3. The **Storage** section can be left at `10 GB`, which should be plenty.

4. In the **Username** section, I've chosen `mbAppDB`.
5. In the **Password** section, choose a password for this database. Note that you will likely never need to connect to it. In fact, the way the application is set up, you will not be able to connect to it from the public internet.
6. In the **Retention** section, it's recommended to choose `Create Snapshot`. This way, when your environment is terminated, a snapshot of your database will be kept in storage.
7. In the **Availability** section, I recommend choosing `Low (one AZ)`. By choosing this option, your database will only be provisioned in one Availability Zone in your data center region. This means that if that Availability Zone were to have an outage, your database would be unavailable during it. Personally, I feel like that is an acceptable risk to take since I don't believe Metabase needs to be available 100% of the time; outages are rare anyway. Alternatively, you could pick `High (Multi AZ)`, but if you do, your database costs will be higher once your free tier period ends.

> **Important Note:**
>
> Recently a bug in AWS was introduced that may cause the Database card section to malfunction. If you are unable to select values in the Database card form, please visit `https://github.com/PacktPublishing/Metabase-Up-and-Running/tree/master/chapter2` for alternative instructions that will unblock you.

Tags

Optionally, you can add a **Tag**, which will help you tie all the resources that will be created together. A Tag is a key-value pair. You may use something like `app` as the key and `metabase` as the value.

App creation

Finally, with the configuration done, you are ready to launch. Click **Create app** and your environment and app's creation process will start. You'll see messages in a terminal-like window as various components of the app are created. This generally takes around 10 to 20 minutes, so go have a coffee or tea while you are waiting.

Once the app has been created, you can visit the unique URL you created and see your newly created Metabase instance.

Overview of the Metabase app infrastructure

Now that we have Metabase properly running, it may be helpful to summarize what has actually been created and see where these resources live in AWS. This is just for our understanding:

- We created a VPC, or Virtual Private Network, to run our app in. This consists of two subnets running in Availability Zones A and B with internet gateways.
- Our app environment consists of one compute instance, called an EC2 instance, running in one of our public subnets in an Availability Zone. According to our configuration, if the app comes under heavy usage, it can scale up to as many as four of these instances. To view the EC2 instances in the AWS console, visit the EC2 service and click **Running Instances** in the dashboard.
- Our app environment also has a load balancer, currently running in the same Public Subnet as our EC2 instance. This is what will distribute traffic to each of the EC2 instances, should our app scale to multiple instances. A load balancer is a type of EC2 instance itself, so to see it in the console, go to the EC2 dashboard and click **Load Balancers**.
- We have a Postgres database acting as our application database. This could be running in either subnet. In my deployment, it is running in Availability Zone B. To see your database in the AWS console, visit **RDS** (**Relational Database Service**) and click **DB Instances**. Note that you cannot connect to this database from your computer; at this point, only the Metabase app itself can connect.
- We also have a number of security groups. As your app environment was created, you may have noticed in the logs that several security groups were created. Security groups are an important concept in AWS and something we'll use later. For now, all you need to know about them is that they limit what types of traffic can visit the resources you've deployed. For example, one security group opens up HTTP traffic to your app's URL from any IP address. Another one only allows your Postgres database to accept traffic over port `5432` from resources with a specific security group themselves.

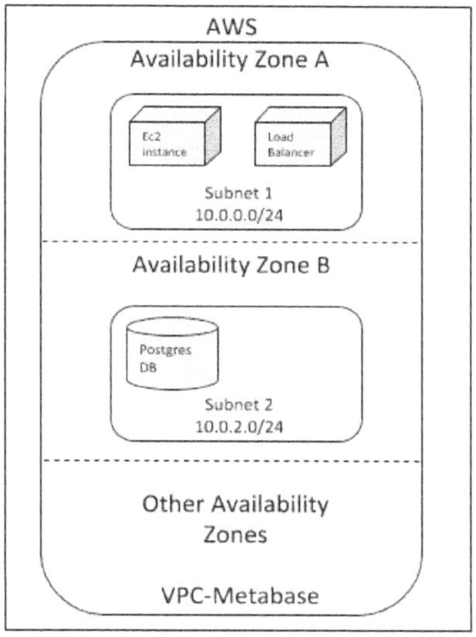

Figure 2.11 – A diagram of what our app environment looks like

Your Metabase environment is now completely set up! In the next section, we'll learn how to terminate the environment, so that, if required, you can start all over again.

Terminating your environment

After all that work setting up your environment, probably the last thing on your mind is trashing all your work. However, sometimes mistakes happen and bad deploys occur. If you want to stop running your Metabase app, perhaps because you want to try re-deploying with a different configuration, just do the following:

1. In the AWS console, find the Elastic Beanstalk service.
2. Click **Applications**. You should have an application called `Metabase`. Click it.
3. Find your Metabase environment. If you have been following along with the tutorial, your environment should be `Metabase-env`. Click it.
4. Towards the upper right-hand corner of the page, find the **Environment actions** drop-down menu and choose **Terminate Environment**.

5. A modal will appear asking you to confirm that you would like to permanently delete your environment. It will list some of the resources that will be deleted or released, including the URL you created. To confirm termination, type the name of your environment at the bottom and click **Terminate**. Again, this is likely going to be `Metabase-env`.

Once your environment has been terminated, it will still temporarily appear in your list of environments as `Metabase-env (terminated)`. It will remain visible for about an hour after termination.

Deleting your application

Recall that Elastic Beanstalk considers an application a "folder of environments." In the previous step, we terminated our environment, so now let's learn how to delete the application that contained our environment:

1. In the AWS console, find the Elastic Beanstalk service.
2. Click **Applications**. You should have an application called `Metabase`. Click the radio button next to it.
3. In the **Actions** drop-down menu, select **Delete application**.
4. You will see a modal explaining which environments will be permanently deleted should you delete your application. To confirm, type the name of your application in the textbox at the bottom of the modal. This name should be `Metabase`.

Now let's see how to upgrade Metabase to newer versions.

Upgrading Metabase on Elastic Beanstalk

As mentioned in *Chapter 1*, *Overview of Metabase*, Metabase is constantly launching new versions with new features, bug fixes, and improvements to the current product. To upgrade Metabase on Elastic Beanstalk, I recommend first visiting their guide as it contains the link to the latest version. Their guide can be found here: `https://www.metabase.com/docs/latest/operations-guide/running-metabase-on-elastic-beanstalk.html#deploying-new-versions-of-metabase` Then, follow these steps:.

1. Download the latest version of Metabase. The link will look like this, but with the latest version in place of `<latest_version>`: `https://downloads.metabase.com/<latest_version>/metabase-aws-eb.zip`.

2. Open the Elastic Beanstalk service in the AWS Management Console.
3. Click **Applications**. Find your application, which should be called `Metabase`, and click it.
4. On the left side of the screen, you should see your application's name with a toggle arrow next to it. Underneath that will be a link to **Application versions**. Click that.
5. In **Applications versions**, click the **Upload Button**.
6. Click **Choose file** and select the `.zip` you just downloaded with the latest version. Give the version label a name, preferably with the new version number in it.
7. Click **Upload**.
8. Now, click the checkbox next to the new version label you just created.
9. Once it's checked, click the **Actions** drop-down menu and select **Deploy**.
10. You will be given the option of which environment you would like to deploy this new version to. If you have been following along, you should only have `Metabase-env`. Select that and click **Deploy**.

This will trigger the deploy process all over again, using the same configuration you had for your original environment. Next, let's see how we can monitor costs in AWS in case we decide to use more than the free tier allows.

Monitoring costs on AWS

At any time, if you want to see how much of your free tier allotment you have used, you can do so in the **Billing Dashboard**. You can find it by clicking on your username in the AWS Management Console and selecting **Billing Dashboard**. However, because we did not give our `metabase-admin` IAM user permissions to view this, you will get a message explaining that you don't have permissions. Sign back in with your root user credentials.

On the **Billing Dashboard**, you can see multiple views of the costs your account is incurring. It is good to check on this, if you truly want to avoid spending any money. Sometimes you may forget to turn something off, or accidentally use a resource that's not on the free tier, and end up getting charged a few dollars at the end of the month. The easiest way to see what you have consumed and how much you have been charged for it is to click **Bill details** in the upper right-hand corner of the page.

Remember that most enterprise analytics software costs tens of thousands of dollars a year. Metabase's entry level cloud hosted version is much less, at $1200 a year. This self-hosted option, however, is free! So paying a little for better tech resources to ensure it runs well is well worth it.

Now that we know how to monitor our spend on AWS, let's move on to learn how to monitor our app's performance.

Monitoring app performance

On the Elastic Beanstalk dashboard, we can see the overall health of our environment. Most of the time it should have the green checkmark, as in *Figure 2.11*. If you deploy using the smaller `t2.micro` EC2 instances, it may occasionally be in the **Warning** state (although I've noticed the actual app works fine in those cases):

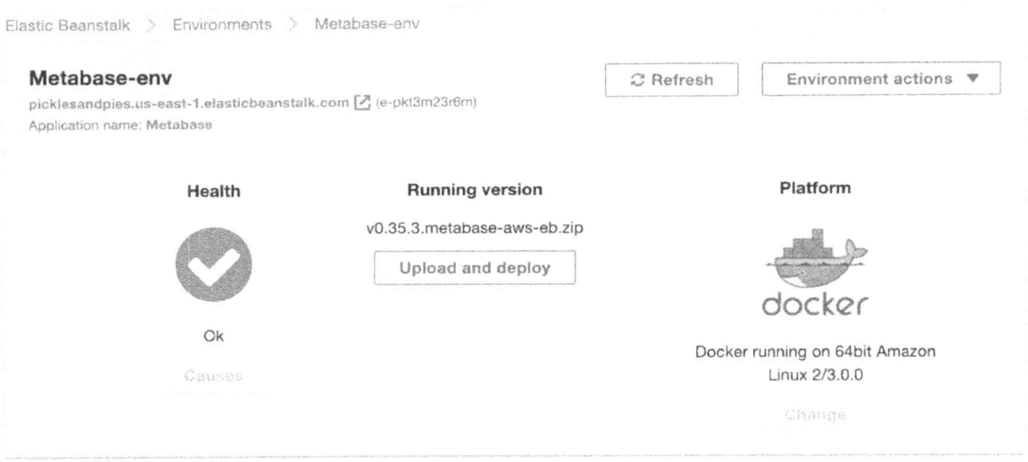

Figure 2.12 -

In addition to the overall health check, we can drill into specific performance-related statistics around the resources we've deployed. Let's learn how to do that.

From the Elastic Beanstalk dashboard, click **Monitoring** on the left rail. This will bring up the performance monitoring overview, where you can view several high-level statistics about your app.

Rather than going over all the statistics presented on the dashboard, let's just learn how to create a chart of the average `NetworkOut` for our EC2 Instances. Recall that in the *Scaling Triggers* section of our environment configuration, we created rules based on this metric to decide whether or not we should add additional compute instances to handle increased traffic:

1. In the **Monitoring** section, click **Edit**. An **Add Graph** section will appear on the screen. In this section, choose the following:

   a. **AWSEBAutoScalingGroup** as **Resource**.

   b. **Average** as **Statistic**.

   c. **NetworkOut** as **CloudWatch metric**.

2. Click **Add**.
3. Next, scroll back down to the **Monitoring** section and click **Save**.

Now your metric should appear in the **Monitoring** section of the page. To drill down into it, click the chart.

The chart presents you with a time series of the average **NetworkOut** value. In the upper right-hand corner of the page, you can adjust the period. Recall that we set out autoscaling rules based on a 5-minute period, and we chose 2 MB as the threshold value. Now you can monitor this statistic and see how close it gets to that threshold value based on the number of users using your Metabase instance.

Summary

In this chapter, we learned best practices for deploying Metabase using AWS. We learned how to sign up for a free AWS account and create both root and IAM users to log in with. We created a VPC with the necessary network setup for our application to exist in. Finally, we deployed Metabase using best practices for scalability, availability, cost, logging, and health monitoring.

In other words, we covered a lot in this chapter. If you came into it with no knowledge of AWS, you may feel overwhelmed by all the information covered. If you feel that way, do not worry! Deploying Metabase is a lot more complicated than using it, especially for people with backgrounds in analytics. If you have gotten this far, congratulations! Now we'll get to the fun part, where we will actually set up Metabase to work with our data. We will be covering all of that in the next chapter.

Section 2: Setting Up Your Instance and Asking Questions of Your Data

In this section, you will learn how to set up Metabase. This includes connecting to the various databases and data sources Metabase allows and building your data dictionary (adding metadata to the columns of your tables). You'll also learn about all the core functionality of Metabase: questions, the various visualization options, dashboards, pulses, collections, adding users and setting permissions, and using the SQL editor.

This section contains the following chapters:

3
Setting Up Metabase

We now know all the ways to get an instance of Metabase up and running. What we have not done yet is actually *used* Metabase. That will change with this chapter. However, before we start to use Metabase to explore data, we need to do some setting up so that it's ready for others to join.

In this chapter, we are going to familiarize ourselves with the **Admin** section of Metabase, and we'll cover the following main topics:

- Signing up for Metabase
- Using a subdomain
- Setting up email
- Allowing others to use Metabase
- Setting up Google sign-in
- Integrating Metabase with Slack

Technical requirements

To use a subdomain, you will need to own a domain and have the ability to create record sets for it. To implement Google sign-in, you need a Google G Suite account with access to the Admin console. To send emails on behalf of Metabase, you need an SMTP server, which you can provision either with your AWS account or through Gmail.

Signing up for Metabase

Before we get started, if you have not done this already, let's sign in to our Metabase instance. In the previous chapter, we deployed Metabase using Elastic Beanstalk on AWS and we now have a dedicated URL for our instance that looks something like this:

```
picklesandpies.us-east-1.elasticbeanstalk.com
```

Visit the URL you created for your instance and we will finish the sign-up process:

1. From the **Welcome to Metabase** screen, click the blue button reading **Let's get started**.
2. On the next page, you will select your language and click **Next**.
3. On the next page, fill in your name, email, password, and organization's name.
4. On the **Add your data** step, for now, choose **I'll add my data later**. We will be covering all the different ways to add data in the next chapter, *Databases*.
5. Keep the toggle on or off, depending on whether you want to allow Metabase to anonymously collect usage events.
6. Optionally, subscribe to receive email updates from Metabase. These can be handy if you want to learn when the next version is available.
7. Finally, click **Take me to Metabase**.

This will take you to what I'll be referring to as your Metabase home screen, pictured in *Figure 3.1*. It includes a section at the top reserved for your team's most important dashboards, a section of items called x-rays, and a section called **Our Analytics**. The x-rays are precomputed dashboards based on the sample dataset that Metabase ships with. Feel free to explore them if you like. We'll cover x-rays in *Chapter 10*, *Advanced Features*:

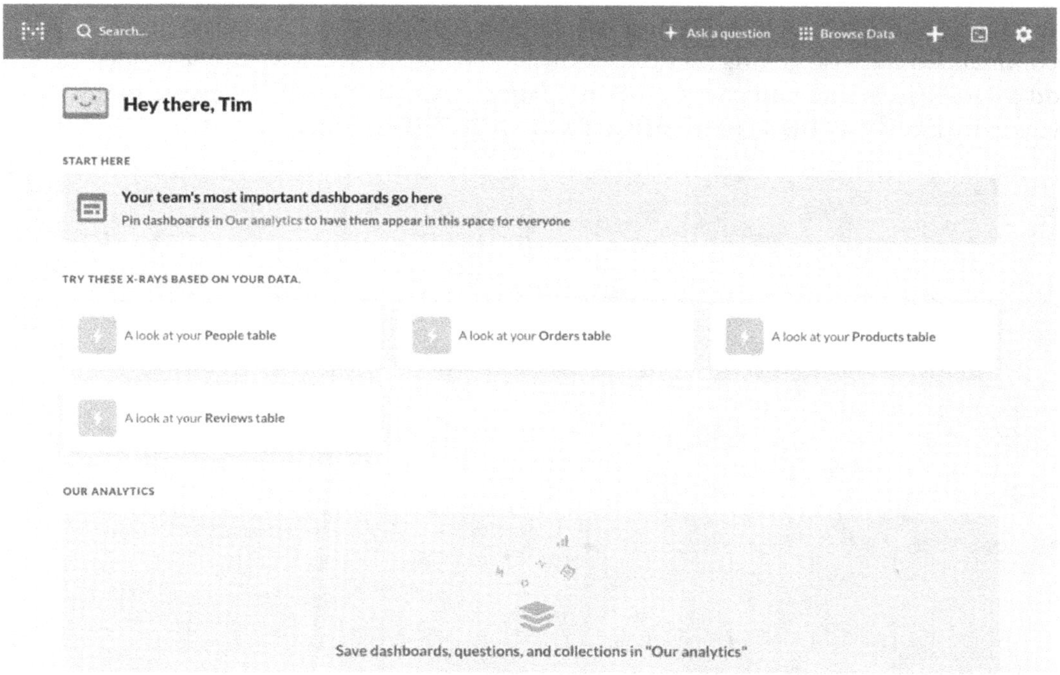

Figure 3.1 – The Metabase home screen

Now that we've signed up for Metabase, note that if another person opens your Metabase URL, they won't be able to get past the sign-in page. Going forward, we'll either have to invite others or implement some sort of sign-in policy to let others use Metabase.

As the first user to sign up, your account is the only account and has full **admin privileges**. Let's take a quick look at the admin panel so that we can learn what privileges admins have.

Getting to the admin panel

To reach Metabase's **admin panel**, click the gear icon in the upper-right corner. Select the **Admin** option. You should see the top bar change color from blue to purple.

The admin panel has a lot in it. To steer users in the right direction, Metabase gives recommended steps on getting set up, as shown in *Figure 3.2*. The first recommended step, **Add a database**, is something we'll cover in *Chapter 4, Connecting to Databases*. In this chapter, we'll cover all the steps in the **GET CONNECTED** section:

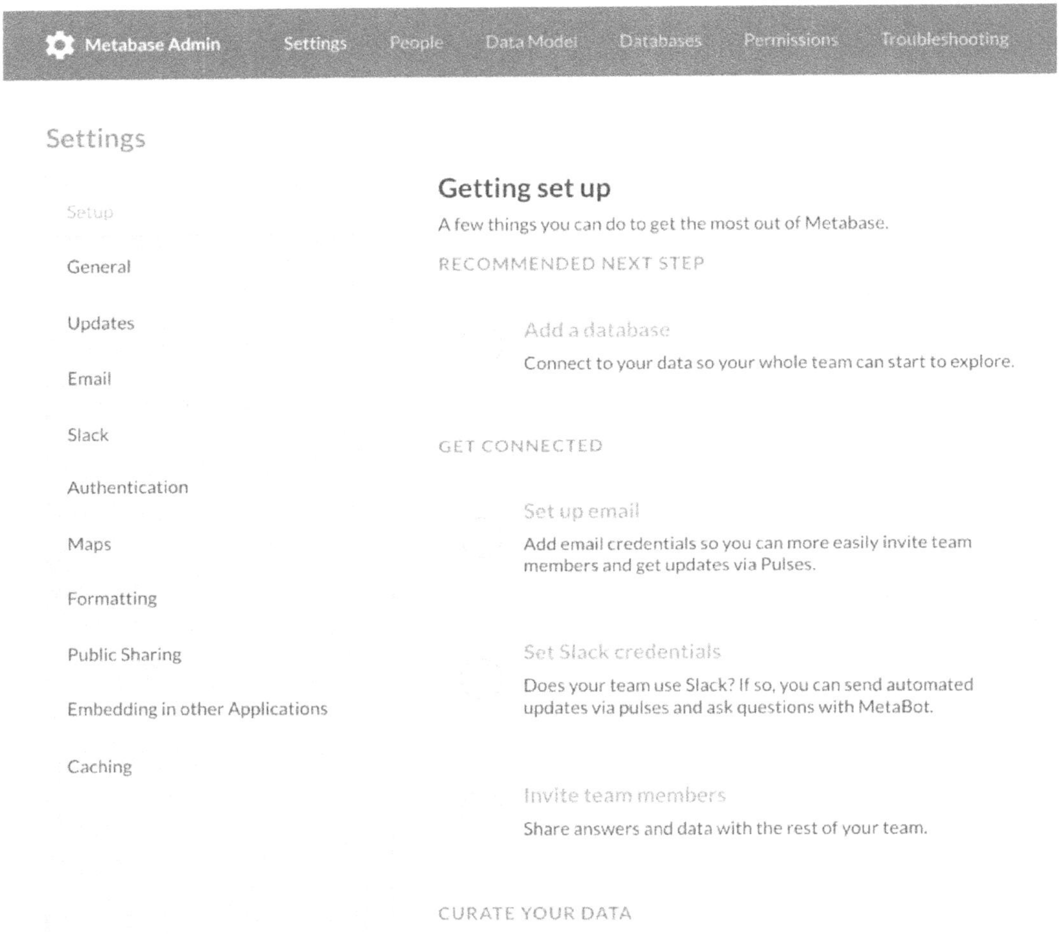

Figure 3.2 – The Metabase admin panel. We will focus on the GET CONNECTED section

For now, click on **General** under the **Settings** menu. Note that the **Site URL** field is populated with the URL created by Elastic Beanstalk. In the next section, we'll learn how to create a subdomain for our instance and use that URL instead.

Using a subdomain

At this point, our Metabase instance is hosted at a subdomain of `elasticbeanstalk.com`. It works just fine, and we could absolutely start handing it out to other people in our organization. However, many people prefer using a **subdomain** to host their Metabase instance. If your domain is `mydomain.com`, a subdomain is something like `subdomain.mydomain.com`. A common subdomain pattern I've seen people use for Metabase is `metabase.mydomain.com`, which is a lot easier to remember, shorter, and looks more official. With a subdomain, our Metabase instance will still live at the `elasticbeanstalk.com` URL, but our subdomain will act as an alias for that URL.

Let's learn how to use a subdomain and create an alias for it.

First, you will have to log in to your **DNS** provider. Once you are logged in to your DNS provider, you will want to create an **ALIAS** record. An ALIAS record simply lets you point a subdomain to an external domain name (the `elasticbeanstalk.com` domain, in our case). This will work the same across any DNS provider:

1. In the **Name** field, pick the value for your subdomain. As I mentioned previously, `metabase` is a good option.
2. In the **Content** (sometimes called **Target**) field, enter the Elastic Beanstalk URL for your Metabase instance. You do not need to add the `http://` part.
3. As a check, assuming your subdomain is `metabase`, your domain is `mydomain.com`, and your Elastic Beanstalk URL is `picklesandpies.us-east-1.elasticbeanstalk.com`, your ALIAS record's preview should look like this:

```
ALIAS metabase.mydomain.com resolves to picklesandpies.
us-east-1.elasticbeanstalk.com
```

4. Save the record.

Now you can visit your Metabase instance at `metabase.mydomain.com`.

> **Important Note**
>
> The preceding steps will work for `metabase.<your_domain.com>` but not www.`metabase.<your_domain.com>`. For the latter, you will need to add an additional ALIAS record. To do so, follow the same steps as previously except choose www.`metabase` in *Step 1*. It's good to have both, since some of your users might want to type the www prefix out of habit.

Most DNS providers are the same, so the preceding steps should work for the majority of them. However, if you use the **AWS Route 53** service for your DNS management, it will be *slightly* different. Here's how:

1. Instead of an ALIAS record, you will create an **A record**.
2. You will then have the option to make it an ALIAS record by clicking the **Yes** radio button. Click it.
3. In the **Alias Target** field, you will be able to select your Elastic Beanstalk environment from the drop-down menu.
4. Select your Elastic Beanstalk environment and click **Create** to make the record.

Now we have created a much nicer looking URL for our Metabase. The next thing we need to do is tell Metabase we'll be using this URL going forward. This is important because later in the chapter, we will configure Metabase to send out emails to other invited users, and we want the link in that email to be the new one we've just created. We already saw where the **Site URL** field lives in the last section, so let's return there:

1. In Metabase, visit the admin panel.
2. From the **Settings** menu, click General.
3. Under **Site URL**, enter the new URL with the subdomain you just created – for example, `metabase.mydomain.com`. You can leave the `http://` value in the dropdown alone momentarily. We'll learn more about this in the next section.
4. You do not need to click save, so you're done.

Now we have a great looking URL for our Metabase. This is the link Metabase will send to new users that you invite to join. As you may have noticed, though, we're sending traffic to Metabase using HTTP, not HTTPS. In the next section, we'll learn how to serve our application over the secure HTTPS.

Serving Metabase over HTTPS

In *Chapter 2, Hosting Metabase on AWS*, when we deployed Metabase using Elastic Beanstalk on AWS, we set everything up so that our traffic is served over HTTP. Nowadays, almost all websites use HTTPS over HTTP. HTTPS is a secure version of HTTP, where traffic is encrypted using public-key encryption and SSL certificates. That means that HTTP is not encrypted, which means that requests and responses are sent in plaintext and can be eavesdropped on by third parties.

Since HTTPS is the industry standard these days and we're going to be dealing with sensitive data in Metabase, we should definitely use it. Let's learn how to set it up.

Creating an SSL certificate in AWS

AWS has a service called AWS Certificate Manager that lets you create **Secure Sockets Layer** (**SSL**) certificates. What these certificates actually are is beyond the scope of this book. Before creating one, check to see whether your domain and subdomain already have one. If not, search for `Certificate Manager` in the AWS console. Once there, take the following steps:

1. Click **Get Started** under **Provision certificates**.
2. On the next page, you'll want to select **Request a public certificate**.
3. On the **Add domain names** page, add the domain and subdomain you created in the last section in two different records. Following our example, one record would be `mydomain.com` and the other `metabase.mydomain.com`.
4. On the **Select validation method** page, choose **DNS validation**. This assumes you have the ability to modify the DNS records for your domain. Since we did that in the last section, I'm assuming you have that ability.
5. You may optionally add tags to your certificate, but I chose to leave this blank.
6. Finally, review your work and click **Confirm** and **request**.

The certificate will be created but needs to be validated first by creating CNAME records with your DNS provider. If you've registered your domain with AWS Route 53, this can be done in a single click. Simply expand the dropdown next to your domains and click the **Create record in Route 53** button. If you use a different DNS provider, you'll need to copy and paste the names and values into a CNAME record yourself.

We now have our SSL certificates created and a record in our DNS for them, which means we can open up our Metabase instance to HTTPS traffic. To do that, we'll need to change our load balancer settings in our Elastic Beanstalk configuration, so let's do that.

Adding an HTTPS listener to the load balancer

We now need to set up our Metabase instance so that the load balancer knows to listen for HTTPS traffic. The way we set it up back in *Chapter 2, Hosting Metabase on AWS*, was to only listen for HTTP traffic. To make these changes, start in the Elastic Beanstalk service in AWS:

1. Open up your Metabase environment. In our example, this is called `Metabase-env`.
2. From the menu on the left sidebar, click **Configuration**.
3. Under **Configuration Overview**, click **Edit** next to **Load Balancer**.

4. Now, scroll up to the top of the **Modify Classic Load Balancer** page. In the **Listeners** section, click the **Add listener** button.
5. Configure the listener as follows:

   a) **Listener port**: `443`

   b) **Listener protocol**: **HTTPS**

   c) **Instance port**: `80`

   d) **Instance Protocol**: **HTTP**

   e) **SSL Certificate**: Pick the certificate you created in the last step from the dropdown.
6. Click **Add**.
7. Now, scroll down to the bottom of the page and click **Apply**.

It will take a minute or so for Elastic Beanstalk to update your settings. Once that's complete, you can test whether it worked by prepending your Metabase instance's URL with `https://`. For example, since my URL is `metabase.picklesnpies.com`, I would type `https://metabase.picklesnpies.com`. If you are using Google Chrome as your browser, you can click the lock icon next to the URL, as in *Figure 3.3*, to verify that your connection is secure:

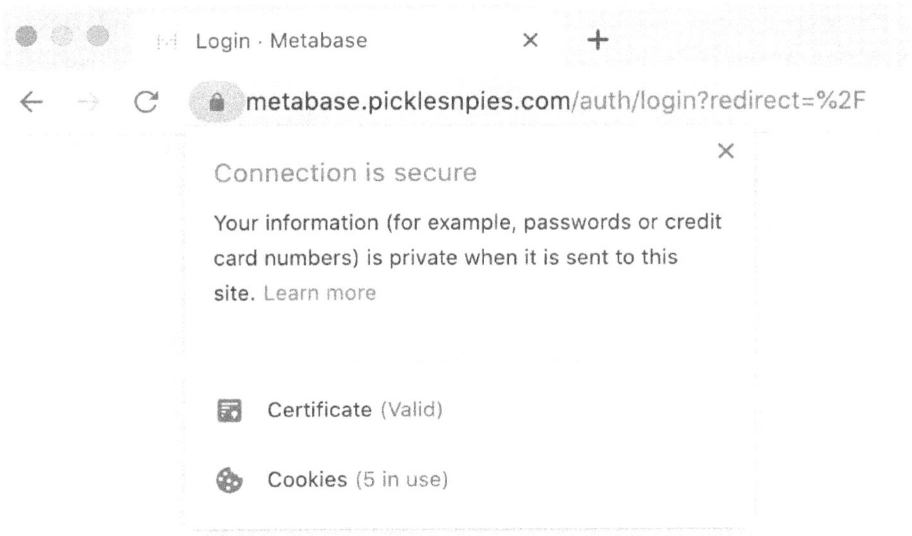

Figure 3.3 – Confirming your HTTPS connection is working

Of course, needing to type `https://` every time you want to visit a URL isn't ideal, and if you were to simply type in the URL alone, it would default to HTTP. So, the next thing we'll want to do is force all traffic to default to HTTPS.

Defaulting all traffic to HTTPS

We're now able to send and receive requests to and from our instance using the secure HTTPS protocol. We can now configure our application environment so that all traffic is forced to go over HTTPS. This means that any request to our URL, even if it's prepended with `http://`, will force it to HTTPS. To do this, open up Metabase and head to the admin panel:

1. On the left-side menu, click **General**.
2. Under **Site URL**, using the dropdown, choose `https://`.
3. Enable the **Redirect to HTTPS** toggle.

Try to force an HTTP request to your Metabase instance. It should automatically redirect to an HTTPS request.

Now that we have a proper-looking subdomain and are serving traffic using HTTPS, the next item of business is setting up Metabase to send emails.

Setting up email

To get started, choose **Setting up email** from either the **Getting set up** section or the **Email** option on the left rail of the **Settings** menu in the admin panel.

To have Metabase send emails, you need an **SMTP** server. SMTP stands for **Simple Mail Transfer Protocol**. Just as we have been using cloud-based services to provision our web servers, we will also rely on them for our SMTP server.

The fields Metabase asks you to fill out are as follows:

- **SMTP Host**
- **SMTP Port**
- **SMTP Security**
- **SMTP Username**
- **SMTP Password**
- **A From Address**, which will be the email address that Metabase sends the email from

Let's learn how to fill in all of these. There are two common ways to go about this. One is using AWS, which we have already familiarized ourselves with. The other is to use **Gmail**, or their professional offering, **Google G Suite**. If your organization uses Google products, such as Google Mail and Google Calendar, you probably have a Google G Suite account. If so, setting up email and allowing users in your organization to sign in with their email address is a lot easier. We will first learn how to send emails with AWS, but if you know you have Google G Suite, then I recommend skipping ahead.

Setting up email with AWS

Let's learn how to fill all the required fields in using AWS. The email service within AWS is called **SES**, or **Simple Email Service**. You will want to log in with your root credentials to complete these steps, so if you are logged in as your `metabase-admin` IAM account, I recommend switching to root first.

Next, find the SES service in the AWS Management Console. SES will allow us to send emails, but to prevent bad actors from using it to send spam, your account will start in a sandbox state with very limited email-sending privileges. In fact, at the beginning, you need to verify *all email addresses* you wish to both send and receive from. That is clearly not ideal for sending emails to many users in your organization, but it's okay for now. To begin, we'll just learn how to send an email to ourselves.

> **Important Note**
>
> If your organization relies on AWS, it's likely that they already have much of this set up.

Because all of the email addresses we send and receive from need to be verified, the first thing we will learn to do is verify our own email address:

1. From the SES home page, click the **Email Addresses** option on the left rail.
2. Click the **Verify a New Email Address** button.
3. Add your email address, and click **Verify this Email Address**. For simplicity, use the same email here as the one you used to sign up for Metabase. This is because AWS will only let you send and **receive** emails from verified email addresses. If you really want to use two different email addresses, verify them both.

> **Important Note**
>
> These steps may not work if the email you use is a forwarding email. I recommend using a non-forwarding email to minimize complexity.

4. You will receive a confirmation email in your inbox. Clicking the link in that email will successfully verify your email address.

At this point, the verification status for your email should read **verified** in green font. You are now able to send an email from Amazon SES on behalf of your email.

Next, we will learn how to access an SMTP server that we can use to send emails. It turns out that to do this, AWS requires you to create a unique IAM user with special privileges. However, you can create this user without actually needing to log in as it. Let's learn how:

1. If not there already, using the AWS Management Console, navigate to SES.
2. On the left rail, find the **SMTP Settings** option.
3. On the **Using SMTP to Send Email with Amazon SES** page, click the blue button reading **Create My SMTP Credentials**.
4. You will see a default IAM username in the text box. Whatever is there will be fine for this IAM user. We will never actually log in with this account, unlike our `metabase-admin` user.
5. Click **Create**.
6. On the next screen, download the credentials file.

> **Important Note**
> This is the *only* time you will be able to download these credentials, so if you miss this step, you will have to start all over again and create a different IAM user.

7. Click **Close**. This will take you back to the IAM service.
8. Return to SES and again click the **SMTP Settings** option.
9. Copy the server name, which should look something like `email-smtp.us-east-1.amazonaws.com`.

You now have an SMTP server that you can use, as well as user credentials. Now you can go back to Metabase and fill in some of the fields:

1. Return to the email settings in Metabase's admin panel. Paste the server name in the **SMTP Host** field.
2. Choose `587` for **SMTP Port**.
3. Choose `TLS` for the **SMTP Security** option.

4. The SMTP username can be found in the `credentials.csv` file from *Step 6* of the previous exercise. It is the second of the three comma-separated values. Copy and paste it.
5. The SMTP password is the third field in the `credentials.csv` file. Copy and paste it as well.
6. For **From Address**, use the email address you verified in the previous flow.
7. Click on the **Save changes** button at the bottom of the flow. If successful, it will turn green.
8. Next, click **Send Test Email** and check your inbox to see whether it worked. If successful, you will get an email with the subject and mailed-by fields identical to *Figure 3.4*.

By doing this, you will, in effect, receive an email from yourself on behalf of Amazon SES:

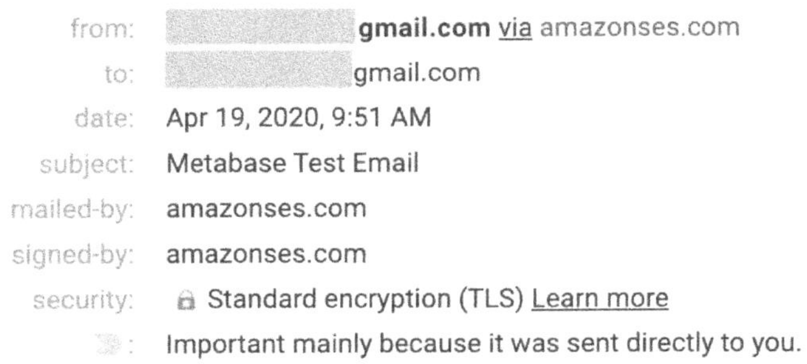

Figure 3.4 – You should receive an email like this, from your email but mailed by Amazon

Now, Metabase can send emails via our SMTP server on AWS. However, we're not ready to invite the rest of our team yet. There are two issues we need to address:

- We might prefer to have our emails sent from an email address such as `metabase@mydomain.com`, rather than our personal or work email address.
- Because we are in the sandbox state, we can only send emails to verified email addresses. We have also only verified our own email address.

Let's learn how to address these issues, starting with the first.

Sending an email with SES from your domain

At this point, all emails that Metabase sends will be from your email address. If your organization owns a domain name and you would like to use a generic email address from that domain name to send Metabase emails, follow the steps in this section.

The first thing you need to know is how your domain is registered. Earlier, we mentioned that AWS has a service for registering domains called **Route 53**. If your organization uses Route 53, the email verification process is a lot easier as AWS will handle a lot of the passing of records for you. If you use another DNS provider, you will just have to copy and paste all the records back and forth.

Let's quickly check whether your domain is registered via Route 53:

1. Visit the Route 53 service in the AWS Management Console.
2. Check whether your domain is there on the Route 53 dashboard.

If your domain is registered with Route 53, you only need to follow *steps 1* through *6* of the following steps. Otherwise, follow all the steps. This will allow you to send emails on behalf of your domain:

1. Return to the SES service.
2. On the left rail, under **Identity Management**, click **Domains**.
3. In the **Verify New Domain** popup, enter your domain name.
4. Click **Generate DKIM Settings**.
5. Click **Verify this Domain**.

The **Verify a New Domain** popup will appear. It will have information around various records you need to add to your DNS settings. However, at the bottom of the popup, you will see that as an Amazon Route 53 customer, these records can be added automatically. Click the button reading **Use Route 53** to complete the verification process. Ensure that the **Domain Verification Record**, **DKIM Record Set**, and **Email Receiving Record** set boxes are all checked. Click **Create Record Sets**.

If you use another DNS service, you will have to manually add these records as follows:

1. In another browser tab, log in to your DNS service and navigate to the page in that service where you manage DNS records.
2. Add the **TXT**, **CNAME**, and **MX** records that AWS provided you with.

Within 1 hour, your domain will be verified. Now, you can change the **From** email address from your personal email to something like `metabase@mydomain.com`.

Now that we can send emails from a more official-looking email address, we still need to address our sandbox status so that we can actually send emails to unverified addresses. Let's learn how to get out of the sandbox environment.

Getting out of the SES sandbox environment

Getting out of the SES sandbox is a surprisingly manual and human process. Rather than just clicking a few buttons, we actually have to send a request to a real person who will determine whether or not we have a valid case. Let's learn how to submit a case to AWS to get out of sandbox mode:

1. From the SES home page, click on **Sending Statistics** on the left rail.
2. At the top of the page, you will see a notification about the sandbox status of your account. Click **Request a Sending Limit Increase**. You will be taken to a form where you can create a case.
3. In the **Limit type** drop-down box, make sure **SES Sending Limits** is populated.
4. For **Mail Type**, select **System Notifications**.

   You can leave the rest of the fields in the **Case Classification** section blank.
5. In the **Requests** section, choose your AWS region. We have been using **Northern Virginia**.
6. From the **Limit** dropdown, select **Desired Daily Sending Quota**.
7. Enter a value in **New limit value** that represents the maximum number of emails you think you will be sending per day. A good default value here is `1000` if you don't know.
8. Finally, for **Case description**, write a short note about why you want the rate increase, as shown in *Figure 3.5*. Remember, we do not want to send a lot of emails, we just want the verified-only restriction lifted:

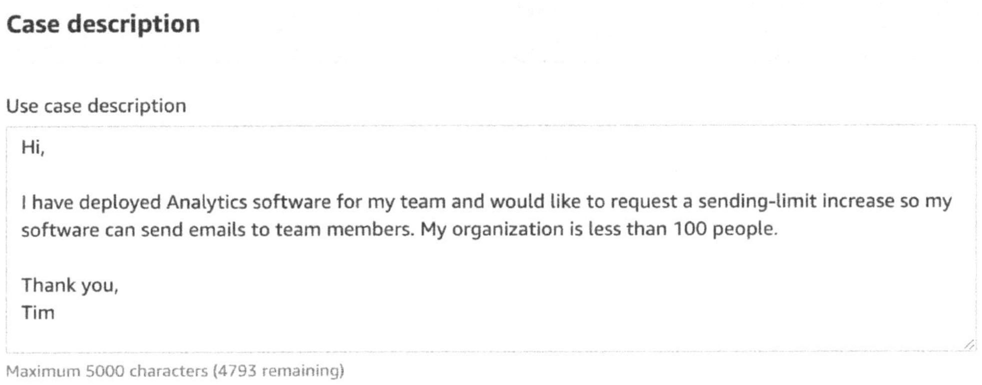
Case description
Use case description
Hi,
I have deployed Analytics software for my team and would like to request a sending-limit increase so my software can send emails to team members. My organization is less than 100 people.
Thank you,
Tim
Maximum 5000 characters (4793 remaining)

Figure 3.5 – An example of what to write in the Use case description field

9. Click **Submit** to submit the case.

Now we wait. It can take up to 24 hours for the case to be reviewed. Remember, this is done by an actual human. Once it is approved, you will be out of the sandbox environment and be able to send emails to others in your organization.

Setting up email with Google Gmail or G Suite

If your organization uses **Google G Suite** (formerly known as Google Apps) to create and manage email addresses, calendars, and docs for team members, you can use Google's SMTP server to configure email as well. This requires much less setup than with Amazon. Let's get started. This will also work for a regular Gmail account.

To allow Metabase to send emails on behalf of your Google account, you will use Google's SMTP server, as well as your Google username and password to authenticate. However, for security reasons, it is not possible (or a good idea) to use your Google password for anything except signing in to your Google account. Also, if you have two-step verification turned on, which is recommended or required by many organizations, using a second factor each time Metabase wants to send an email purely doesn't make sense. The solution here is to create something called an **app-specific password**. According to Google's documentation, an app-specific password is "a 16-digit passcode that gives a non-Google app or device permission to access your Google account" (`https://support.google.com/accounts/answer/185833`). Let's learn how to make one.

> **Important Note**
>
> App-specific passwords can only be created for accounts that have two-step verification turned on. If you do not have this turned on, you can also turn it on in your Google Security settings.

To get started, go to your Google account at `www.myaccount.google.com`:

1. From the menu of options on the left, click **Security**.
2. In the **Signing in to Google** section, click **App passwords**.
3. Now, you can create the app-specific password. There are two dropdowns: one called **Select app** and one called **Select device**.
4. Choose **Mail** from the **Select app** dropdown.
5. Choose **Other** for **Select device** and write in `Metabase`.
6. Click **Generate**.
7. A modal will pop up with your 16-digit password. You need not make note of it, as the idea is that it will only be used one time. Copy the password to your clipboard and leave the tab open for now.

Now that we've created our app-specific password, we can return to Metabase and fill out the form in the email settings:

1. From the Metabase admin panel, click **Email** from the list of settings on the left rail.
2. Set the SMTP host to `smtp.gmail.com`.
3. Set the SMTP port to `587`.
4. For **SMTP Security**, choose `TLS`.
5. The SMTP username will be your Gmail or G Suite email address.
6. The SMTP password will be the app-specific password you just created.
7. For now, the **From** address will be your Gmail or G Suite email address.
8. Click the **Save changes** button at the bottom of the flow. If successful, it will turn green.
9. Next, click **Send Test Email** and check your inbox to see whether it worked.

> **Important Note**
> If you try this from your G Suite account, as opposed to your Gmail account, and get a **No Matching Clause** error when you try to send the test email, you might have to change a security setting in your G Suite admin settings. To do so, from Google Admin, select **Security** | **Settings** and click the **Allow users to manage their access to less secure apps** radio button.

Metabase is now able to send emails on your behalf. If you do not want emails from Metabase to be addressed from you, and would rather them be from a more Metabase-branded email address, there are two options. The easiest is to simply create a `metabase@mydomain.com` account in G Suite. Depending on what tier of G Suite your organization is on, that might be the best option. For some accounts that only have a limited number of accounts to spare, the better route is to create an **alias**. You can create up to 30 email aliases per user account, so you should not have any limitation issues. Let's learn how to do that.

You will need admin access to your G Suite account to create an alias:

1. Click **Users**.
2. Select the user you want to create the alias for to open up their profile.
3. From the user's profile, find the **User information** section and click **Email aliases**.
4. Add your alias – for example, `metabase@mydomain.com`.

This will let you receive mail addressed to `metabase@mydomain.com`, but not send it. To send emails, we need to take an additional step:

1. Go to the Gmail account that you attached the alias to.
2. Click the settings gear icon.
3. Click the **Accounts** tab.
4. Under the **Send mail as:** section, click **Add another email address**. A pop-up window will open.
5. In the pop-up window, enter a name for this alias (for example, `Metabase`) and enter the email alias in the **Email address** field, as shown in *Figure 3.6*:

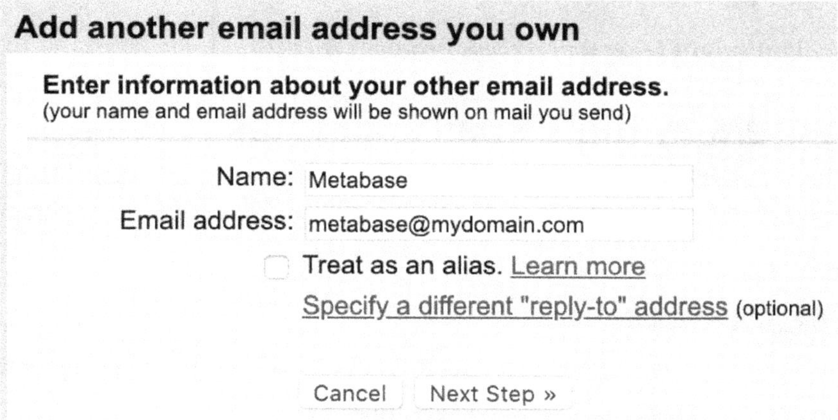

Figure 3.6 – A screenshot of the pop-up window

6. Uncheck the **Treat as an alias** box. This will allow you to send emails as this email address but not receive any emails to this address.
7. Click **Next step**, which should just close the window.

Now, you can return to the email form in Metabase's admin panel. The only thing you need to change is the **From** address field. Enter the new email alias you created:

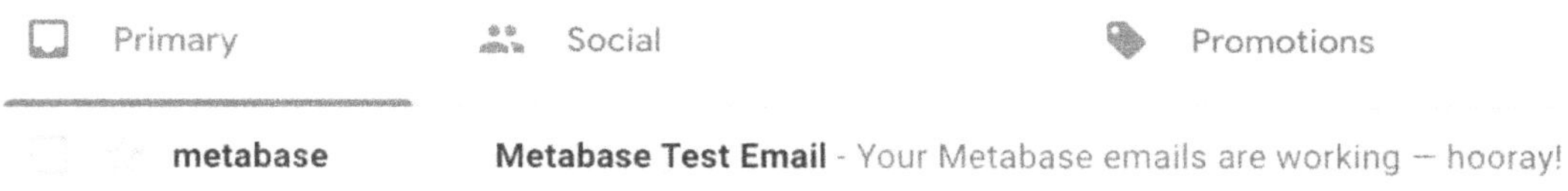

Figure 3.7 – A screenshot of the confirmation email

Now, your test email will come from your new `metabase@` email alias, as in *Figure 3.7*, instead of from your email.

Allowing others to use Metabase

Now that our Metabase instance can send emails out with our nicely branded Metabase URL, it's finally time to invite others in our organization to join the party.

There are a few different ways to do this, depending on how your organization manages identities. In this section, we will learn three ways to add users in your organization:

- Manually, by sending individual emails out
- Integrating with **Google sign-in**
- Using **Lightweight Directory Access Protocol** (LDAP)

Inviting users by their email addresses

Let's learn the simplest way to invite users to Metabase – sending individual emails out. This is a great option if you have a small team. To get started, visit the admin panel:

1. On the top purple bar, click on **People**.
2. Click the **Add Someone** button.
3. Fill out the form, entering the first and last name as well as the email address.
4. Optionally, you can add this user to the **Admin** group.
5. Click **Create**.

The user you invited will receive an email with a call to join Metabase. When they first visit Metabase, they will be asked to create and confirm a password for their account.

While this is by far the easiest way to invite users to Metabase, it could get tedious entering email after email if you have a lot of people in your organization. If most people in your organization have an email address from your organization's domain, using Google sign-in allows them all to sign up for an account without you needing to create it first. Let's learn how to set this up.

Setting up Google sign-in

To set up Google sign-in, first visit `https://developers.google.com/identity/sign-in/web/sign-in`:

1. Click the link to go to the **Credentials** page.
2. If you already have a project created, you'll be taken to the **Create Credentials** page. If not, you'll have to create a project. Give it a meaningful name like `Metabase Sign-In`.
3. Now click the **CREATE CREDENTIALS** link towards the top of the page.
4. From the dropdown menu of options, choose **OAuth client ID**.
5. On next page, under **Application Type**, choose **Web** application.
6. Choose a Name. This will not be shown to end users, so it can be anything meaningful to you.
7. Now, under the **Authorized JavaScript Origins** section, click + **ADD URI**.
8. In the **URI**s field, add the URL for your Metabase Instance.
9. Click **Create** at the bottom of the form.

The next screen will present you with your **client ID**. Copy the client ID and return to Metabase:

1. From Metabase, go to the admin panel and click **Authentication** in the **Settings** menu.
2. Click **Configure** in the **Sign in with Google** box.
3. Add the client ID you copied to the first field.
4. Finally, add the domain name that you want to allow sign-ins from. This is just the `@mydomain` tag your organization uses for email addresses.
5. Click **Save Changes**.

Now, when a logged-out user visits your Metabase URL, they will see the **Sign in with Google** option, as in *Figure 3.8*. It will only allow accounts at the domain you specified in *Step 10* to successfully sign in:

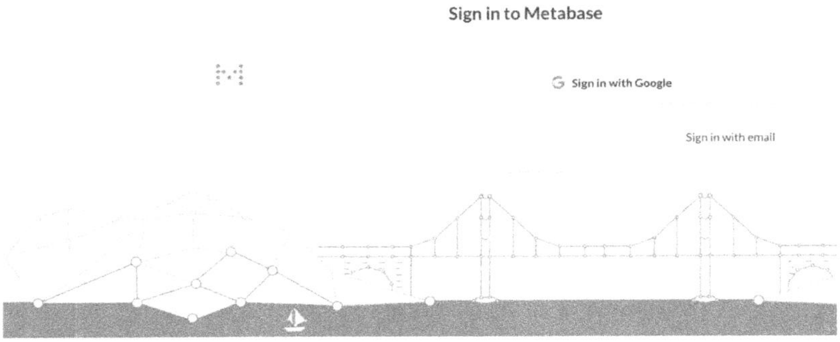

Figure 3.8 – The Metabase sign-in page with Google sign-in

> **Important Note**
> Many organizations work with consultants or other third-party groups and may want to use Google sign-in for internal users but also grant access to select external users. If you have Google sign-in activated, you can still send individual invites to users with external email addresses.

Authentication with LDAP

If your organization uses LDAP to manage its directory of users, you can configure Metabase to allow users to authenticate with their LDAP credentials.

LDAP tends to be used by larger organizations – the overhead is too much for small teams. LDAP can also be set up in many different ways. Setting up LDAP is beyond the scope of this book, but the following shows you how to set up Metabase's authentication with LDAP under general conditions. Let's jump in:

1. Start in the admin panel and click **Authentication** in the **Settings** menu.
2. On the LDAP card, click **Configure**.
3. In the **Server Settings** section, click the toggle to turn **LDAP Authentication** to **Enabled**.
4. Enter your LDAP server name in the **LDAP Host** section.
5. Enter `389` for **LDAP Port**, unless you use SSL to connect to your LDAP server, in which case use `636`.

6. Choose the type of security you use to connect to your LDAP server.
7. Next, add your username or **Distinguished Name** (**DN**) and password.
8. Under **User Search Base**, enter the objects, separated by commas, that define the starting point in your directory that you want to search from.
9. Next, add any filters you like.
10. Enter the appropriate attributes for **Email**, **First Name**, and **Last Name**. Generally, these will be as follows:

- **Email Attribute**: `mail`
- **First Name Attribute**: `givenName`
- **Last Name Attribute**: `sn`

11. Finally, if you have groups in your LDAP directory that logically correspond to groups you'd like to use in Metabase, click the toggle to enable them. We will learn how to construct groups in the next section.

Now that we've learned all the ways that you can add users to Metabase, let's learn how we can configure Slack and complete the **GET CONNECTED** section in the admin panel.

Integrating Metabase with Slack

If your organization uses Slack, you can easily create a Slack bot for Metabase. This lets you ask Metabase questions directly in Slack, as in *Figure 3.9*:

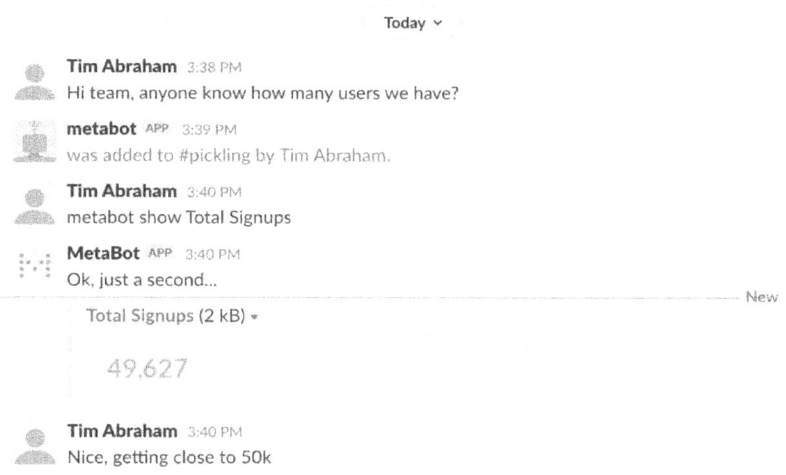

Figure 3.9 – Asking questions to MetaBot, Metabase's Slack bot

Let's learn how to set this up:

1. Open the admin panel.
2. Under the **Settings** menu, click **Slack**.
3. Click the blue **Create a Slack Bot User for MetaBot** button.
4. This will take you to your Slack instance in a new browser tab, as in *Figure 3.10*, where you'll give a name to your bot. I recommend using the name `metabot`.
5. Once you've given your bot a name, click **Add bot integration**:

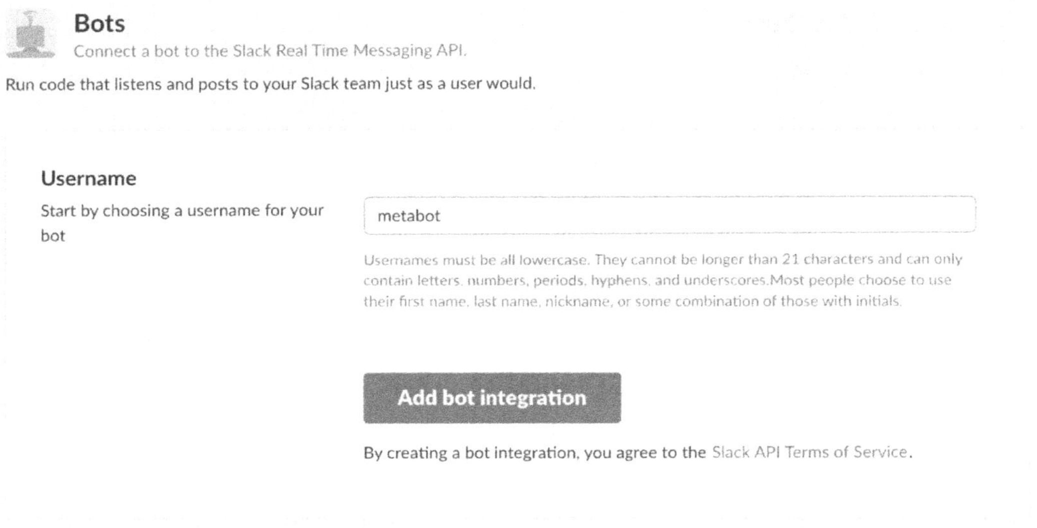

Bots
Connect a bot to the Slack Real Time Messaging API.
Run code that listens and posts to your Slack team just as a user would.
Username
Start by choosing a username for your bot
metabot
Usernames must be all lowercase. They cannot be longer than 21 characters and can only contain letters, numbers, periods, hyphens, and underscores.Most people choose to use their first name, last name, nickname, or some combination of those with initials.
Add bot integration
By creating a bot integration, you agree to the Slack API Terms of Service.

Figure 3.10 – Adding the metabot Slack bot

6. After clicking **Add bot integration**, you will be taken to a new page with an API token. Copy this token and return to Metabase.
7. Once back in Metabase, paste the API token in the **Slack API Token** field.
8. Slide the **metabot** toggle to **Enabled**.
9. Click **Save changes**.

Now, head to Slack and create a new channel – name it `metabase_files`. It's important that you give it this exact name. You should also have an app in Slack called **metabot**, as in *Figure 3.11*:

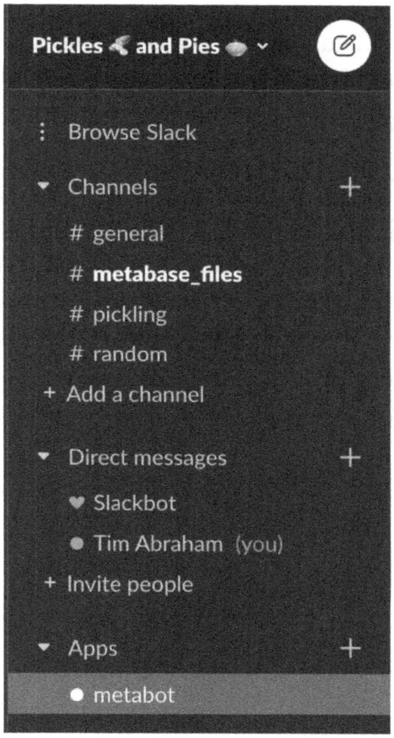

Figure 3.11 – After adding the Slack integration, you will get the metabot app

To test that the integration is working, click on the **metabot** app in Slack and type `metabot help`. You should see a response as in *Figure 3.12*:

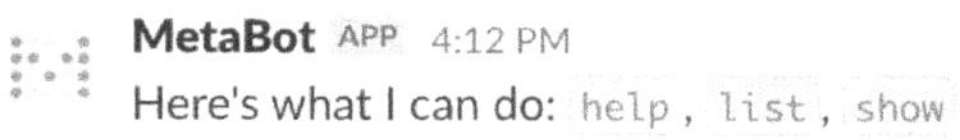

MetaBot APP 4:12 PM
Here's what I can do: help, list, show

Figure 3.12 – MetaBot responding to our query in Slack

We'll learn more about what MetaBot can do in the upcoming chapters. As of now, we've successfully finished all the **GET CONNECTED** steps required to set up Metabase.

Summary

In this chapter, we learned how to set up our Metabase instance and invite others to join. We picked out an attractive subdomain to host our app, and configured Metabase to send emails through an SMTP server. We learned how to make an email alias so that our emails look like they are coming from Metabase and not our personal email addresses. Finally, we started inviting users to join our instance. We learned how to implement Google sign-in and LDAP so that any user in our organization can join without a personal invite.

Next, we finally get to the data part. In the next chapter, we'll be learning about all the databases you can connect Metabase to. If you have your own database that you've been anxious to start exploring with Metabase, you will finally get to in the next chapter.
For those of you without a database, don't worry. In the next chapter, I'll be sharing a dataset and giving instructions so that you can learn how to create your own PostgreSQL database, load data into it, connect it to Metabase, and explore it throughout the rest of the book.

4
Connecting to Databases

In this chapter, we will finally connect a database to Metabase and start exploring data. This chapter is all about **databases**. Metabase is designed to connect to most of today's most popular relational, NoSQL, and analytical databases, and we will learn a little about each one.

We will also learn how to launch our own **PostgreSQL** database and load it with the sample data we will be exploring throughout the rest of the book. In addition to preparing us with a dataset to use in future chapters, this chapter is intended to help you learn the best practices when working with databases.

We will cover the following topics in this chapter:

- What is a database?
- Creating a PostgreSQL database in AWS
- Connecting to our PostgreSQL database in Metabase
- Connecting to a database with best practices
- Connecting to other types of databases in Metabase

Technical requirements

This chapter is the most technically challenging chapter in the book. As in the last two chapters, we will be mostly using **Amazon Web Services** (**AWS**). We will also be using the terminal a lot, making use of utilities such as `ssh`, `psql` and `git`. Finally, we will be connecting to a PostgreSQL database, both in Metabase and via the terminal.

What is a database?

While a thorough overview of databases is beyond the scope of this book, let's learn (or for some readers, refresh ourselves) about what databases are. According to Wikipedia, "*a database is an organized collection of data, generally stored and accessed electronically from a computer system*" (`https://en.wikipedia.org/wiki/Database`). Databases have been around for decades, and today, there are many different types of databases for different use cases.

Traditionally, the most common type of database has been the **relational database**. Relational databases are made up of **tables**, which can be thought of as spreadsheets. Tables are rectangular, meaning they have rows and columns. The relational part comes from how the tables link to one another, as depicted in *Figure 4.1*. Note how in *Figure 4.1*, we have an `orders` table and an `users` table, linked together by `id_user`. Rather than store all the user information for each order (such as `name` and `location`), a relational database saves space by keeping them separate but explicitly declaring the relationship between the two. Some of the most popular relational databases are **PostgreSQL**, **MySQL**, and **Microsoft SQL Server**:

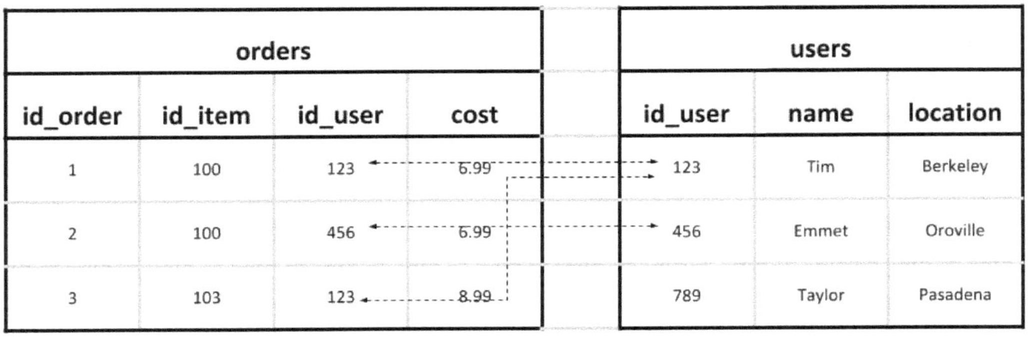
orders
id_order
id_item
id_user
cost
1
100
123
6.99
2
100
456
6.99
3
103
123
8.99
users
id_user
name
location
123
Tim
Berkeley
456
Emmet
Oroville
789
Taylor
Pasadena

Figure 4.1 – A users and orders table in a relational database

Relational databases are often referred to as **SQL** databases. SQL, or **Structured Query Language**, is the programming language used to get data from relational databases. In the early 2000s, **NoSQL** databases started to become popular. NoSQL databases discard the relational paradigm and instead allow more flexible schemas, which makes them a popular choice for software developers who want to rapidly iterate on features. They tend to not be as friendly for analytics and data science as relational databases, but Metabase handles both. Some of the most popular NoSQL databases are `MongoDB`, `Redis`, and `Cassandra`.

Along with the rise of big data over the last 15–20 years, we have seen new types of databases, referred to as **analytical databases**, become popular. The main use case for a relational or NoSQL database is to store information and serve it to an application quickly. When you log in to your email, for example, a database is working behind the scenes to serve records to the application based on your needs. As such, databases tend to be very fast at looking up individual rows. Where they tend to not perform as well is in doing tasks such as aggregating columnar data across many rows. This, however, is exactly what people in analytics want to do – aggregate and summarize data. Analytical databases were created to address this use case. These databases are used only for analytics and tend to be very scalable in terms of size. That means they can grow and grow to store more data without suffering in performance or exploding in cost. Not all analytical databases are relational, but the two most popular relational ones are Google's **BigQuery** and Amazon's **Redshift**.

While databases have matured and specialized over the years to address increasingly specific business needs, the traditional SQL-based relational database is still the standard in the majority of organizations. While we will cover NoSQL and analytical databases briefly in this chapter, the majority of the content will use the relational database PostgreSQL. Even if you use a different database in your organization, the lessons learned using PostgreSQL are easily applicable to most databases.

Now that we've learned an overview of databases, let's move on and learn how to create our own PostgreSQL database. We'll then load data into it and connect it to Metabase.

Creating a PostgreSQL database in AWS

In this section, we'll be creating a PostgreSQL database in AWS, downloading a utility called `psql` to connect to it, and finally, loading some sample data into it. Let's get started.

PostgreSQL is a popular open source database. It's actually what is running behind the scenes in our Metabase instance as the application database. In that case, it was created automatically by the Elastic Beanstalk configuration. Here, we will create one from scratch, using **Relational Database Service** (**RDS**) in AWS. Let's get started:

> **Important Note**
>
> You get 750 hours of RDS a month on the Free Tier. Since we're already using one of these to power our Elastic Beanstalk app, you will now be charged if you leave both running all month long. As of the time of writing, a `db.t2.micro` instance costs around USD 0.03 per hour.

1. Log in to AWS as the `metabase-admin` IAM user and find the **RDS** service in the AWS Management Console.
2. Click the orange **Create Database** button.
3. For **Choose a database creation method**, click **Standard Create**.
4. For **Configuration**, choose **PostgreSQL**.

   You can keep the default version number.
5. For **Templates**, choose **Free tier**. We will not be working with huge amounts of data in our examples, so this is more than enough.
6. Moving on to **Settings**, enter a name for your database instance in the **DB instance identifier** field. I've chosen `datadb`.
7. **Master username** can be kept as `postgres`.
8. Enter a good password and make note of it.
9. For **DB Instance size**, keep `db.t2.micro` to stay on the free tier.
10. For **Storage**, keep **General Purpose SSD** and **20 GB**.
11. Uncheck **Enable storage autoscaling**, since the amount of data we are working with is static and won't grow.
12. Under **Connectivity**, choose the VPC we have been working with, `vpc-metabase`.
13. Next, click the **Additional connectivity configuration** toggle to expand it.
14. Change your database to be **publicly available** by clicking the **Yes** radio button.
15. In **Additional configuration**, enter `pies` as your initial database name.
16. Keep **Enable automatic backups** checked.
17. Scroll down to the bottom and click **Create database**.

It generally takes a few minutes for a database to launch. While we're waiting for our database to launch, we can do a few other things to get ready to use it. We will start by downloading the `psql` PostgreSQL client.

Downloading the PostgreSQL client on macOS

While our PostgreSQL databases are created by AWS, we'll need something on our local computer that allows us to establish a connection to it. The simplest way is by downloading PostgreSQL locally. If you have Homebrew installed on your Mac, you can download PostgreSQL by simply running the following on the command line in your Terminal:

```
brew install postgresql
```

If you do not have Homebrew installed, visit `https://brew.sh/` and follow the instructions to install it first.

Downloading PostgreSQL on Windows

You can download the latest version of Postgres for Windows at `https://www.postgresql.org/download/windows/`.

Connecting to your database with psql

Once you've downloaded PostgreSQL on your Mac or Windows PC, you can test to see whether you have `psql`, the interactive PostgreSQL terminal client, by running the following in your terminal:

```
which psql
```

If you see an output looking something like `/usr/local/bin/psql`, then you have it.

To connect to your database, go back to RDS in the AWS console. By now, your database creation should be done:

1. Click on **Databases**.
2. Click on the new database you created, which we named `datadb`. Note that you should have two databases on your dashboard, the other being your Metabase application database.
3. Scroll down and make note of the endpoint. This is the host address of our database. It should look something like `datadb.abc1234567.us-east-1.rds.amazonaws.com`.

4. Return to your terminal and enter the following command, replacing the endpoint with the value in *Step 3*:

```
psql -h <endpoint> -p 5432 -U postgres -d pies
```

5. On the next line, you'll be prompted for the password you made when you created your database in the last section. Enter it.
6. You are now connected to your PostgreSQL database, using the `pies` database. Your terminal prompt should look something like this:

psql (11.2, server 11.5)
SSL connection (protocol: TLSv1.2, cipher: ECDHE-RSA-AES256-GCM-SHA384, bits: 256, compression: off)
Type "help" for help.
pies=>

Figure 4.2 – A screenshot of the terminal prompt

Congratulations! You've created a database that we can connect Metabase to. However, there are no tables or data in this database, so before we connect it to Metabase, let's add them.

Introducing Pickles and Pies, our fictional business

Metabase comes with a sample dataset that you can play around with, but I've also created a unique dataset for readers of this book that we'll be exploring throughout the rest of the chapters.

The dataset is based on a fictional e-commerce business called **Pickles and Pies**, where, as you can guess, we sell pickles and pies. Our fictional business is based in the San Francisco Bay Area, but will gladly ship products anywhere in the US. We started this business at the beginning of 2019 and have seen good growth in both users and orders since then. At the same time, growth has been so fast that we feel we lack a basic understanding of our business. How are we doing? What are the most popular items? Are we getting much repeat business, or are most of our users one-time customers? Are there unique segments of users or products that we need to understand? Answering these questions is key to running our business, and we'll be exploring them all in Metabase in later chapters. For now, though, let's learn how to load this dataset into our PostgreSQL database.

Loading data into our PostgreSQL database

To get started, we'll use `git` to clone a repository containing our data. We first used `git` back in *Chapter 1, Overview of Metabase*. To get started, open your terminal and navigate to wherever you keep your Git repositories. If you do not have something like that, I'd recommend creating a directory called `repos` or `workspace` in your home directory. You can do so with the following command:

```
mkdir ~/repos
```

Then, change directories into it:

```
cd ~/repos
```

Now you can clone the repository:

```
git clone https://github.com/PacktPublishing/Metabase-Up-and-Running.git
```

Next, change directories into the newly cloned repository with the following:

```
cd Metabase-Up-and-Running
```

Run the `psql` command again to connect to your database:

```
psql -h <endpoint> -p 5432 -U postgres -d pies
```

Then, from the `psql` command-line prompt, which should look like `pies=>`, run the following command to load data into your database:

```
pies=>\i data/create_pies_db.sql
```

To check whether it worked, reconnect to your database and try selecting one line from the newly created `users` table:

```
pies=>\c pies;
pies=> SELECT * FROM users limit 1;
```

If everything worked out, you should see the first user who signed up for our fictional business. Don't worry: that's not my actual credit card number!

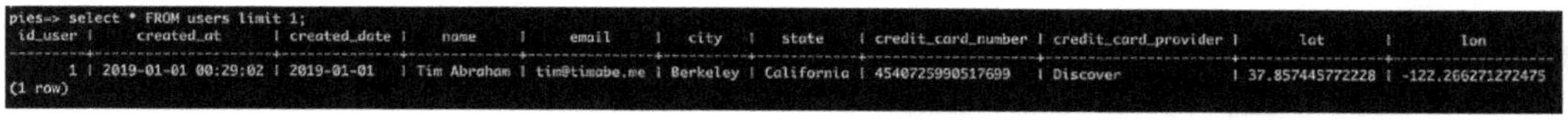

```
pies=> select * FROM users limit 1;
 id_user |     created_at      | created_date |    name     |      email      |   city   |   state    | credit_card_number | credit_card_provider |       lat        |        lon
---------+---------------------+--------------+-------------+-----------------+----------+------------+--------------------+----------------------+------------------+-------------------
       1 | 2019-01-01 00:29:02 | 2019-01-01   | Tim Abraham | tim@timabe.me   | Berkeley | California | 4540725990517699   | Discover             | 37.857445772228  | -122.266271272475
(1 row)
```

Figure 4.3 – A screenshot of the database

Now that we're able to connect to our database from the terminal, let's learn how to connect to it in Metabase.

Connecting to our PostgreSQL database in Metabase

Connecting to our database in Metabase is very similar to how we connected to it on the command line, except it is more user-friendly. To get started, open the admin panel in Metabase:

1. From the top menu bar, click **Databases**.
2. You should have one database already, the sample dataset that comes with Metabase.
3. Click **Add Database**.
4. **PostgreSQL** should be the default option from the dropdown. If not, choose it.
5. For **Name**, enter `Pies`. This is just a user-friendly name that Metabase will use.
6. Under **Host**, enter the endpoint from RDS.
7. For **Port**, use `5432`, which is the standard port for PostgreSQL traffic.
8. The database name will be `pies`.
9. The database username will be `postgres`.
10. Enter the password you made when you created the database.
11. Keep the **Enabled** slider on.
12. Click **Save**.

At this point, Metabase will store the connection parameters for our database. It will automatically start scanning our database tables. This will happen quickly, and you should see a modal as in *Figure 4.4* saying that your database has been added:

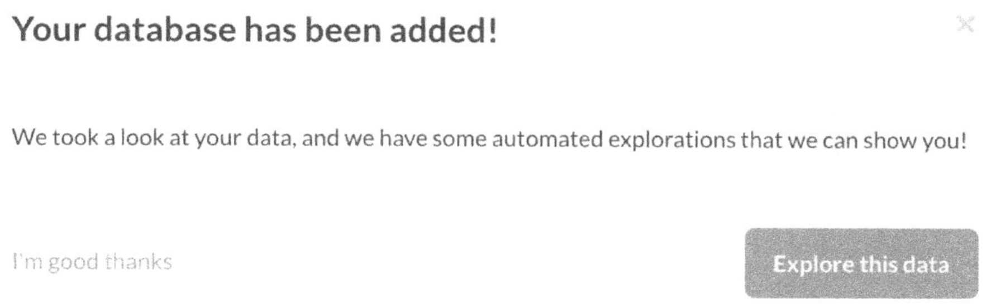

Your database has been added!
We took a look at your data, and we have some automated explorations that we can show you!
I'm good thanks
Explore this data

Figure 4.4 – A screenshot of the database success window

Not only has the database been added, but here we can see that Metabase has already created some automated explorations based on our data! Metabase has a feature called **x-rays**, where the program proactively guesses some of the questions you might have based on your data. Let's take a look at what they come up with.

Click **Explore this data**. Clicking this will bring up another modal, with a smiley avatar called **Metabot** introducing itself:

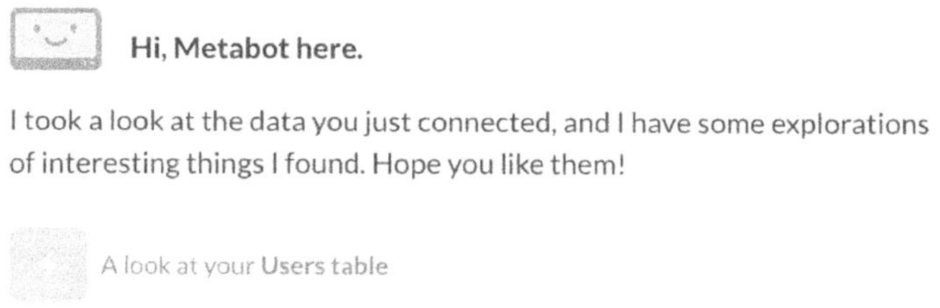

Figure 4.5 – A screenshot of metabot introducing itself

Let's have a look at our **Users** table. Metabase has already answered several key questions about our users, including overall figures such as the following:

- Total users
- New users in the last 30 days
- Growth in the last 30 days

There are also a few attractive-looking charts on this dashboard. Scrolling down the page, we see a map of US states shaded by how many users we have. Let's click on that:

Figure 4.6 – A screenshot showing the database geographical breakdown

We can see that most of our users are in California. That makes sense because our business is based in California. Also, California is the most populous state in the US. Let's click on it and zoom in to see exactly where our California-based users live:

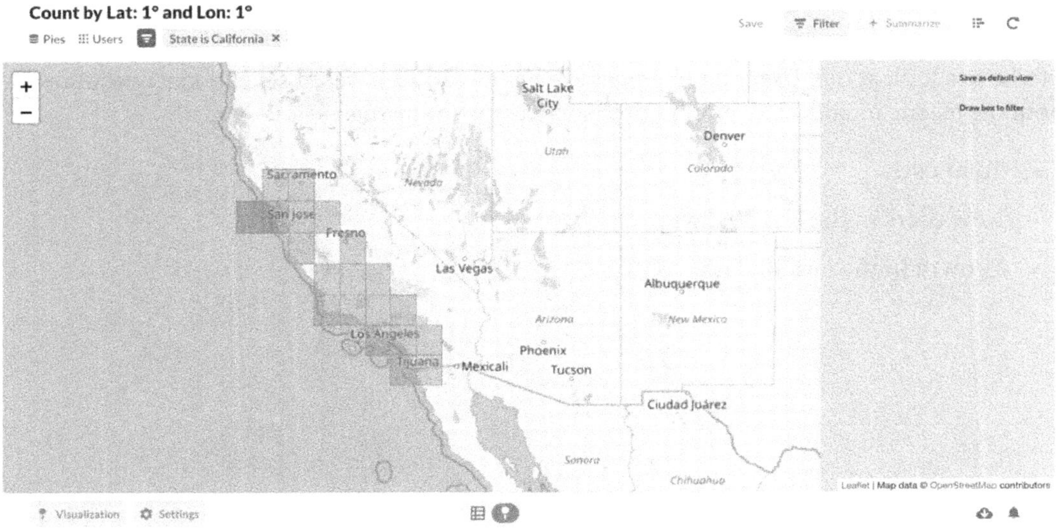

Figure 4.7 – A screenshot showing the database's map of California

As *Figure 4.6* tells us, most of our California-based users live in the San Francisco Bay Area, which makes sense given that is where we are headquartered.

Feel free to play around a bit more with the x-rayed data in Metabase if you like, but know that we will come back to this dataset many times before the book is done and thoroughly explore it. In *Chapter 7, Creating Visualizations*, we'll learn more about how these maps are made, and even make our own customized map. In this next section, we'll learn some best practices for using databases.

Connecting to a database with best practices

Up to this point, we've learned how to launch a PostgreSQL database with AWS, load data into it, and connect it to Metabase. If you plan on using Metabase in an existing organization, chances are that there will already be a database full of data for you. At the same time, it's unlikely that the database your organization uses to store data can be connected to in the same way as we learned previously. This is unlikely for two main reasons:

- *Most databases are not publicly accessible*. Recall that in the last section, we made our database publicly accessible. That was to make loading data and connecting it to Metabase easy. Generally, it's a bad idea to make a database publicly accessible, as it lets anyone attempt to connect to it.
- *Doing analytics on a production application database is dangerous*. Your application database is what is serving critical information to your application. Sending queries to it for analytical purposes can slow down the database response time, or in the worst case, crash your entire database, especially if you are writing queries with joins or other expensive computations.

The standard way to avoid these problems is to make your database **private** and create what is called a **read replica**. Let's learn about what both of these concepts mean.

Making your database private

Databases often contain very sensitive information, such as email addresses, full names, physical addresses, credit card numbers, and passwords. Even though databases are password-protected, exposing them to the public internet is an unnecessary risk. Imagine if you knew there was a public address such as our PostgreSQL endpoint that contained all your social media or banking data; even if the password was hard to guess, you would probably be a bit nervous with that setup. To avoid this risk, databases are generally restricted to only allow connections from authorized addresses, generally in a single network or VPC.

When we created our database, we gave it a special configuration to make it publicly accessible. The main reason we did that was that it made loading the sample data easier. However, the default configuration has the database set as private. Let's learn how to alter our database to make it private:

1. From the AWS Management Console, select the **RDS** service.
2. Click **Databases** on the left menu.
3. Click the radio button next to the database we want to make private: `datadb`.
4. Click the **Modify** button.
5. Scroll down to the **Network & Security** section and change the **Publicly Accessible** radio button from **Yes** to **No**.
6. Scroll to the bottom of the page and click **Continue**.
7. Next, you'll be asked when you want to schedule this modification. Click the radio button next to **Apply Immediately** and click the **Modify DB Instance** button at the bottom of the page.

Now, you will not be able to connect to this database via the public internet. To test this, open your terminal and try to connect with `psql` the way you were able to before:

```
psql -h <endpoint> -p 5432 -U postgres -d pies
```

The command should hang for 30 seconds or so before timing out with an error. Now, even if someone knows your database password, they cannot connect to it. In fact, the prompt to enter the password won't even appear. This is because the request from the terminal is unable to reach the endpoint. This is great for the security of our data, but presents challenges when *we* want to connect to our databases to analyze it in Metabase. Let's see what happens if we try to connect to it in Metabase.

Open Metabase back up. If you still have the tab open from before, where we looked at users in California, even better. Try to interact with data from your `pies` database. You will notice that you are able to connect to it just fine. How can this be when we just restricted connections from the public internet and confirmed it by failing to connect with `psql`?

The answer is that by making the database private, we restrict connections from the public internet but not from resources in our VPC. Since all our Metabase infrastructure was deployed in the same VPC as our database, those resources are allowed to connect.

We have now learned how to avoid the first cardinal sin of databases: do not make them publicly available. Now, let's learn how to avoid the second one, by using a read replica for analytics, rather than your production database.

Creating a read replica

Early in my career, I worked as a data analyst at a company that foolishly allowed me to query their production database. One day, I wrote a SQL query with a JOIN clause but left out a critical join condition. The query ended up taking down the whole database for the website, effectively taking down the site as well.

Over the years, we have learned that analytics should never be done on a production database. Instead, the best practice today is to query what is called a read replica of the production database. A read replica is a **read-only** copy of your database. Read-only means you can query the database, but not write new records to it. As such, it is isolated from the master database, and any operations sent to it will not affect the performance of the database in production.

Creating a read replica in AWS is very easy. Let's learn how:

1. From the AWS Management Console, select the **RDS** service.
2. From the RDS dashboard, select the database we just created, `datadb`.
3. On the next screen, click the **Actions** drop-down menu and select **Create read replica**.
4. In the **Create read replica** database instance flow, you can leave everything as is except the **DB Instance Identifier** field. When we created our master database, we used `datadb` in this field. Here, we can use something similar – for example, `dbreplica`.
5. Scroll down to the bottom of the page and click **Create read replica**.

This will trigger a creation process that will take a few minutes. When it is done, we will have a read-only clone of our main database that we can query in Metabase, knowing that anything we do to it will not affect the performance of our main database.

This database will have the same configuration as the main one, meaning it will also be private.

Now, let's go back to Metabase and change the database connection parameters to use our read replica instead. Start in the admin panel:

1. From the top menu bar, click on **Databases**.
2. You should have one database already, the sample dataset that comes with Metabase.
3. Click **Pies**, or whatever you named your database.

4. Remove the value from the host, and in its place, add the endpoint for your read replica. If you named your read replica `dbreplica`, you can just replace the `datadb` part of the connection string with `dbreplica`, as the rest of the string will be identical.
5. The rest of the connection parameters can be left as they were. It's only the host endpoint that has changed.
6. Click **Save Changes** at the bottom.

Now you will be querying your read replica database, and keeping your "application" database safe from errant queries. I put application in quotes because our application database is not a real application database, but we are pretending that it is.

I recommend this as the ideal setup for connecting your database to Metabase. That is, to summarize, the following:

- Make sure your databases are not accessible from the public internet. Ideally, launch your databases in the same VPC that hosts your Metabase instance.
- Use a read replica of your application database for analytics.

While this is how most organizations will likely set things up, there is another common setup that we need to learn about. In this setup, the database and read replica are private, but are launched either in a different VPC or in such a way that Metabase cannot connect to it. To allow Metabase to connect to the database in a setup such as this, you need to deploy what is called a **bastion host**. Let's learn about what bastion hosts are and how to create one.

Creating a bastion host

A bastion host is defined as "*a server whose purpose is to provide access to a private network from an external network, such as the internet*" (`https://en.m.wikipedia.org/wiki/Bastion_host`). That means that the bastion host can connect to the private resource – in our case, a database – and it can also accept traffic from the public internet.

There is no official AWS bastion host service, but creating one is still relatively straightforward. To create one, we will use the **EC2** service. We have already familiarized ourselves with EC2 instances, deploying them in *Chapter 2, Hosting Metabase on AWS*. However, that was done automatically with Elastic Beanstalk. This time, we will use the actual EC2 service. Let's get started:

1. From the AWS Management Console, search for **EC2** and select it.
2. Within the EC2 service, find the **Launch Instance** button and click it.

3. This will take you to a wizard-like flow, starting with **Step 1: Choose an Amazon Machine Image (AMI)**. You could pick any of the free tier eligible options, but for the sake of this tutorial, pick the first one, **Amazon Linux 2 AMI**.
4. On **Step 2: Choose an Instance Type**, choose the `t2.micro` option. This is the size we have been using and is part of the free tier.
5. Click **Next: Configure Instance Details**. In this form, you can leave almost everything as default; just make note of the following:

   a) Make sure that the network is `metabase-vpc`, or whatever VPC your database is in.

   b) In the dropdown next to **Auto-assign Public IP**, choose the **Enable** option. This will give your instance a public IP address that you can connect to.
6. Click **Next: Add Storage**. You can leave the default **Add Storage** configuration as is.
7. Click **Next: Add Tags**. You can either leave this section blank or if you would like, add a tag with the key set to `Name` and the value set to `Bastion Host`.
8. Click **Next: Configure Security Group**.

   We were first introduced to security groups in *Chapter 2, Hosting Metabase on AWS*. Security groups are firewall rules that let us specify what kinds of traffic we want to allow to what resources. Here, we want to create a new security group that will allow our bastion host to accept traffic from the public internet and also connect to our PostgreSQL database in our VPC. Let's learn how to do that.
9. Next to **Assign a Security Group**, click the **Create a new security group** radio button.
10. Next to **Security Group Name**, enter a name for the security group, such as `bastion-host-sg`.
11. Give a description for your security group, such as `Security Group for connecting to Postgres in metabase-vpc`.
12. Now, we can specify the rules for our security group. Notice that one rule is already there by default. Let's break down the components of this rule:

    a) **Type: SSH**: This is declaring that the rule is for the `ssh` protocol. SSH, or secure shell, is a protocol that allows secure command-line execution on remote servers.

    b) **Port range: 22**: This is the standard port for SSH traffic, just like `80` is the standard port for HTTP.

c) **Source: 0.0.0.0/0**: This defines the range of IP addresses that can send traffic to the EC2 instance in CIDR notation. The address `0.0.0.0/0` will cover all addresses.

To summarize, the rule will allow incoming SSH traffic over the standard SSH port `22` from any IP address. This is needed to send commands to the bastion host, so we need not alter it. Optionally, for extra security, you could put a range of IP address that your organization uses into **Source**, which will limit traffic to only those addresses.

13. Click **Add Rule**, as we are going to make one more rule in this security group. For this rule, we want the bastion host to be able to access our PostgreSQL database:

    a) For **Type**, select **PostgreSQL** from the dropdown.

    b) **Protocol** and **Port Range** should read **TCP** and **5432**, respectively. Leave these as they are.

    c) Next, in **Source**, we want to add our PostgreSQL database's security group. To find it, go to the RDS dashboard and select the read replica database. From the **Connectivity and Security** tab, you will see the VPC security group. It should look something like `default (sg-1234abc4321def)`. Enter that in the **Source** field, and it should auto-populate.

14. Click **Review and Launch**.
15. On the next page, if you chose `0.0.0.0/0` in the last step, you will see a warning letting you know that your instance is open to the world. To be clear, that means that anyone can try to connect to your bastion host. If they are able to, they can then try to connect to your database. However, unlike your database password, which is maybe 20 characters long, your bastion host can only be logged into using a 2,048-bit RSA key, which is an adequate amount of security as the amount of computing power needed to guess this key using brute force is astronomical. And then they would still need to guess your database password!
16. Click **Launch**. This will bring up a modal asking you to choose a key pair to connect to your instance. This is the public and private RSA key mentioned previously. You can choose to create a new key pair and give it a name such as `bastion_key_pair`. Download the file; it contains your private key. AWS will add the public key to the host automatically. This is the only time you will have the chance to download it.
17. Finally, click **Launch Instances**.

In a minute or two, your bastion host will be ready to connect to. Let's learn how to connect to it.

Connecting to your bastion host

Let's connect to the bastion host we deployed in the last section. Start from the AWS Management Console:

1. Navigate to the **EC2 dashboard**.
2. From the EC2 dashboard, click **Running Instances**. If you've been following along, you should have at least two instances, at least one for your Metabase environment and another for the newly created bastion host. It should look as in *Figure 4.8*:

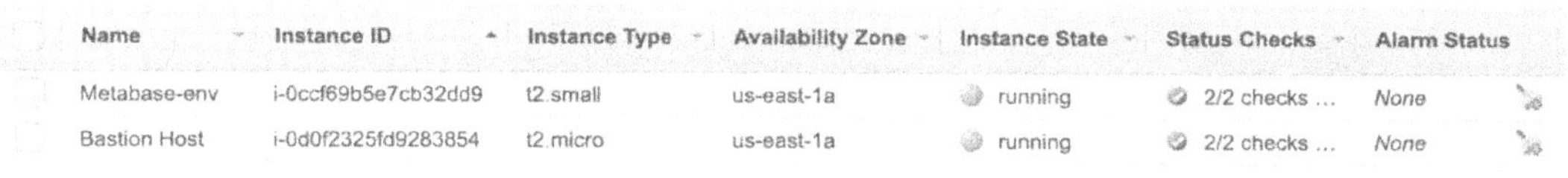

Name	Instance ID	Instance Type	Availability Zone	Instance State	Status Checks	Alarm Status
Metabase-env	i-0ccf69b5e7cb32dd9	t2.small	us-east-1a	running	2/2 checks ...	None
Bastion Host	i-0d0f2325fd9283854	t2.micro	us-east-1a	running	2/2 checks ...	None

Figure 4.8 – A screenshot showing the EC2 dashboard

3. Click the button next to your bastion host to highlight it.
4. The **Connect** button at the top of the page should go from grayed out to solid. Click the **Connect** button.
5. A modal should pop up with instructions on how to connect to your bastion host. Make note of the example given, which should look something like this:

```
ssh -i "bastion_key_pair.pem" ec2-user@ec2-34-224-31-60.
compute-1.amazonaws.com
```

6. Before we run this command from our terminal, we need to alter the file permissions on `bastion_key_pair.pem`, which contains our private key. To do so, first navigate in your terminal to your `Downloads` directory:

```
cd ~/Downloads
```

7. Your `Downloads` directory is not a great place to keep this file, so let's move it somewhere else. I recommend moving it to the `.ssh` directory if you have one. If you do, it would be in your home directory:

```
mv ~/Downloads/bastion_key_pair.pem ~/.ssh/.
```

> **Important Note**
> In Unix-like systems, files and directories that start with a period are referred to as **dotfiles**. These files and directories are hidden in applications and utilities that let you explore your filesystem, such as Finder on macOS and `ls` in Unix and Linux. The `.ssh` directory is an example of a hidden directory.

8. Now, we are going to change the file permissions with the **chmod** command so that you have read access only:

```
chmod 400 ~/.ssh/bastion_key_pair.pem
```

9. Finally, we can connect to our bastion host with the following command, replacing what comes after `ec2-user@` with whatever DNS name AWS gives your host. This will be in the modal in *Step 5*:

```
ssh -i ~/.ssh/bastion_key_pair.pem ec2-user@ec2-34-224-
31-60.compute-1.amazonaws.com
```

10. The first time you connect, you may have to type `yes` when it prompts whether you want to continue connecting. After that, you should see your command prompt change, looking as in *Figure 4.9*:

Amazon Linux 2 AMI
https://aws.amazon.com/amazon-linux-2/
No packages needed for security; 9 packages available
Run "sudo yum update" to apply all updates.
[ec2-user@ip-10-0-0-25 ~]$

Figure 4.9 – Terminal prompt on the bastion host

You are now connected to your bastion host. This host is able to connect to your PostgreSQL database as well. Recall that because we made our database private, we are no longer able to connect to it from our terminal. With the bastion host in place, we can now connect to it again. To do so, we just need to slightly alter the SSH command we used previously to give the proper port forwarding. Let's learn how to do that.

Connecting to a private PostgreSQL database via a bastion host

To connect to our private PostgreSQL database, we need to do what is called **SSH port forwarding**, or **SSH tunneling**. In that, we basically forward a port from our local machine to the bastion host. Practically, what we need to have ready to do this is the following:

- The path to our `pem` file, containing our RSA private key.
- The default port for PostgreSQL, `5432`.
- The host or endpoint for our `dbreplica` PostgreSQL database.
- The user (`ec2-user`) and DNS for our bastion host.

Putting everything together, the command you'll type is as follows:

```
ssh -i <step1> -fN -L <step2>:<step3>:<step2> ec2-user@<step4>
```

For me, it looks like this:

```
ssh -i ~/.ssh/bastion_key_pair.pem \
-fN -L 5432:dbreplica.ci7btk9552i7.us-east-1.rds.amazonaws.
com:5432 \
ec2-user@ec2-34-224-31-60.compute-1.amazonaws.com
```

Here, `-fN` forwards the port in the background, and `-L` specifies the port forwarding. Running this command will not connect you to the bastion host. Instead, it will create an SSH tunnel in the background.

After running the preceding command, you can now connect to your PostgreSQL database with the following command from your local terminal:

```
psql -p 5432 -h localhost -U postgres -d pies
```

This may seem like a lot of work to connect to a database when we were able to easily connect to it at the beginning of the chapter. However, many organizations using best practices will be making their databases private, so having a bastion host is often the only way to connect to these databases.

Now that we've learned how to set up our bastion host and use it to connect to a private database, let's learn how to connect to our database through the bastion host in Metabase.

Connecting to a private database via a bastion host in Metabase

Now, let's use the bastion host to connect to our private database:

1. SSH into your bastion host:

   ```
   ssh -i ~/.ssh/bastion_key_pair.pem ec2-user@<ec2_dns>
   ```

2. Next, we will add a password for `ec2-user`. This will allow us to SSH into the bastion host without the private key. For the next three commands, we need to preface them with `sudo` because they require root access:

   ```
   sudo passwd ec2-user
   ```

3. You will be prompted to enter a password and confirm it. Give a strong password, as this host is your line of defense against attacks to your database.
4. Now, we need to change our `sshd_config` file to allow password authentication, which by default is off. To edit the file, open it with your favorite text editor. `nano` is a good option, but you can also use `vim`:

```
sudo nano /etc/ssh/sshd_config
```

5. Find the line in the file that reads `#PasswordAuthentication yes`. It should be about 60 lines down. The # character, in this case, is used to comment out the line. Remove the symbol and exit the file by typing *Ctrl* + *X*, typing *Y* to save it.
6. Finally, restart the SSH service:

```
sudo service sshd restart
```

You can now SSH into your bastion host with a password as well as your private key. Now, go back to Metabase.

7. Start in the **admin panel** and click **Databases**.
8. Click our **Pies** database to edit the connection parameters.
9. Scroll down to the bottom of the page, where the toggle for **Use an SSH-tunnel for database connections** is. Toggle it on, and a new form will appear.
10. In the **SSH tunnel host** field, add the DNS name of your bastion host.
11. In the **SSH Port** field, enter `22`.
12. In the **SSH tunnel username** field, enter `ec2-user`.
13. Enter the password you created in *Step 3* for the **SSH tunnel password**.
14. Click **Save Changes**.

Metabase is now able to connect to the database via an SSH tunnel through the bastion host. Note that this may slow down performance, so if you are able to connect to your database directly (without the bastion host), you should continue to use that method.

> **Important Note**
> Allowing SSH access to the bastion host via a password is far less secure than with the private key. Restricting the range of IP addresses in your security group that has SSH access to the host is a good way to balance this and keep things secure.

In this section, we learned all the best practices and ways to connect Metabase to a PostgreSQL database. The good news is that everything we just learned will work for other types of databases in RDS, including MySQL, Amazon Aurora, and Microsoft SQL Server. They will just have different default port numbers. In the next section, we'll learn about the other types of databases that can be connected to Metabase, and how connecting them differs from PostgreSQL.

Connecting to other types of databases in Metabase

Let's get to know all the other types of databases we can connect to in Metabase.

Relational databases

Besides PostgreSQL, which we've already covered extensively, the other relational databases you can connect to with Metabase are as follows.

MySQL

To connect to a **MySQL** database, choose MySQL from the list of database types in the **Database** section of the Metabase admin panel. Connecting to MySQL is nearly identical to PostgreSQL. The standard port for MySQL is `3306`.

MariaDB

Although not listed in the database types, you can connect to a **MariaDB** database with Metabase using the MySQL option.

Microsoft SQL Server

To connect to **Microsoft SQL Server**, choose SQL Server from the list of database types in the **Database** section of the Metabase admin panel. Connecting to SQL Server is nearly identical to PostgreSQL. The standard ports are `1433` and `1521`.

Amazon Aurora

Amazon Aurora is a relational database available in RDS. It can be deployed with either MySQL or PostgreSQL compatibility. Depending on which one you deploy it with, use either the MySQL or PostgreSQL connection in Metabase's database types.

NoSQL databases

The main **NoSQL** database you can connect to in Metabase is **MongoDB**. Although MongoDB is quite different from a relational database, connecting to it is very similar. The default port for MongoDB is `27017`.

Analytical databases

As mentioned at the beginning of the chapter, analytical databases have become popular in recent years. These databases are solely for analytics, so there is no need to create read replica versions of them. They tend to be more expensive to use and are scalable for querying large amounts of data (think terabyte scale and beyond).

Because they are more expensive to run, we will not learn how to create them. Rather, we will just cover how to connect to them in Metabase.

Amazon Redshift

Amazon Redshift is one of the most popular analytical databases in use today. It is based on PostgreSQL, and you can even connect to a Redshift database with `psql`. To connect to a Redshift database in Metabase, choose Amazon Redshift from the list of database types in the **Database** section of the Metabase admin panel. The default port for Redshift is `5439`.

Like most resources in AWS, Redshift instances have an hourly price and are not available on the free tier.

Google BigQuery

Google BigQuery is Google's version of Amazon Redshift. One major difference between the two is that with Redshift, you are charged by the hour, while with BigQuery, you are charged by the amount of data you query. Connecting to a BigQuery database is slightly different from the standard way we've learned about in this chapter. Let's learn how to connect to BigQuery:

1. Choose **BigQuery** from the list of database types in the **Database** section of the Metabase admin panel.
2. The project ID and dataset ID will come from your Google Cloud Platform account.
3. Next, right-click on the **Click Here** link to open a new window, allowing you to create a client ID. In the list of **application types**, click the radio button for **Other**.
4. Paste the **client ID** and **secret** into the fields in the form.

5. Next, right-click on the **Click Here** link under **Auth Code** to get the auth code. A tab will open with a success code that you can copy and paste into the field.
6. Click **Save**.

Presto

Presto is a distributed SQL engine for big data. It is most commonly used alongside the **Hadoop Distributed File System** (**HDFS**) to query large amounts of data distributed across commodity hardware. Connecting to a Presto database follows the same conventions as connecting to a PostgreSQL database.

Snowflake

Snowflake is a company that offers a data platform that helps manage an organization's data. Connecting to a Snowflake database is similar to PostgreSQL, although Snowflake has a few additional layers of information to include, such as a **region ID**, a **schema**, and a **role**.

Spark SQL

Spark SQL is an abstraction on top of **Apache Spark**, which is an open source distributed cluster computing framework. Connecting to a Spark SQL database follows the same conventions as connecting to a PostgreSQL database.

Druid

Druid is another analytical database that is specially geared toward metrics and fast aggregations. It is not a relational database, but Metabase's functionality works well on it. Connecting to a Druid database only requires a host and port number.

Other databases and sources

In addition to all the databases we've already covered, you can connect Metabase to **H2** and **SQLite**, which are both local databases, as well as **Google Analytics**. Let's learn about them.

Local databases, such as H2 and SQLite, are great for prototyping and local applications, but because they are local, they stop running once you shut down your computer. They can be used in larger web applications, but are not designed for that. As such, they have narrow use cases in Metabase.

H2

H2 is an open source, Java SQL database. The sample dataset that comes with Metabase is in an H2 database. If you look at the **Databases** tab in the admin panel, you'll see that we already have a connection set up for it. Metabase also uses an H2 database as its application database for local installations, such as the one we did all the way back in *Chapter 1, Overview of Metabase.*

SQLite

SQLite is similar to H2. It's widely used as an application database for locally running applications. In analytics, I've seen SQLite used for local analysis on datasets that are either larger or more complex than, say, a CSV file. Since Metabase doesn't currently support CSV files, SQLite can be used as a workaround.

Google Analytics

Google Analytics is not actually a database, but rather a set of interactive and aggregated reports and dashboards that Google offers for free at `https://analytics.google.com/`. You can use Google Analytics to track various things about a website or application, including key metrics, such as the number of logged-in and logged-out visitors to your product, the number of page views, and the sources of your referral traffic. This is information that normally wouldn't get captured in your application database. I recommend most organizations use Google Analytics or something similar, such as Segment (`https://segment.com/`), to capture this kind of event-based information.

While Google Analytics is not a database, all the aggregated reports it offers can be pulled into Metabase via the Google Analytics API and treated like data tables. Let's learn how to connect Google Analytics to Metabase:

1. Choose **Google Analytics** from the list of database types in the **Database** section of the Metabase admin panel.
2. Give a name to your Google Analytics database – for example, `Google Analytics`.
3. Under **Google Analytics Account ID**, enter the account ID for your Google Analytics account.
4. Under **Client ID**, right-click on the **Click here** link to open a new window, allowing you to create a client ID. In the list of **application types**, click the radio button for **Other**.
5. The **project ID** and **dataset ID** will come from your Google Cloud Platform account.
6. Paste the **client ID** and **secret** into the fields in the form.

7. Next, right-click on the **Click Here** link under **Auth Code** to get the auth code. A tab will open with a success code that you can copy and paste into the field.
8. Click **Save**.

You will now be able to treat Google Analytics as if it were a connected database.

Summary

In this chapter, we learned the best way to connect a database to Metabase. We learned specifically how to create our own PostgreSQL database, fill it with sample data, and connect that database to Metabase. We then covered database best practices and learned how to set up a bastion host to connect to a private database.

In addition to looking deep into PostgreSQL-related examples, we learned about the other types of databases that Metabase can connect to.

In the next chapter, we'll learn how to build a data model and dictionary in Metabase for our newly connected database. This will make our data easy to understand and explore for our less technical users.

5
Building Your Data Model

Metabase has several features that allow you to create helpful layers of **metadata** on top of your database to make it more user-friendly to work with. Metadata is data about data. If you have ever struggled with ugly or oddly formatted fields in a database, or been perplexed by a certain data type, you know this pain point. You can imagine that these pain points are all the worse for the less technical users in your organization. By investing a little time upfront to properly define your columns, data types, table relationships, descriptions, and permissions, you can greatly improve comprehension and usability for others in your organization.

In addition to adding metadata to enhance your database, Metabase also allows you to hide parts of your data that are either irrelevant or highly sensitive. This will all be covered in this chapter.

Specifically, in this chapter, we're going to cover the following main topics:

- Editing your data model
- Specifying foreign key relationships
- Defining segments and metrics
- Building your data dictionary
- Applying data permissions

Technical requirements

For those getting tired of AWS, I have good news: this chapter has no AWS requirements. It is fully focused on Metabase. You will need a running instance of Metabase with a connection to the `pies` database we learned about in *Chapter 4, Connecting to Databases*. The link to the data for that database is `https://github.com/PacktPublishing/Metabase-Up-and-Running/blob/master/data/create_pies_db.sql`.

Editing your data model

In *Chapter 4, Connecting to Databases*, we created a database with data about our fictional business and connected it to Metabase. If you followed along with everything in *Chapter 4, Connecting to Databases*, you should have two databases connected to Metabase, just like in *Figure 5.1*:

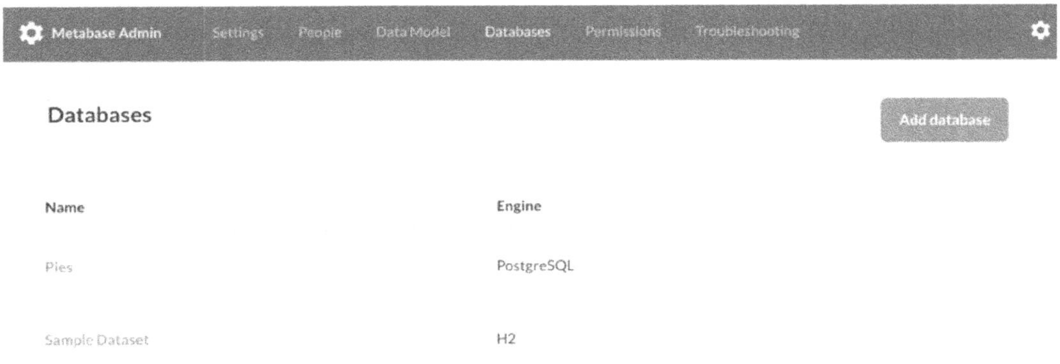

Figure 5.1 – The two databases connected to Metabase

In this section, we will learn how to customize our database's data model. Before we do that, it might be helpful to take a quick tour of our database in Metabase so that we gain some familiarity with it. Let's get started.

Touring the Pies database in Metabase

In *Chapter 4, Connecting to Databases*, we only spent a little time exploring the actual data in our `Pies` database. Before we go ahead and refine our data model, let's get to know the tables and contents of this database. To get started, have Metabase open:

1. Click **Browse Data** on the top blue bar.
2. Select the **Pies** database.

You'll see that the database has just four tables:

- **Menu**
- **Orders**
- **Reviews**
- **Users**

These are typical tables for an e-commerce business. Note that Metabase has capitalized these table names (in our PostgreSQL database, they are in all lowercase). Capitalizing table names is one of the many transformations Metabase does automatically to make the contents of our database more user-friendly. Let's explore these tables one by one, starting with the **Menu** table.

The Menu table

To explore the **Menu** table, simply click it. You'll be taken to a screen with the entire **Menu** table printed out, just like in *Figure 5.2*:

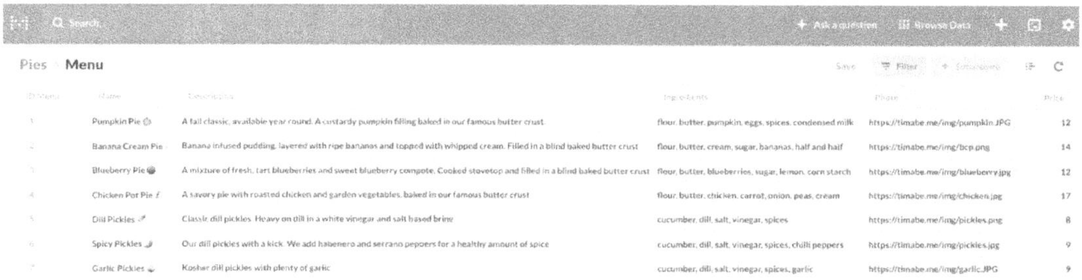

Figure 5.2 – The Menu table in our database

The **Menu** table holds the items that are available for sale, and some information about them, such as a description, ingredients, and price. Were we to connect to our database in `psql` and describe the **Menu** table using `\d menu`, we'd see the exact same columns:

```
pies=> \d menu
Table "public.menu"
Column       |        Type          | Collation | Nullable | Default
-------------+--------------------+-----------+----------+-----
----
 id_menu     | integer            |           | not null |
 name        | character varying  |           |          |
 price       | double precision   |           |          |
 ingredients | text               |           |          |
 description | character varying  |           |          |
 photo       | character varying  |           |          |
Indexes:
"menu_pkey" PRIMARY KEY, btree (id_menu)
```

You can pick whatever column orderings you like by clicking the **Settings** gear icon at the bottom of the page. Later in this chapter, we'll learn how to get Metabase to automatically reorder the columns in a smart way. Also, note that Metabase has taken our **snake_case** column names and given them human-readable names – for example, **id_menu** appears as **ID Menu**.

Metabase has also highlighted the entries in the **ID Menu** column, indicating that they are clickable. Let's try clicking the first ID, for **Pumpkin Pie**. Doing this will bring up a detailed record of the **Pumpkin Pie** entry, as shown in *Figure 5.3*:

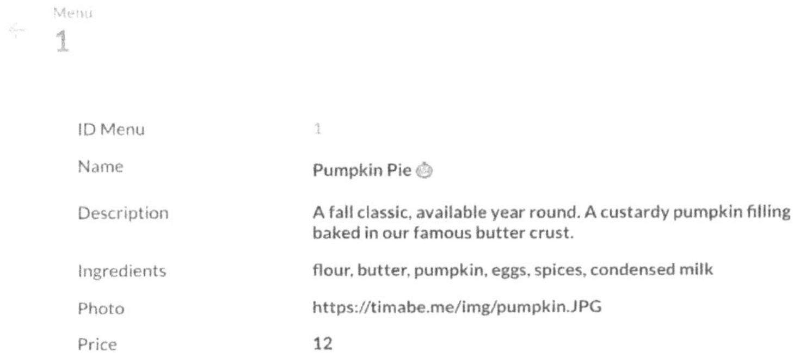

Figure 5.3 – A detailed record of our database's Pumpkin Pie Menu entry

Right off the bat, we can see that exploring our data in Metabase is more user-friendly than exploring it directly from the database. The organization of columns, the readability, and the ability to click on records to drill deeper into them are all helpful. Let's continue and explore the **Orders** table.

The Orders table

To explore the **Orders** table, click **Browse Data** | **Pies** | **Orders**.

Unlike the **Menu** table, we cannot see this entire table on one screen. Depending on your screen size, you will be able to see one to two dozen rows of this table, and Metabase allows you to scroll down to see the first 2,000 by default. Let's click the first **ID Order** field to understand what sort of data we capture for each order. You can see the order description in *Figure 5.4*:

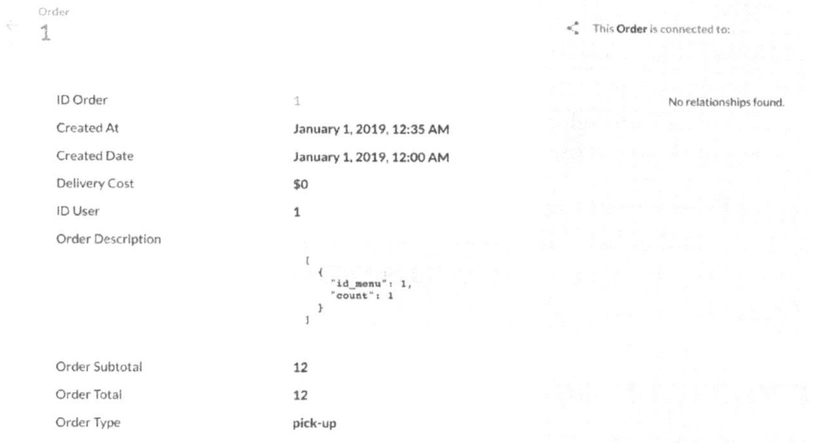

Figure 5.4 – Detailed description of an order in our database

Some of the transformations Metabase has already done are recognizing the delivery cost as a dollar value and representing a date, which appears in our database as `2019-01-01` for **January 1, 2019, 12:00 AM**. However, Metabase has not recognized **Order Subtotal** or **Order Total** as dollar values. That's okay because we'll learn how to customize the format of all our columns later in the chapter. Next, let's explore what the **Reviews** table has.

The Reviews table

Just like most other e-commerce businesses, our fictional business allows products to be reviewed on a 5-star scale. Let's have a look at the contents of our **Reviews** table. Click **Browse Data | Pies | Reviews**.

Go ahead and click on the first **ID Review** item to see the contents of the record. It should look exactly as in *Figure 5.5*:

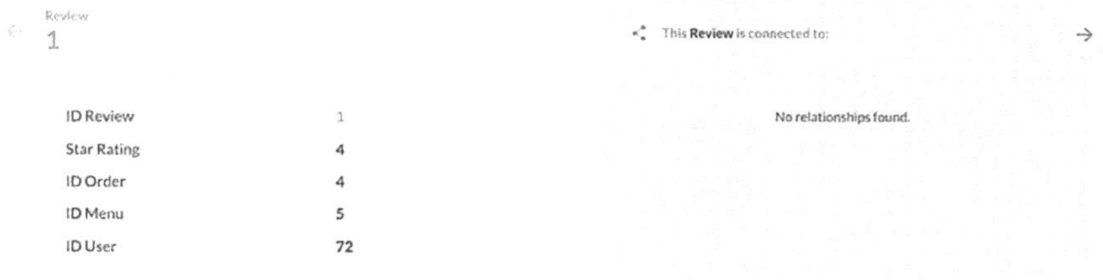

Figure 5.5 – A detailed record of a review in the Reviews table

Aside from the star rating and the ID for the review, everything else is an ID from another table (**Menu**, **Order**, and **User**). Finally, let's have a brief look at our **Users** table.

The Users table

To explore the **Users** table, click **Browse Data** | **Pies** | **Users**. Select the first User ID. We can see that Metabase has automatically recognized the **Email** column as an email address, and the **Lat** and **Lon** fields as latitude and longitude coordinates. You may recognize the name of the user, too.

We've now taken a brief tour of the tables in our database and learned what sort of useful data transformations and enhancements Metabase has already done by adding metadata. In the next section, we'll learn how we can add our own metadata in the **Data Model** section of the Admin Panel.

Editing the data model's metadata

As mentioned at the beginning of the chapter, adding metadata to our tables is beneficial to anyone using Metabase as it adds clarity around our data model. To edit your data model's metadata, do the following:

1. Enter the Admin Panel and click **Data Model** on the top purple bar.
2. **Current Database** should be showing **Pies**, but if it is showing **Sample Dataset**, just change it to **Pies** in the dropdown.
3. Click **Menu** to start with the **Menu** table.

You should see a screen as in *Figure 5.6*. I've added some numbers to point out specific areas we will address:

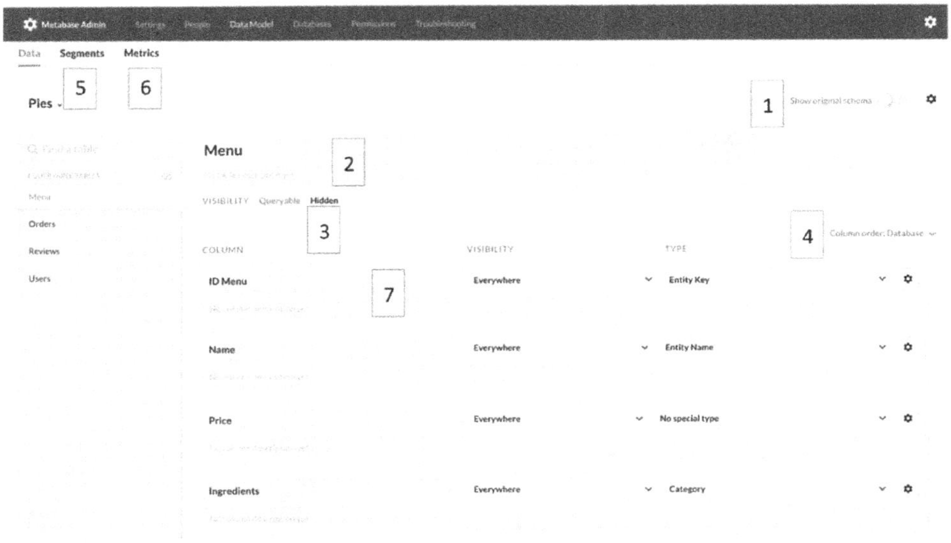

Figure 5.6 – The data model for our Menu table

Following along with the number labels in *Figure 5.6*, let's learn what each section does:

1. **Show original schema**: Toggling this on will show the schema of the **Menu** table exactly as it appears in our database, just as if we executed a `DESCRIBE` or `\d` command. Give it a try.
2. **Table description**: We can write a helpful description of our **Menu** table here, to make it clear to users that this table holds all the items we have for sale with information about ingredients and prices. In this section, write `Contains all items for sale at Pickles and Pies as well as descriptions, ingredients, and prices.`
3. **Visibility**: Some tables in an application database contain technical data that won't ever be useful for analytics. An example would be a table with information about schema migrations. Metabase allows you to easily hide these tables by changing **Visibility** to **Hidden**. With this table, it should be clear that we want to keep it **Queryable**.
4. **Column order**: Clicking this gives us three other options for how our columns should be ordered. You can choose to have them in the same order as **Database**, or arrange them in **Alphabetical** order, a **Custom** order, or a **Smart** order – where Metabase tries to guess the best ordering for you! Let's pick **Smart** order.
5. **Segments**: A segment is a named set of commonly used filters for a table. We will cover **Segments** thoroughly later in this chapter.
6. **Metrics**: A metric is an alias for an aggregated numeric column with an optional filter and grouping. We will cover **Metrics** thoroughly later in this chapter.
7. **Columns**: These are the columns in the **Menu** table. We already saw them in *Figure 5.2* and *Figure 5.3*. In this section, though, we can add more useful metadata to our columns.

Now, let's learn what we can do to enhance the metadata of the columns in our table.

Enhancing column metadata

Still focusing on the **Menu** table, let's see how Metabase has chosen to represent the columns. I've reproduced it in *Figure 5.7*. We can see that for each column in the table, there are four fields:

Figure 5.7 – The options to edit our columns' metadata in the Menu table

Let's understand what each of these sections in *Figure 5.7* mean:

- **Column**: This is simply the name of the column in the table, although by default, Metabase has transformed it from **snake_case** to something more friendly. A column such as `my_column` will be transformed to `My Column`. In Metabase, this transformation is called **Friendly Table and Field Names**. To turn this off, go to **Settings | General | Friendly Table and Field Names**.
- **Visibility**: Earlier, we learned that you can hide entire tables in Metabase. You can also do this with individual columns. This can be helpful if you have a column containing information that you want to keep secure, perhaps one containing passwords or credit card numbers. To exclude a column from a table, change the **Visibility** option to **Do not include**. There is a third option called **Only in detail views**, which will only show the column contents in views of a single record, as in *Figure 5.3*, but hide it otherwise.

- **Type**: This is the data type of the column. If you come from a background in databases, you are probably familiar with the standard data types: `int`, `varchar`, `float`, `date`, and so on. Metabase has a far richer set of data types than a standard database and will try to guess the right column types for each column. Note that Metabase has recognized **ID Menu** as the **entity key**, or **primary key**, in our table. It has also inferred that the **Name** column is the name of each entity.
- **Column description**: Here, you can write out a good description of your column so that users in your organization can better understand what it is to be used for. Some columns are more self-explanatory than others, but I think it's a good idea to err on the side of being overly pedantic.

Now that we understand what these fields are for, let's edit our schema appropriately. You have some freedom here, especially on the column descriptions. *Figure 5.8* shows one recommended version. Aside from adding descriptions, I've left most of the values as is:

Figure 5.8 – An example of properly specified column metadata for the Menu table

> **Important Note**
>
> I've given default table and column descriptions to the other three tables in our database at the Postgres level, so you only need to fill out the values for the **Menu** table.

Note, in *Figure 5.8*, how I've changed the visibility of the **Description** column so that it will only show up in detail views. This is because it's a text-heavy column that I don't need to see rendered in table views, where it might not fit nicely. I've also changed **TYPE** for **Ingredients** and **Photo** to be **No special type**, and the **Price** column to have a type of **Price** as well. Changing its type to **Price** allows you to specify the currency of your choice as well.

By adding column types and descriptions and setting visibility options, we are able to make our table look friendlier and more intuitive. This will prove to be beneficial to you and other users of Metabase when it comes to exploring the data. It turns out that we can go even further, by telling Metabase how we want the fields in our columns to look, and how we expect to interact with them. Let's learn how.

Editing a column's field settings

Notice the gear icon next to each of the columns. Clicking the gear opens the column's **field settings** and allows you to enhance the metadata for your columns even further. Let's look at two examples, starting with the **Ingredients** column:

1. Click the gear corresponding to the **Ingredients** column.
2. Scroll down to **Filtering** on this field section.
3. Change the option to **Search box**. This will allow you and your users to filter the **Menu** table based on items that contain certain ingredients.
4. Next, click the gear icon corresponding to the **Photos** column.
5. If you haven't done so already, change **Field Type** to **No Special Type**. You may have already done this in the last section when we set up our column data types.
6. From the left rail, click **Formatting**.
7. In the **View as link or image** section, choose **Image** from the dropdown.

Alright, now let's go back and view our table to see what sort of changes took place. Leave the Admin Panel and click **Browse Data | Pies | Menu**. You should see something just as in *Figure 5.9*:

Pies › Menu

ID Menu	Name	Ingredients	Photo	Price ($)
1	Pumpkin Pie	flour, butter, pumpkin, eggs, spices, condensed milk		12.00
2	Banana Cream Pie	flour, butter, cream, sugar, bananas, half and half		14.00
3	Blueberry Pie	flour, butter, blueberries, sugar, lemon, corn starch		12.00
4	Chicken Pot Pie	flour, butter, chicken, carrot, onion, peas, cream		17.00
5	Dill Pickles	cucumber, dill, salt, vinegar, spices		8.00
6	Spicy Pickles	cucumber, dill, salt, vinegar, spices, chilli peppers		9.00
7	Garlic Pickles	cucumber, dill, salt, vinegar, spices, garlic		9.00

Figure 5.9 – The Menu table after editing its metadata

You will notice the following:

- The description has been hidden but is viewable when you click on an ID.
- There are images of our menu items in the **Photo** column, rather than just links.
- The **Price** column is properly formatted for USD.

This is a far more user-friendly view of our table than what we had seen originally in *Figure 5.2*. It feels like we are actually looking at a menu, not just a table of data. While it might not be a huge improvement to a seasoned data analyst's user experience, you can bet that the data consumers that we learned about in *Chapter 1*, *Overview of Metabase*, will feel far more comfortable with this view.

Let's drill down further into this table and see the effect of editing our **Ingredients** column's field settings:

1. Click the **Ingredients** column header.
2. Select the **Filter** option.
3. Change the dropdown to **Contains**.
4. In the open text box, type `flour`.

You will see a filtered version of our menu, with just the menu items that have **flour** in their ingredients. The filter is rendered in purple at the top of the table, with an **X** that you can click to remove it.

You can already see that investing time to add metadata and specify column field settings pays off in the long run by making tables easier to view, comprehend, and filter. Now that we've seen how to take these actions on a single table, next we'll look at how we can tell Metabase how tables relate to one another.

Specifying foreign key relationships

Recall in *Chapter 4, Connecting to Databases*, how we learned that the relational part of a relational database comes from how records in one table relate to other records. One of the benefits of this is to save space. To see an example of this, let's have another look at our **Reviews** table, or simply turn back to *Figure 5.5*. Notice that aside from the review ID and star rating, all other columns in our **Reviews** table relate to other tables:

- The **ID Order** column relates to **ID Order** in the **Orders** table.
- The **ID Menu** column relates to **ID Menu** in the **Menu** table.
- The **ID User** column relates to **ID User** in the **Users** table.

Recall that when we first viewed our metadata for the **Menu** table, we saw that Metabase had determined that **ID Menu** was an **Entity** (or **Primary**) key. The same is true for **ID Order** in the **Orders** table and **ID User** in the **Users** table – they are all **Entity** keys. When we see an **Entity** key in a different table, as we do here in the **Reviews** table, we call it a **foreign key**. For example, in the first record in our **Reviews** table, we see that **ID User** is `72`. That means that if we wanted to know more information about the user who made this review, we could find out by looking up user `72` in our **User** table. Normally, in software applications and data analysis, this is done using a **SQL JOIN**, joining the `id_user` foreign key in the **Reviews** table to the `id_user` entity key in the **Users** table. In Metabase, we can accomplish the same thing without any SQL, simply by specifying the foreign key relationships in the data model. Let's learn how:

1. Open the **Data Model** tab in the **Admin** panel.
2. Select the **Reviews** table.

   Now, we will explicitly specify the foreign key relationships, starting with **ID Menu**:

3. For **ID Menu**, select **Foreign Key** as the type from the dropdown menu.
4. An additional dropdown menu will appear below. Clicking it will reveal the four possible primary keys that the foreign key can relate to.
5. Select **Menu | ID Menu** from the dropdown.
6. Now do the same for the **ID Order** and **ID User** columns, linking them to the **Order** and **User** tables, respectively.

By doing this, Metabase now understands that when we see **ID User** `72` in our **Review** table, we are referring to **ID User** `72` in our **Users** table. Let's see it in action. Go back to the **Reviews** table view by exiting the **Admin Panel** and clicking **Browse Data | Pies | Reviews**. Again, let's click on the first review ID.

Unlike in *Figure 5.5*, now all the foreign keys are clickable. If we click on **ID User 72**, we are taken to the detailed record of that user in the **Users** table. Furthermore, now the detailed view shows that this user is connected to three reviews. If we click on that, we are taken back to the **Reviews** table, where we can see that in addition to being the first reviewer, this user also made review numbers `454` and `19172`.

Having the ability to click on a foreign key value in a table and be taken to its primary record is pretty useful, and certainly not something you can do with most database software. However, there is even more that we can do here. In the next section, we'll learn how we can customize the information we see for a foreign key.

Editing foreign key field settings

Previously, we learned how to edit the field settings for columns in our **Menu** table. There are some special actions we can do when we edit field settings specifically for foreign keys. Let's learn about them:

1. In a new tab, open the **Admin Panel** and click **Data Model**.
2. Choose the **Reviews** table.
3. Click the gear icon on the **ID Menu** row.
4. Scroll down to **Display Values**.

   This field, **Display Values**, allows us to specify what kind of value from the **Menu** table we want to see when a menu ID is referenced in our **Reviews** table. The default is to use the original value, which is simply the integer value in our **Menu** table. However, it might be more informative to use the actual name of the **Menu** item. People in our organization might have a hard time remembering that ID `1` is `Pumpkin Pie` while ID `2` is `Banana Cream Pie`. It might be easier if we just used the actual menu item names instead of the integer value, so let's do that.
5. Change the value in **Display Values** from **Use original value** to **Use foreign key**.
6. Now, select the value you want from the **Menu** table. In our case, it will be **Name**.

Now, go back to the tab you had open where you were browsing the **Reviews** table and refresh the page. You'll see that the **ID Menu** column in the **Reviews** table has had the integer values replaced with the much more informative **Name** column.

We can now make these types of enhancements for the other foreign keys in our **Reviews** table. Here are my recommendations:

- For **ID Order**, I recommend sticking with the integer value. The reason is that reviews are for specific menu items, not overall orders, which may contain multiple menu items.
- For **ID User**, I recommend using **Name** in the **Users** table. This just makes the view more user-friendly.

After all of this, your **Reviews** table should look just as in *Figure 5.10*:

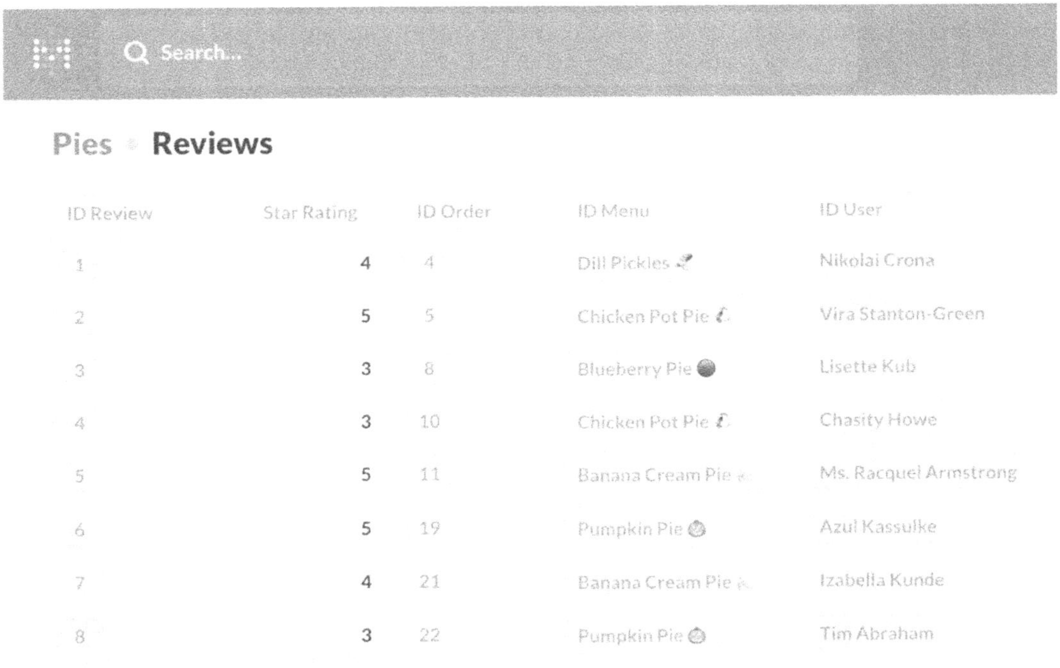
Search...
Pies
Reviews
ID Review
Star Rating
ID Order
ID Menu
ID User
1 4 4 Dill Pickles Nikolai Crona
2 5 5 Chicken Pot Pie Vira Stanton-Green
3 3 8 Blueberry Pie Lisette Kub
4 3 10 Chicken Pot Pie Chasity Howe
5 5 11 Banana Cream Pie Ms. Racquel Armstrong
6 5 19 Pumpkin Pie Azul Kassulke
7 4 21 Banana Cream Pie Izabella Kunde
8 3 22 Pumpkin Pie Tim Abraham

Figure 5.10 – We've edited our foreign keys for ID Menu and ID User to show the entity names instead

Now that we've learned all the powerful ways to edit metadata and connect our tables' foreign keys, let's move on and learn about more of Metabase's powerful admin features.

Defining segments and metrics

In the last section, we learned how to edit the metadata for our columns and define our foreign key relationships. The main purpose of all of that work was to make for an easier and more intuitive user experience for people less technical than us. In this section, we'll expand on that, using two useful features that Metabase offers: **segments** and **metrics**. Let's learn about segments first.

Defining segments

Simply put, a segment in Metabase is a named **filter** on a table. They can be quite powerful, though, as often, a name is much easier to remember than the filtering logic behind it. Let's explain this with an example.

Consider our fictional business, Pickles and Pies. Internally, we may have teams that only focus on the pickle part of the business, and other teams that handle the pie side of things. When looking up stats about sales, review ratings, and repeat orders, people in our organization may only care about the stats for either pickles or pies, but not both.

Metabase makes it easy to filter tables, and we've already seen a little of that in this chapter. For example, if we wanted to filter our **Reviews** table to only show pickles, we could do the following:

1. Click **Browse Data | Pies | Reviews**.
2. In the upper right-hand corner, click the purple **Filter** button.
3. Scroll down to **ID Menu** and click **Name**.
4. From here, you can click on the three pickle menu items.
5. Finish by clicking **Add Filter**.

You'll now see a filtered version of your table that only has reviews of the three pickle options on the menu. While this is easy, it may be a bit tedious to do this every time – especially if this is going to be a common filter used by the pickle team. This is where segments are useful. Let's learn how to make one to create the same filtering logic:

1. Go to the Admin Panel and click **Data Model**.
2. At the top of the screen, below the purple bar, click the **Segments** tab.

3. Click the blue **New segment** button. This will take you to the **Create Your Segment** page. A segment is a set of filters and a name and description that describes what the filters do.
4. Click the + button under **Filtered By**. Remember that we want to filter by **Menu Name**. **Menu Name** is linked to this table by the **ID Menu** foreign key. Click **ID Menu** to expand its dropdown and click **Name**. You should see the seven names of menu items. Do not click **ID Menu** under the **Review** table dropdown, since these IDs are only the integer values.
5. Click the three pickle items: **Dill Pickles**, **Garlic Pickles**, and **Spicy Pickles**.
6. Click **Add Filter**.
7. Now, let's give our segment a good name and description that will make sense to our users. For **Name**, I've chosen `Reviews of Pickle Products` and for **Description** I've chosen `This segment only returns reviews for dill, garlic, and spicy pickles.`
8. Click **Save Changes**.

Now, the new segment appears in the **Segment** section. Take note of the three dots, or ellipsis, in this row under **Actions**. Let's learn what these actions are, starting with **Edit Segment**.

Editing a segment

Choosing **Edit Segment** from the **Actions** dropdown will allow you to change the filtering logic, the name, and the description of your segment. It's quite possible that in the future, our business will add new kinds of pickles – perhaps a fermented half-sour pickle. When that happens, we will want to include it in our segment. Adding it is as simple as editing the **Filtered By** section. However, before you save the changes, Metabase asks for a short description of what you changed. This is helpful for other **Admins**, as they can view the version history of the segment to understand its evolution.

Since we haven't introduced any new pickle products yet, but want to be well prepared for pickle expansion, let's edit this filter and add a general filter that simply searches for the string `pickle` in the menu name. Generally, I don't recommend creating filters based on string matching as it can give a false sense of security. Imagine we introduce a new product and name it `Sour Dills`; it would not be captured by this filter and we would have a false negative. We also might do something creative at some point and have the pie team introduce a pie with pickled ingredients and `pickle` in the name. This would produce a false positive in our segment. However, for the tutorial's sake, this is fine. Let's edit our filter:

1. Click the + sign in the **Filtered By** section.
2. Again, pick **ID Menu | Name**.
3. In the filter modal, find the dropdown in the upper right-hand corner. The default value will be **Is**, which indicates that the filter will look for exact matches.
4. Change the dropdown to **Contains**, which indicates that the filter will look for string matches.
5. In the text box, type `pickle`. Keep the case-sensitive box unchecked, since we want to capture any occurrence of the word regardless of capitalization.
6. Click **Add Filter**.
7. Remove the first filter we created (based on exact matches) by clicking the **x** next to it. Multiple filters in segments use the **AND** Boolean operator, and there is currently no option to use **OR** instead. The filter based on exact matches will restrict any menu items that aren't in its list, regardless of whether they have the word `pickle`.
8. The name of our segment is fine, but the description is no longer true. Change it to something that captures the filter logic – for example, `This segment only returns reviews menu items with the word "pickle" in them (not case sensitive)`.
9. In the **Reason for Changes** box, write a short description of the change – for example, `Replacing the list of exact menu names in favor of a catch-all method based on string matching of the word "pickle"`.
10. Click **Save Changes** to update the segment.

As I mentioned, I don't recommend using string matching for segments. So, now that we've learned how to edit our segment, let's learn how to view its revision history and revert it.

Viewing a segment's revision history

The second option in the **Actions** dropdown in the **Segments** section is **Revision History**. Clicking it will show you all the version history of your segment. Let's go ahead and click it. Provided you have been following along, you should see something exactly as in *Figure 5.11*:

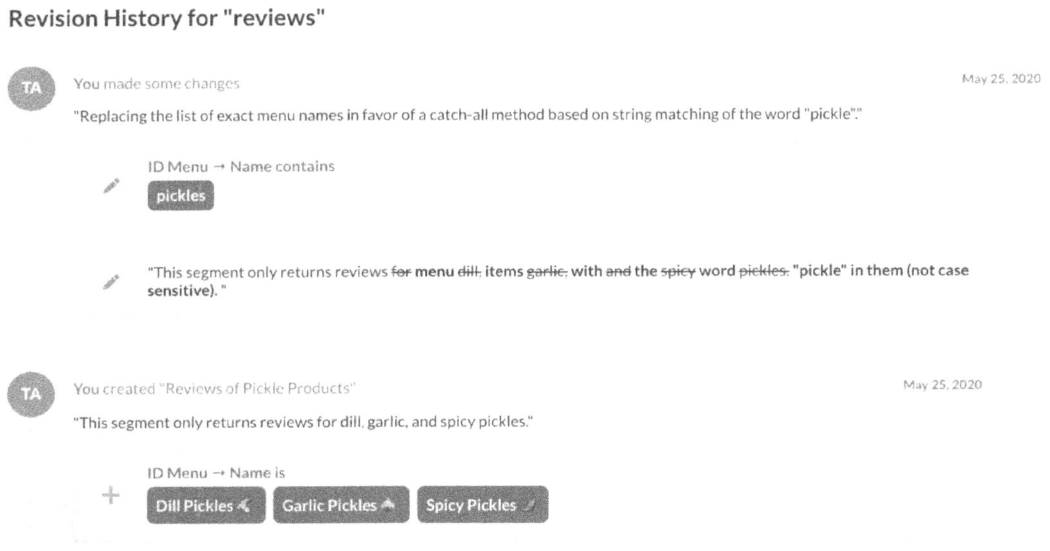

Revision History for "reviews"
TA
You made some changes
May 25, 2020
"Replacing the list of exact menu names in favor of a catch-all method based on string matching of the word "pickle"."
ID Menu → Name contains
pickles
"This segment only returns reviews for menu dill, items garlic, with and the spicy word pickles. "pickle" in them (not case sensitive). "
TA
You created "Reviews of Pickle Products"
May 25, 2020
"This segment only returns reviews for dill, garlic, and spicy pickles."
ID Menu → Name is
Dill Pickles
Garlic Pickles
Spicy Pickles

Figure 5.11 – Our segment's revision history

The main value of this page is to see how other admins have changed a segment's definition over time. Since segments live under the Admin Panel, only **admins** can create and edit them. However, if we want to revert our changes, this page is a good way to put the pieces back together. We can learn what our original filter and description looked like, and go back through the **Edit Segment** flow to have it match up again.

The final option in the **Actions** dropdown is **Retire Segment**. This is for when we want to get rid of a segment altogether. Let's see how to do that.

Retiring a segment

Sometimes, a segment will become obsolete. Imagine we decide that our menu is going to only have pickles going forward. We wouldn't need this segment anymore. In this scenario, we would want to delete our segment. Metabase favors the word `retire` over `delete`. A retired segment will still work on **Saved Questions**, but the option to use them in new **Saved Questions** will go away. We will learn more about **Saved Questions** in *Chapter 6, Creating Questions.*

If you decide to retire a segment, Metabase will ask you to write a brief explanation as to why you are removing it.

Now that we've learned how to create, edit, and retire a segment, let's learn how to apply them.

Using a segment

To apply our newly created segment, recall that the table we created, it was for the **Reviews** table:

1. Click **Browse Data | Pies | Reviews**.
2. Click the purple **Filter** button in the upper right-hand corner.
3. You will see your new segment, **Reviews of Pickle Products**, called out with a star symbol. Click it.

The table will immediately apply the segment, and filter for only reviews of pickles.

In summary, creating segments requires a bit more upfront work than just manually filtering the table, but this upfront work is often worth it if the filter is going to be a commonly applied one. This is especially true if the consumers of the filtered data tend to be less data literate, or if the filtering logic is complex.

Now that we've covered segments, let's learn about metrics.

Creating metrics

Like segments, which are names for commonly used filters, metrics are names for commonly aggregated numbers. I like to think of them as user-friendly aliases for certain numerical columns. For example, our **Orders** table has a column called **Order Total**, which stores the price paid for a given order. Is **Order Total** the same thing as revenue? As power users, we know that they are, but regular consumers in our organization may not. That's why it is helpful to explicitly call it out as **revenue** in a metric.

There are three components to a metric, although only one is required. The three components are as follows:

- **Filters** (optional): If there are records in your database that for any reason you need to filter out, you would add them. Otherwise, you just leave this blank.
- **View** (required): **View** is the column that contains your metric and the aggregation associated with it. Counting, adding, taking the average, or finding the maximum are all examples of aggregations. You can think of them as functions that take one or more numbers and reduce them to a single statistic.
- **Group By** (optional): If your metric is commonly grouped by a dimension in your database, you would add it here. We will learn more about **Group By** in *Chapter 6, Creating Questions*. Generally, I would avoid adding **Group By** for a metric, since a metric can have **Group By** applied to it after it has been created.

An example might help us understand these components better. Let's create our **Revenue** metric. Remember, **Revenue** should represent the sum of **Order Total.** Do we need to filter any orders out? Actually, we do. It turns out that the orders associated with **ID User** `1` were not actually paid for, or in some cases were test orders. While normally we wouldn't care about leaving these orders in our reports, our accounting team has told us that they need exact revenue numbers and would prefer to filter these out:

1. From the Admin Panel, click **Data Model**.
2. At the top of the screen, below the purple bar, click the **Metrics** tab.
3. Click the blue **New metric** button. This will take you to the **Create Your metric** page.
4. Under **Select a table**, click the **Orders** table.
5. Under the **Filtered by** section, click the + button to add a filter.
6. Select **ID User**.
7. In the modal, change the value in the dropdown from **Equal to** to **Not equal to**.
8. In the text box, type `1`. This is the user ID we want to filter out.
9. Under **View**, click the green text. Change it from **Count of rows** to **Sum of**. Choose **Order Total** as the value to be summed.
10. Leave the **Grouped By** section blank.
11. Give a name to your metric – for example, `Order Revenue`.

12. Give a description. Here, it's good to be as detailed as possible. A good description might be `The sum of the price of menu items ordered, plus delivery cost. Test and employee orders are removed. This metric is safe for accounting to use.`
13. Click **Save Changes**.

We now have a metric called **Order Revenue** associated with our **Orders** table that our accounting team, among others, can use.

Editing, viewing the version history, and retiring metrics all work exactly the same ways as they do with segments. Now, let's see how to view our metric.

Viewing a metric

To view our metric, we'll want to use our **Orders** table. Let's open it up, by exiting the **Admin Panel** and clicking **Browse Data | Pies | Orders**:

1. Click the green **Summarize** button.
2. The default option will be **Count**. Click that and find the new metric we just created, **Order Revenue**. Click it.
3. The table will be replaced by the metric, showing our total order revenue is `2,801,178`, as in *Figure 5.12*. Not too bad, right?

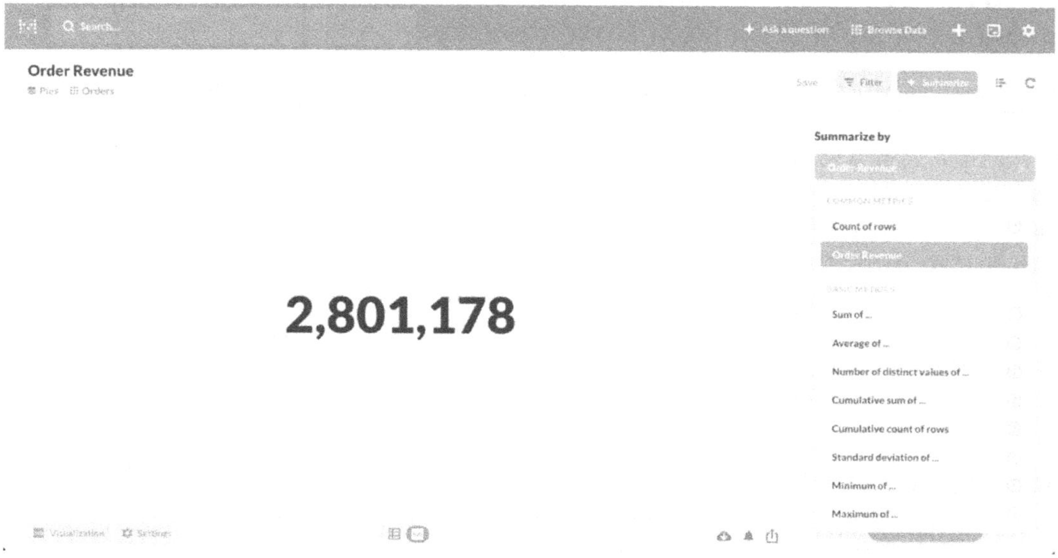

Figure 5.12 – Our order revenue metric

Note that **Order Revenue** is not rendered as a dollar value. This is because we have not yet edited the metadata. We only edited the metadata for the **Menu** table. If you like, you can go back and edit the metadata for the **Orders**, **Reviews**, and **Users** table, including calling out the foreign key relationships.

All of this upfront work we've done on our tables is like preparing a plot of land for a garden. Sure, we could plant our flowers and vegetables anywhere, but they will thrive and produce better yields if we weed our plot and add compost before planting. In the end, it will be worth it.

Now that we know how to edit our metadata, as well as make metrics and segments, we have built a strong foundation for our data model. You may be wondering how our users, especially those without admin access, can see all this rich metadata we've enhanced our database with. That's exactly what we'll be covering in the next section, when we learn about a feature in Metabase called the **data reference**.

Building your data dictionary

To discover all the metadata, table descriptions, and column descriptions we've added, Metabase uses a feature called the **data reference**. In addition to showing most of the metadata we've added, the data dictionary has room to enrich user comprehension about our database, tables, segments, and metrics even more. The idea behind the data reference is that if a new user creates a Metabase account but has no context about what any of the databases or tables are, they should be able to easily look up key information to help them get started.

Our `Pies` database is relatively easy to understand, but you can imagine how this is an exception rather than the rule. Organizations store all kinds of data, often in strange ways. For example, I once worked at a company that stored all of its most important analytical data in a database called `temp`. They had a difficult time explaining to new hires that the `temp` database was the one with the actual important data in it. Many companies today prefer to store daily snapshots of some of their production tables as **dimension** tables in their analytics databases. Looking up a particular ID in these databases will often kick off expensive full-table scans and return the entire historical snapshot. This is all to say that databases and tables often have nuances that end users need to know about. The data reference is where we make those nuances explicit – let's learn how to put it into practice.

Viewing and editing the data reference for a database

To find the data reference, click **Browse Data**. In the upper right-hand corner, there is a book icon and text reading **Learn about our data**; this takes you to the data reference, so go ahead and click it.

Inside the data reference, you'll notice that it already has entries for **Metrics**, **Segments**, and **Our Data**. Clicking through each of these, you'll see the metric and segment we created, as well as our databases (`Pies` and `Sample Dataset`).

Let's drill deeper and look at what exactly lives in the data dictionary for our `Pies` database:

1. From the **Data Reference** menu, click **Our Data**.
2. Select the **Pies** database from the list.

This brings up the **Pies** database's entry in the data reference. Although we've already given descriptions to all our tables and columns, we don't have any descriptions at the database level, so the **Description** field here is blank. Additionally, there are two extra blank fields that, if we want, we can fill in to add more context about our database. Unlike **Description**, which can be populated at the database level, these fields are unique to Metabase. They are as follows:

- **Why is this database interesting**
- **Things to be aware of about this database**

These fields are especially relevant if you plan on having multiple databases connected to your Metabase. Let's fill them out:

1. For **Description**, write `A read replica of our production application database.`
2. For the **Why is this database interesting** field, write `This database contains tables containing orders, users, review, and the menu of items we sell.`
3. For **Things to be aware of about this database**, it might be good to tell our users that `Because this is a Read Replica database, you may query it at will without worrying about the performance of our actual business' website.`
4. Click **Save**.

Now, when your users view the data reference for the `Pies` database, they will see something as in *Figure 5.13*:

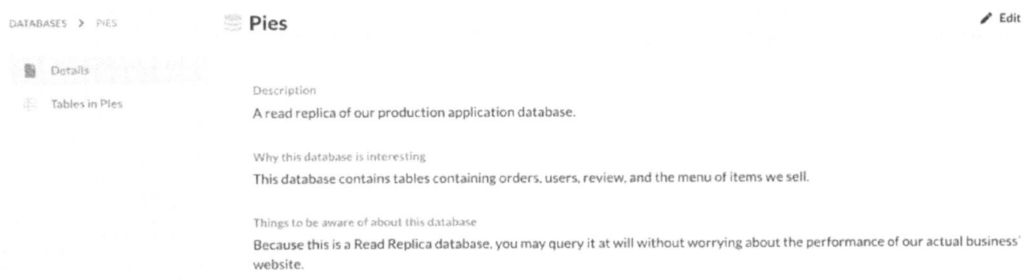

Figure 5.13 – Updated data dictionary for our Pies database

Now that we've filled out the data reference for our database, we can move on to the tables.

Viewing and editing the data reference for tables

You can also add information to your data reference at the database table level. To view the data reference for a table, assuming you are on the page depicted in *Figure 5.13*, look to the menu on the left rail. Click **Tables in Pies**.

You will see the four tables in our `Pies` database, along with their descriptions. Click on one of them, perhaps the **Menu** table since that is the table we've worked with most in this chapter.

The data reference's information schema at the table level will look a lot like it did at the database level. The fields you are able to fill out, **Why this table is interesting** and **Things to be aware of about this table**, are very similar.

To edit the fields in this table, click the **Edit** button in the upper right-hand corner. Alternatively, if you do not feel like there is anything to add that will improve comprehension of this table, feel free to leave it blank. Again, I'm going to err on the verbose side, and here is what I recommend adding:

1. In the **Why this table is interesting** text box, write `Everything we produce and sell is stored as a record in this table.`
2. In the **Things to be aware of about this table** text box, write `The columns you will most likely use the most are the Name column and ID Menu column. Fields like description and ingredients are text heavy and harder to work with.`

Adding this will give as much information as we can give to our users about this table. As we continue working through the book, objects related to this table will automatically be added to the data reference.

If you like, you can fill out the open text fields for the other tables in our `Pies` database for practice.

We've learned how to edit the data reference for our database and tables. You can also do so for segments and metrics. We'll cover that in the next section.

Segments and metrics in the data reference

From the root of the data reference, which you can get to by clicking **Browse Data | Learn about our Data**, let's have a look at the metric and segment we created. We'll start with our metric – **Order Revenue**:

1. Click **Metrics** from the data reference menu on the left.
2. Click **Order Revenue** from the list of metrics. It should be the only one.

This brings up the **Order Revenue** entry in the data reference. Note that the description we wrote earlier is displayed here. Additionally, there are three extra blank fields that, if we want, we can fill in to add more context about our metric. These fields are similar to what we've seen when working with the data reference.

It may not be necessary to fill out the empty text fields for a metric like **Order Revenue**, since it's relatively straightforward and the one caveat about test orders being removed has already been called out in the description. I don't recommend filling these out for every metric, but they exist because these questions naturally come up.

Below these three open text boxes, there is an option to select the top 2–3 fields that you group this metric by. This is a handy way to point your users to the most common use cases. For a metric such as **Order Revenue**, fields such as **Created Date** and **Order Type** are good choices.

Additional thoughts on the data reference

You may feel that filling out all the fields in the data reference is overkill. Do not feel obliged to do so. Deciding on how much or little to pay attention to these fields when it comes to your data is a personal choice. I recommend trying to put yourself in the shoes of your least technical or least data-literate users. What are some questions they might have? Err on the side of being overly verbose, but there's no need to go completely overboard. The more you add here, the more empowered those users will be to answer their own data questions.

We have now filled out all there is to know about our tables, metrics, and segments. Our users should have everything they need to start exploring our data. However, maybe some will know too much! We might want to take some security precautions around sensitive fields in our tables – think credit card numbers and email addresses. Even granting access to revenue numbers to everyone may make us feel uncomfortable. Fortunately, Metabase allows us to control access to data at the database and table levels. Let's learn how.

Creating permissions

Permissions either allow or prevent groups of users from accessing certain data. Metabase has a simple philosophy around permissions, which they outlined in a blog post back in 2016 when they introduced the feature (`https://www.metabase.com/blog/Permissions/`). Unlike some analytics products, which give extremely fine-grained and complex permission capabilities down to the individual record, Metabase keeps it high level. They do, however, offer more fine-grained permissions in their Enterprise version.

In Metabase, permissions are not applied at the user level, but rather at the group level. So, before we learn about permissions, let's learn about groups.

Creating user groups

Groups allow you to organize sets of users. The purpose of creating groups is to control permissions around the viewing of certain databases, tables, or columns. For example, a good practice is to restrict the access of **Personally Identifiable Information (PII)**, such as full names and email addresses, to the majority of your organization. Meanwhile, some teams, such as customer service, will need access to these fields. In this case, we would want to create a **group** for our customer service team, and then add the necessary permissions. To start out, let's learn how to create groups:

1. Start in the Admin Panel and click **People**.
2. From the menu on the left-hand side, click **Groups**.
3. Notice the two default groups: **All Users** and **Administrators**. Every user you create will go into the **All Users** group. Users with admin access will go into both. These groups cannot be renamed or deleted.
4. Click the blue button to create a group.
5. Give your group a name – for example, `Customer Service Team`.
6. Click **Add**. This will create a group called **Customer Service Team**. Now let's add members to it.

7. Click the newly created group.
8. Click the **Add Members** button.
9. One by one, enter the users you want to be part of this group and click **Add**.

You can create as many groups as you like, and users can be members of multiple groups. The power of groups will become clear when we start creating permissions, which we'll do in the next section.

Applying data permissions

To view permissions in Metabase, start in the Admin Panel. From the top purple bar, click on **Permissions**. You'll see two tabs: **Data permissions** and **Collection permissions**. Since we have not yet covered collections, we'll learn about **Collection permissions** in *Chapter 8, Building Dashboards, Pulses, and Collections*. For now, we'll focus on **Data permissions**.

Metabase's **Data permissions** allows you to restrict a group of users from accessing either an entire database or an entire table. There are ways to restrict column access as well, although it's somewhat of a hack as it involves making changes to the data model.

Additionally, you can choose whether you want a group of users to be able to write SQL queries or only use the UI tools provided by Metabase to explore the data. We've already seen some of Metabase's UI tools, and we'll see more later, but for now, you should think of them as an easier, friendlier subset of what the SQL language offers. The option where you can use the UI tools is referred to in Metabase's permissions as **Data Access**, and the option where you can write SQL queries is referred to as **SQL queries** (who would have thought?).

To summarize, you can restrict a group's access at the entire database level or at an individual table level, and you can limit what that group can do to either **Data Access** (UI tools) and **SQL queries**, or **Data Access** only.

> **Important Note**
>
> Metabase's Enterprise version offers more fine-grained permission options, including **Data Sandboxing**.

Now that we understand how Metabase's **Data permissions** option works, let's learn how these permissions apply to groups.

Understanding how permissions apply to groups

As previously mentioned, we start with two default groups: **Administrators** and **All Users**. **Administrators** will always have full permissions and this cannot be edited. The **All Users** group will have full permissions to start out with but can be edited. Any user added to your Metabase will be part of the **All Users** group, so you can think of that group as the base, or root, group. Any group you add, such as the **Customer Service Team** group we added in *Chapter 3, Setting Up Metabase*, would have any permissions that the **All Users** group has, *as well as any additional permissions that* **Customer Service Team** *is granted*. In other words, Metabase's permissions work in an additive way. Any additional groups you create cannot have fewer permissions than your **All Users** group.

Let's see how this works at the database level. *Figure 5.14* will make this clearer. You can see that we've turned off SQL access for the `Pies` database for the **All Users** group. That means that users in this group cannot use the SQL console to write queries against tables in the `Pies` database. However, the **Customer Service Team** group does have SQL access to the `Pies` database. All users in the customer service group are also members of the **All Users** group, but their customer service-level permissions override the **All Users** permissions:

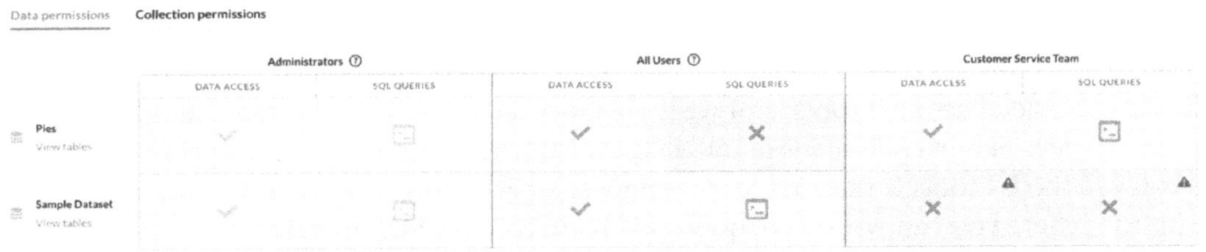

Figure 5.14 – The Customer Service Team group's permissions for the Pies database override that of All Users and they can write SQL queries. For Sample Database, the restrictions on the Customer Service Team have no effect

You can also see, in *Figure 5.14*, that we have a conflict in `Sample Dataset`. The **All Users** group has full permissions, but **Customer Service Team** has both **Data Access** and **SQL queries** removed. Notice the warning icons in the upper right-hand corners of those boxes. Hovering over those icons will reveal the conflict – because the **All Users** group has a higher level of permissions, these **Customer Service Team** permissions will be overridden.

So, in summary, if you would like to restrict data access to some of your users, you must apply those restrictions to the **All Users** group.

Limiting column-level access

While Metabase's permission settings don't offer the granularity to restrict column access to groups (unless you have the Enterprise version), it is possible to hide a column via the **Data Model** section of the **Admin Panel**. We learned about this briefly in the *Enhancing column metadata* section of this chapter, when we changed the **Description** column in our **Menu** table so that it was only visible in detail views.

We could have also hidden that column completely, or any other column for that matter. To do that, instead of choosing **Only in detail views**, choose **Do not include**. Doing that is somewhat akin to removing the column's **Data Access** permission.

> **Important Note**
>
> Any user with SQL query permissions will be able to view all the columns of a table, even if the column's visibility is set to **Do not include**.

So, to summarize, you can use the **Visibility** option in the data model to set **Data Access**-level permissions on an individual column, but not **SQL queries** permissions.

Additional thoughts on permissions

Since there are a lot of ways to configure permissions in Metabase, you might be wondering what the best permission settings are for your organization. While all organizations are different, here is what I generally recommend: if you are a small and open organization, just leave everything open! That means giving the **All Users** group **Data Access** and **SQL queries** access.

If you have sensitive data, or are an organization with a strong hierarchy or division of labor, I recommend using what I call the **Vertical Permissions Framework**. This framework is based on assigning users group membership based on their technical abilities. For example, we might create the following groups:

- **SQL Wizards**: This group has users who are fluent in writing SQL queries. They would have the same data permissions as **admins**, meaning they can use the **Data Access** UI tools and write SQL queries.
- **Inquisitors**: This group has users who are familiar with the data and need to be able to explore it to answer the business-related questions that come up. However, these users would not be allowed to write SQL queries.
- **Data Explorers**: This group can see the work that the SQL wizards and inquisitors have done, but they can't actually do any manipulation of data on their own.

- **All Users**: This is our default group. They have the same data permissions as **Data Explorers**. However, it's still useful to make a distinction as we'll change this when we learn about **Collection permissions** in *Chapter 8, Building Dashboards, Pulses, and Collections.*

The permissions for these groups at the database level is shown in *Figure 5.15*:

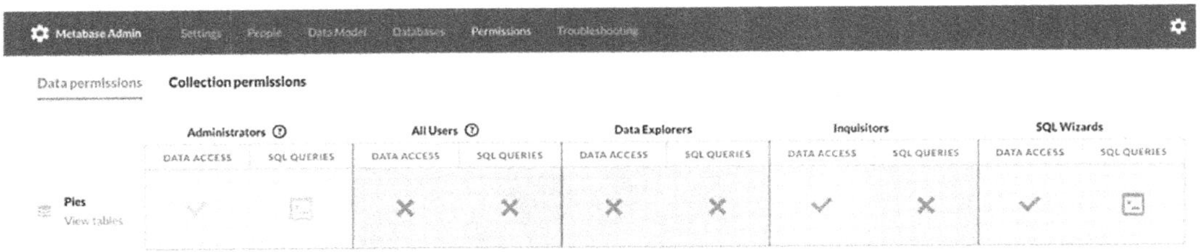

Figure 5.15 – Database permissions for the Vertical Permissions Framework

Figure 5.16 shows the table-level permissions:

Figure 5.16 – Database- and table-level permissions for the Vertical Permissions Framework

This framework works well for top-down organizations with sensitive or complicated data, as it only allows SQL access to an elite group of users. Most users get view-only access. However, as I said, in a small organization, I think it makes sense to give everyone full permissions.

Summary

In this chapter, we finally got to explore our data in Metabase. After a brief tour, we spent a lot of the chapter in the Admin Panel learning how to enhance the metadata of our database and its tables. By adding descriptions, curating our field settings, and specifying foreign key relationships, we give users in our organization a better chance of finding what they want – and help them avoid making mistakes. All they need to do to get started is open the data reference!

We also learned how to restrict access to sensitive databases and data tables using permissions and groups.

Aside from all that, we got several glimpses of what Metabase actually does. Inadvertently, by browsing data, filtering it, and making metrics and segments, we introduced ourselves to some of the basic capabilities Metabase has to offer.

In the next chapter, we'll learn how to create **questions** – the main building blocks for everything in Metabase. Much of it will look familiar to you because of what we did in this chapter.

6
Creating Questions

In the last chapter, we saw what our data looks like in Metabase and laid the groundwork to perform analytics. In this chapter, we will learn how to create **questions**. Questions in Metabase are exactly what they sound like. Are you curious to know how many orders we have at our fictional business? What about the number of users? In this chapter, we'll learn how to ask those questions in Metabase (and get the answers).

Questions are the fundamental building blocks of Metabase. Understanding how to create questions in Metabase will unlock all the actual analytical aspects of the product and open up key insights into our organization. As we work through the rest of the book, we'll learn that features in Metabase, such as dashboards and reports, are simply sets of questions.

There are several ways to create questions in Metabase, and in this chapter, we'll cover them all. The best way to learn about questions is to jump right in and start creating them, so let's get started.

In this chapter, we'll cover the following main topics:

- Asking questions in Metabase
- The three types of questions
- Asking a simple question
- Asking a custom question
- Creating a native question

Technical requirements

As in the last chapter, this one is also fully focused on Metabase. You will need a running instance of Metabase with a connection to the `pies` database. We will also be writing SQL queries toward the end of this chapter. If you don't have a solid understanding of SQL, that is fine. By copying and running the queries from the book, you'll be able to complete all the examples.

Asking questions in Metabase

Let's start by understanding what a question is. A question is anything that causes Metabase to execute a database query on your connected data sources and return data. That means that anything that returns data from our database is considered a question, which also means that we've already created a few questions. Recall that in *Chapter 5, Building Your Data Model*, we spent some time browsing our database tables and applied some filters to them. In the background, Metabase was taking these commands, translating them into SQL queries, executing them, and returning the results. Even those simple actions, since they returned data, would technically be considered questions.

Questions become valuable once they return meaningful data and are **saved**. Let's illustrate this with a simple example, building upon what we learned in the last chapter.

Saving your first question

To get used to creating and saving questions, let's make a very simple one. Imagine we want to know what pies are on our menu. Filtering for pies on our menu is similar to what we did in *Chapter 5, Building Your Data Model*, when we saved a segment based on pickle items:

1. Open Metabase's home screen.
2. Click **Browse Data** | **Pies** | **Menu**.
3. Click the purple **Filters** button in the upper right-hand corner.
4. Scroll down to **Name** and click it.
5. In the list of **Menu Item Names**, click the four items that contain the word `Pie`.
6. Click **Add Filter**.
7. Now, next to the **Filter** button, click **Save**. A **Save question** modal will pop up.

8. In the **Name** field of the modal, enter `Pies on our Menu`.

- In the **Description** field, enter something explaining how our filter works – for example, `Current Pies are Banana Cream, Blueberry, Chicken Pot Pie, and Pumpkin`.

9. The final field asks which **collection** this question should be added to. A collection is like a folder for saved questions and other Metabase objects, such as dashboards. The defaults, for now, should be **Our analytics**, **My personal collection**, and **All personal collections**. For now, let's add this to **My personal collection**. We will learn more about collections in the next section.
10. Click **Done**.
11. You'll see a confirmation modal pop up and be asked whether you want to add this question to a dashboard. We'll learn more about dashboards in *Chapter 8, Building Dashboards, Pulses, and Collections*, so for now, click **Not now**.

If you followed along, your saved question should look as in *Figure 6.1*:

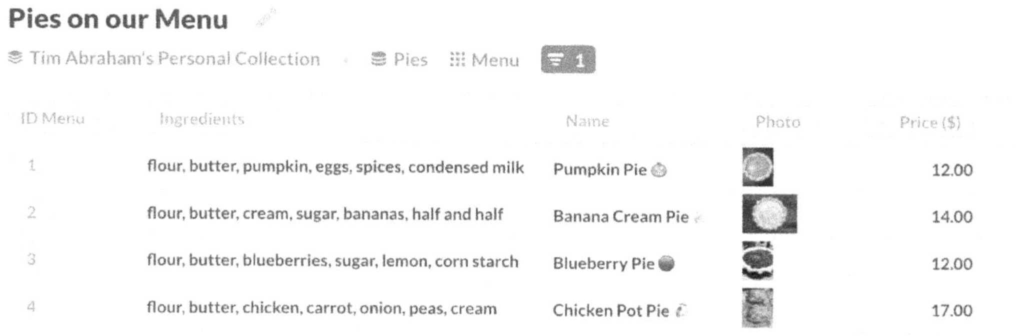

Pies on our Menu
Tim Abraham's Personal Collection
Pies
Menu
1
ID Menu
Ingredients
Name
Photo
Price ($)
1
flour, butter, pumpkin, eggs, spices, condensed milk
Pumpkin Pie
12.00
2
flour, butter, cream, sugar, bananas, half and half
Banana Cream Pie
14.00
3
flour, butter, blueberries, sugar, lemon, corn starch
Blueberry Pie
12.00
4
flour, butter, chicken, carrot, onion, peas, cream
Chicken Pot Pie
17.00

Figure 6.1 – Our first saved question, called Pies on our Menu

We now have a **saved question**, stored in our **personal collection**. Let's learn how we can revisit this question:

1. Open Metabase in a new tab.
2. On the home screen, scroll down to **Our Analytics**.
3. Click **Browse all items**.

4. In the list of **Collections** on the left-hand side, find **My Personal Collection** and click it.
5. You will see the saved question, **Pies on our Menu**, under the **Everything** tab, as well as the **Questions** tab.
6. Click on it to open it back up.

Creating this **Pies on our Menu** question was just a simple example to show how any representation of data can be considered a question and how questions can be saved and stored in collections. In this case, we got to our saved question by simply browsing our data and filtering it until it returned something meaningful to us. That will often be the case, as a big part of doing data analysis is exploring, testing, and tinkering until something meaningful emerges. Metabase makes this kind of exploration and refinement easy to do.

Before we explore more ways to create questions, let's take a quick detour and learn more about collections. Collections are how we keep all our saved questions organized, so it's good to have an understanding of them before we fill up Metabase with too many saved questions.

Creating new collections

In the last section, we learned that collections in Metabase are like folders for saved questions. As you can imagine, if everyone in your organization starts saving questions, your Metabase will quickly become disorganized and bloated. Collections offer a way to keep things tidy. Some organizations like to have a collection for each team in their org chart. For example, there could be a collection for the sales team, the marketing team, the engineering team, the accounting team, and so on.

A new instance of Metabase will have, by default, a collection named **Our Analytics**. Every other collection created will live there, so you can think of it as the root folder. Each user that has a Metabase account will also have their own **personal collection**.

Let's learn how to create a **collection** for the marketing team. To create a new collection, follow the steps listed here:

1. Go to your Metabase home screen.
2. Scroll down and click **Browse all items** in the **Our Analytics** collection.
3. Click **+ New Collection**.
4. Name the new collection `Marketing`.

5. Optionally, give it a description such as `Questions for the Marketing Team`.
6. Save the collection in **Our Analytics** and click **Create**.

We'll learn more about collections in *Chapter 8, Building Dashboards, Pulses, and Collections*, including how to set permissions for them. For now, though, knowing how to create new collections will help us stay much more organized. With that out of the way, let's get back to learning how to create questions.

So far, all the analysis we've done has started with us clicking **Browse Data** and selecting a database and a table. Browsing data is great for when we are in exploration mode. However, sometimes, we know ahead of time what we want to ask, or at least we have a notion of what we want to ask. For these cases, Metabase offers another path. You may have noticed the other option, next to **Browse Data**, that reads **Ask a question**. Let's click it and learn more about it.

Figuring out what questions to ask

Often, the hardest part of analytics is figuring out what to ask. One of the reasons it is so hard is that there are no right or wrong approaches. Figuring out what questions to ask requires more than just data skills; it requires some degree of domain expertise. Fortunately, when you start out with a blank slate, as we are with our Pickles and Pies business, the top questions to ask are usually pretty obvious and high level. As such, they also tend to be relatively simple. For our business, let's imagine that these questions are the following:

- How many orders have been placed?
- Who are our top customers?
- What are our top sellers?

This feels like a good start. Obviously, there is a lot more to know, and that will come later, but for now, let's keep these three questions in mind. By the end of the chapter, we will have answered them all. We'll also see that, while they are simple questions, getting to the answer is not always simple. Metabase is designed to make asking these questions as easy as possible. However, because there is no one-size-fits-all framework in analytics, Metabase offers three paths you can take to create your question. Let's learn about them.

The three types of questions in Metabase

Once you click **Ask a question**, you'll see three options, as in *Figure 6.2*:

Figure 6.2 – The three types of questions

We will learn about all three in this chapter, but we'll start with the **simple question**.

Asking a simple question

Asking a simple question in Metabase will feel very familiar to you since it's nearly identical to what we've already done using the **Browse Data** feature. Simple questions generally have four components to them:

- A single table
- An optional filter
- An optional aggregation to summarize by
- An optional grouping

Let's consider our first question: how many orders have been placed?

The table

A simple question will always start with a single table from our database. In this case, it's going to be the **Orders** table. This is because we want to know how many orders have been placed, and each row in the **Orders** table is an order.

To select the **Orders** table, click **Ask a Question**:

1. Click **Simple question**.
2. Click the **Pies** database icon.
3. Click the **Orders** table.

You should see a full table view, just like when we browsed the data in *Chapter 5, Building Your Data Model.*

> **Important Note**
>
> Although the **Simple question** feature only allows you to choose from a single table, you will also have access to all the columns in tables with a specified foreign key relation. This demonstrates some of the value of setting up your foreign key relationships, as we learned in *Chapter 5, Building Your Data Model.*

An optional filter

Applying a filter to a table will remove records that don't match the filter's criteria. Because every row in the **Orders** table is an order, we will not require any filters to answer our question.

An optional aggregation to summarize by

Summarizations (also called **aggregations**) are functions such as count, sum, mean, and so on. These functions take multiple values and return a single value. To see the summarize options in Metabase, click the green **Summarize** button. The default is **Count of Rows**. Clicking on **Count** should show all the other summarize options, as in *Figure 6.3*. Note that the metric we created in *Chapter 5, Building Your Data Model*, **Order Revenue**, is also a summarize option:

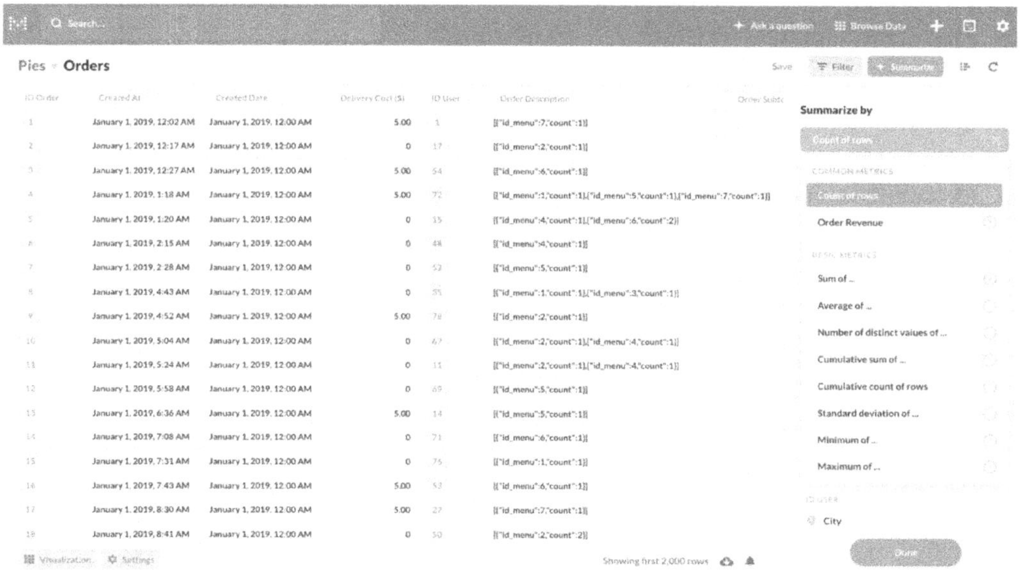

Figure 6.3 – The summarize options

Do we need an aggregation to answer our question about total orders? That depends. If there were only a few orders in our table, we might not need to use one since we would clearly be able to see each row on the screen. However, once we pass a certain threshold, listing them one by one no longer makes sense. We can see, by looking at our table, that Metabase is only showing us the first 2,000 rows of our **Order** table. That means we have more than 2,000 orders, and so an aggregation will be needed to summarize our information. Because each row is an order, to find the number of orders, we'll want to count the rows. That happens to be the default, so all we need to do is click **Done**.

Doing so should return one big number, **131,639**. We have answered the question of how many orders have been placed. Now that we are happy with the state of the question, let's learn how to save it so that you and others can easily find and revisit it:

1. Click **Save**, which is in the upper right-hand corner of the page.
2. Give the question a good name – for example, **Total Orders Placed**.
3. Optionally, give a description if you feel it's necessary. For this question, I think just having the name is adequate.
4. Since this is an important-looking number for our business, let's add it to the **Our Analytics** collection.

An optional grouping

We have answered our question about total orders already, but the single numerical answer may be leaving you with additional questions.

One natural question you may have is whether this number, **131,639**, has been growing over time. After all, a growing business is a healthy business, whereas a shrinking number of orders would be a sign that something is wrong (despite the total number of orders looking pretty good for a small business selling pickles and pies).

This is where grouping becomes valuable. To look at **Total Orders** by time, we'll want to group it by some value in the table that corresponds to time. Let's learn how. Start by opening back up the **Summarize** sidebar:

1. Click the green **Summarize** button.
2. Notice the options under **Group By**. These are all the values we can group this question by.

3. Remember, we want to group by something that corresponds to time. **Created Date** and **Created At** are both appropriate options, as they are records of the day and time an order was made. Hover over **Created Date**. Make sure to hover over the created date under the **Order** section and not the **ID User** section.
4. Notice, as you hover over **Created Date**, that **by week** will appear by default. This is Metabase guessing that we want to see the count of orders grouped at a weekly **time grain** instead of a daily time grain. Clicking on **by week** will give you additional time grains you can use, as pictured in *Figure 6.4*.
5. For now, let's use the **Day** time grain. Click **by week** and select **Day** to change the grouping to the day granularity.
6. Click **Done**:

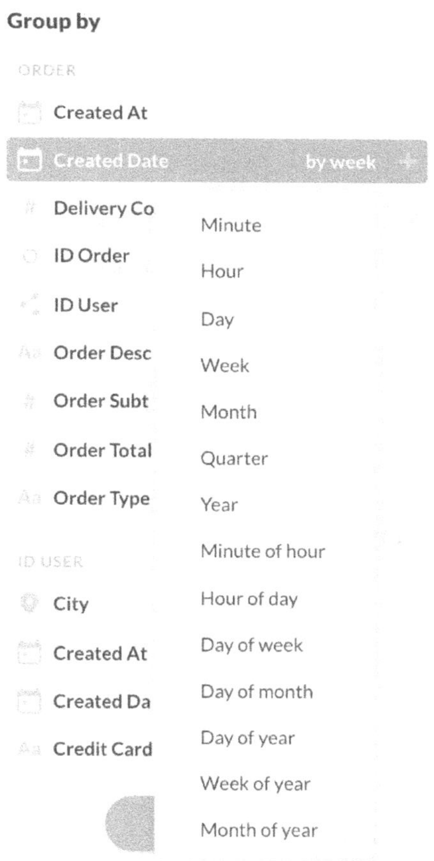

Figure 6.4 – The set of time granularities you can group by

The first thing you'll probably notice is that the single number has turned into a chart, as in *Figure 6.5*:

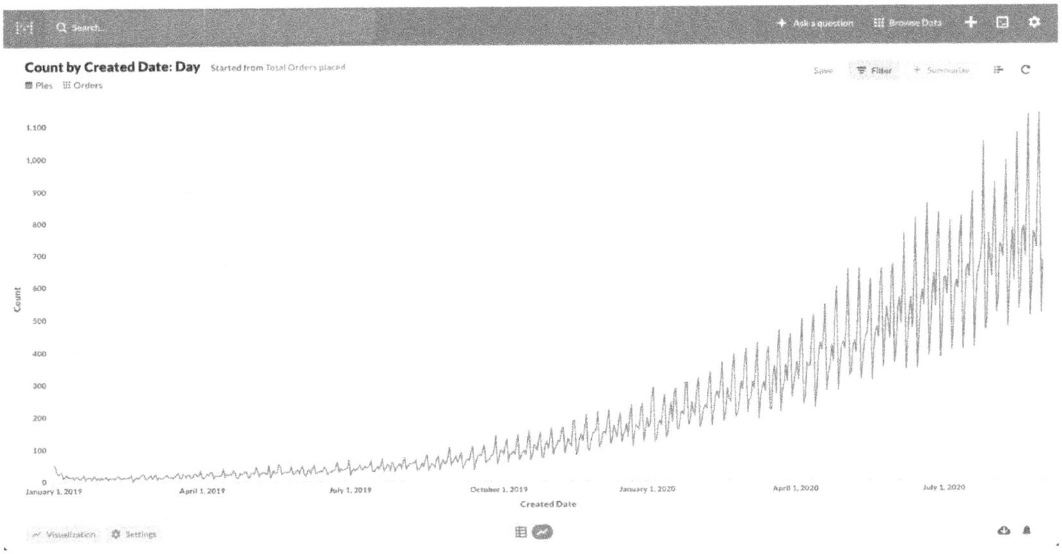

Figure 6.5 – A chart of orders by Created Date

Again, this is Metabase guessing what the best way to visualize this information is. To toggle from the chart view to a view of the raw data, click the table icon at the bottom of the chart.

Playing around with saved questions

In the last section, we took a saved question and made some changes to it. By doing that, we changed the nature of the question – it's no longer telling us how many orders have been placed, but rather how many orders have been placed *over time*. We might want to save this question as an additional question since it feels just as important of a view into our order volume than the single number representing total orders. We can see in this chart that our business looks healthy because orders have been steadily growing over time.

To save this question derived from another saved question, let's do the following:

1. Click the **Save** button in the upper right-hand corner just as we did before.
2. You will be asked whether you want to replace the original question, or **Save as a new question**. Choose the latter.
3. Give it the name **Orders per Day**, an optional description, and designate a collection.

Analytics almost always involves starting with a question, such as *how many orders have been placed?*, and then exploring deeper into the question based on the initial results. As you explore deeper, you discover more interesting representations of the data, such as orders over time. You may also find uninteresting representations of the data - grouping orders by the minute they were created is an example of an uninteresting one (go ahead and try it). Finding uninteresting representations is okay. The point is, when doing analytics, it's powerful to be able to explore and iterate quickly, and when you find an interesting view of your data, you save it so you and others can come back to it. Metabase is designed with this process in mind.

As you use Metabase more, you'll notice that a lot of the most valuable questions you save will be derived from other saved questions. Questions also serve as valuable jumping-off points for other users. Say a less technical user in our organization wants to learn about order volume but doesn't know anything about our data. If we send them our **Orders by Date** question, chances are that by clicking around and trying different groupings, they'll easily be able to find what they want.

Many questions are simple ones and can be handled with the **Simple question** feature. For more sophisticated questions, we can use Metabase's **Custom question** feature.

Asking a custom question

In the last section, we learned that the **Simple question** feature offers ways to build a question based on a single table and an optional filter, summary function, and grouping. This will work great for many of your most important questions, but it will only be a matter of time until the complexities of your question can no longer be addressed by the **Simple question** feature. When that happens, your next best option is the **Custom question** feature. Let's learn about it and answer the second question, *Who are our top customers?*

First off, let's think about what a "top customer" is. Are they our customers with the most orders? The most items ordered? The most money spent? The most money spent in the last 90 days? As analysts and data scientists, we are all too familiar with seemingly simple questions turning out to be too vague and underdefined. For now, let's define our top customers as those with the most orders, and limit those customers to just the top 10.

We know that our customers' names are stored in the **Users** table, but their orders live in the **Orders** table. We also know, because of our work in *Chapter 5, Building Your Data Model*, that our **Orders** table has **ID User** in it and we have called **ID User** out as a foreign key and linked it to the **Users** table. That means that when we use the **Orders** table, we can access any of the columns in our **Users** table. So, to answer this question, we will only need to use the **Orders** table.

To create a custom question, start by clicking **Ask a Question**, just as you did to create a simple question. Next, click **Custom question**. This will bring up a notebook-style editor. Going forward, I will be referring to this editor as the **notebook editor**:

1. Where it reads **Pick your starting data**, select **Pies** as the database and **Orders** as the table. This will cause the notebook editor to display a **Filter**, **Summarize**, and **Group** option, just like in a simple question.
2. Since we're defining top customers by the number of orders, click **Pick the metric you want to see**, and in the **Summarize** section, choose **Count of rows**.
3. To the right of the **Summarize** section, also in green, is the **Grouping** section. Here, we want to group by user. Click **Pick a column to group by**. While **ID User** would be acceptable, you can imagine that we may want to know the names of these users and not just their IDs. Since the users' names are in the **User** table, scroll down to the bottom where you see the **ID User** foreign key symbol represented by a single dot connected to two other dots. Click that and choose **Name**.
4. Note that next to the **Summarize** section, there is a light-gray **Play** button icon. Clicking this will let you preview your data. It's often handy to preview your data as you go along your question building journey to ensure each step is returning what you expect it to.
5. If we were to finish here, we would get *all* users and their count of orders. However, we only want our top 10 users. To find that, we'll need to sort our results. You may have noticed that as soon as we completed the grouping part in *step 3*, our editor populated some additional actions we could take. One of those actions is **Sort**. Go ahead and click **Sort**.
6. Now, we will specify which value we want to sort by. The two options are **Name** and **Count**. Since we want to sort by the number of orders, and the number of orders is the count of rows, it stands to reason that we will sort by **Count**. Click **Count**.
7. Notice that **Count** now appears in the **Sort** section with an upward-pointing arrow. The upward-pointing arrow indicates the results will be sorted in ascending order, from smallest to largest. What we want, though, is descending order. By clicking the arrow, you can switch it to a downward-pointing arrow, indicating a descending sort. Again, feel free to use the **Preview** button to ensure you've got your data sorted the right way.
8. Recall that we only want the top 10 users. To limit the results, click the **Row limit** icon. In the **Enter a limit** text field, enter `10`.

9. Check that your editor looks as in *Figure 6.6*. If it does, then click **Visualize** to see the results:

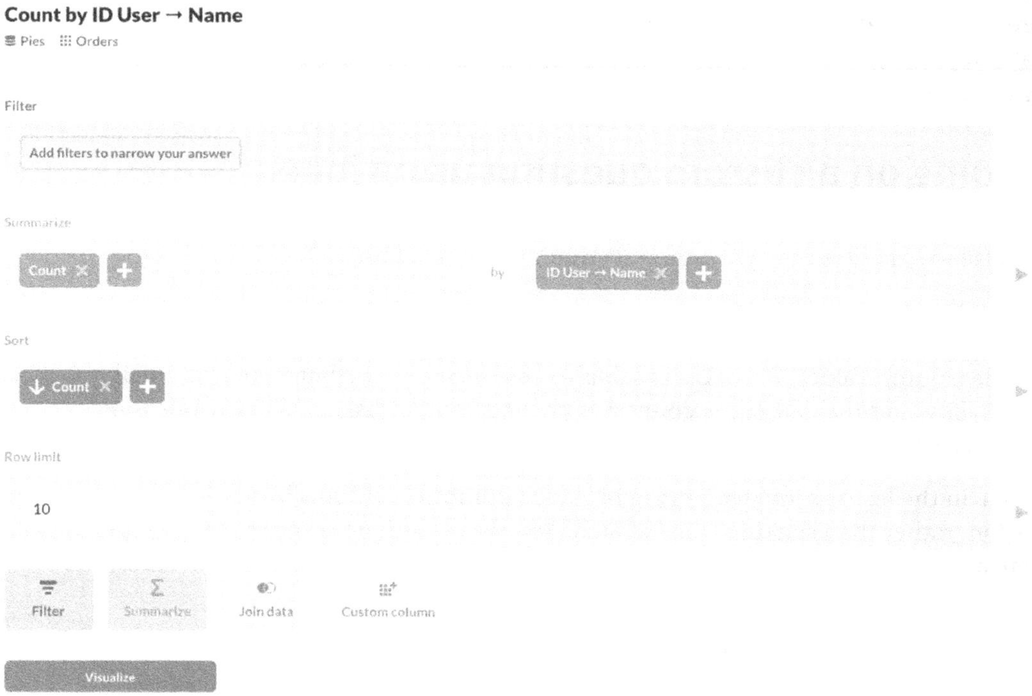

Figure 6.6 – Using the Custom question feature to find the top 10 customers

After clicking **Visualize**, you should see a bar chart with the names of our top 10 customers. The height of the bars corresponds to the number of orders they have placed. Let's save it:

1. For **Name**, write `Our Top Customers`.
2. As mentioned, `Top Customers` is a vague name since it doesn't make clear what metric we are ranking them by and where we apply a cut-off. This is where a good description is invaluable. For **Description**, write `Our top 10 users all time by number of orders placed`.
3. Put the question into the **Our Analytics** collection and click **Save**. We don't need to add this to a dashboard.

You have now created and saved a question using the **Custom question** editor. Unlike the **Simple question** feature, the **Custom question** notebook editor works in more of a step-by-step way, with previews along the way so that you can check your work. It also has far more features than **Simple question**, such as the ability to join a table to other tables and create custom columns and expressions for more advanced computation. Let's learn about them, starting with joins.

Building on a custom question using joins

The custom question we built in the last section was still relatively simple. Let's explore what else we can do in the **Custom question** notebook editor.

Imagine that we have shared our **Top 10 Customers** question with our marketing team and they would like to know more about these valuable customers. The marketing team likes the column values in the **Users** table since it includes attributes such as email address, city, and the date the account was created. They've asked us to include those columns from the **Users** table in this question.

Just like in the last section, we'll bring in these additional columns by editing our saved question, rather than starting from scratch. You should still be at the saved question, but if you aren't, you can get back to it by finding **Top 10 Customers** in the **Our Analytics** collection.

Once you have the question open, click the **Show editor** button in the upper right-hand corner (seen in *Figure 6.7*) to toggle from the visualized results back to the editor:

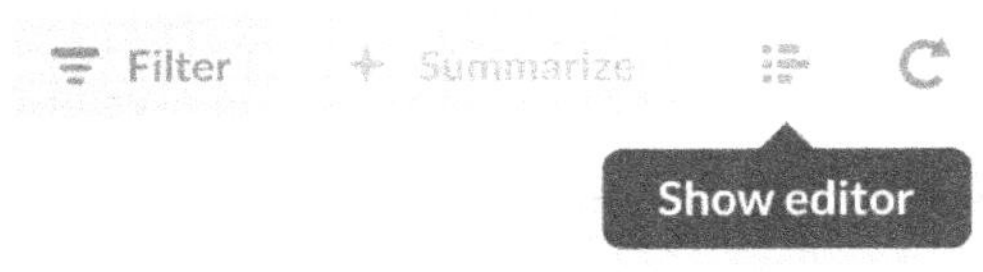

Figure 6.7 – To return to the notebook editor from a saved question, click the Show editor icon

In the editor, notice below the **Row limit** section how you have four additional operations you can do: **Filter**, **Summarize**, **Join data**, and **Custom column**. Since we want to bring in more information from the **Users** table, and the table we're working with is a summary of the **Orders** table, we need to **join** data. You'll see a **Join data** section inserted into your editor, just as in *Figure 6.8*:

> **Important Note**
>
> When you join data from a previously summarized question, you can only join to the columns present in that summarized representation of the data. If you are familiar with SQL, you can think of the summarized question as a subquery.

Figure 6.8 – The Join data section in the question editor

Recall, when we learned about relational databases back in *Chapter 4*, *Connecting to Databases*, how we learned that databases save space by keeping information in different tables linked together by a common value. If you want to unite those tables, you can do so by **joining** them based on a common value. The values we have in our question so far are our users' names and the number of orders they've placed. We want to bring in more of the columns from our **Users** table, so that will be the table we join to. Let's learn how to join it using the notebook editor:

1. Click **Pick a table...**.
2. Choose **Users**, since that table has all the attributes about our customers.
3. Choosing the **Users** table as the table to join to will render an option in the section where you can pick the columns you want to join on. Because the only column both tables have in common is **Name**, that will be the column we join on. So, pick **Name** for both options, just as in *Figure 6.9*:

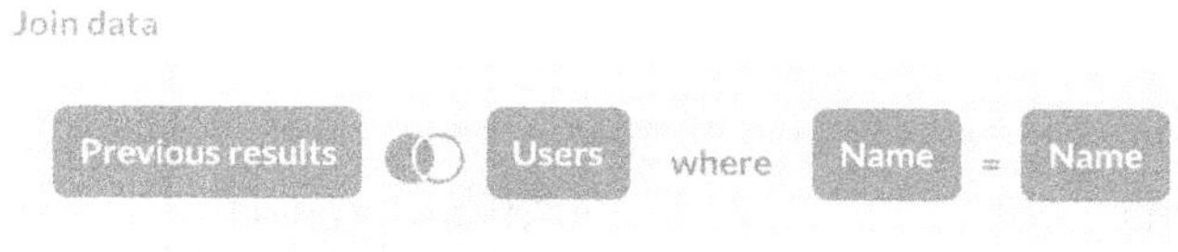

Figure 6.9 – Creating a left outer join with our results and the Users table

4. On the far-right side of the **Join** data step, click the text reading **Columns**. This is where you will select the columns from the **Users** table that you want to see in the final result. Let's say that the marketing team cares only about **City**, **Credit Card Provider**, **Email**, and **State**. Leave those checked and everything else unchecked.
5. Click **Visualize** to see the new results. If you still see the bar chart, click the table icon at the bottom center of the screen to view the results in table form.

Now, as *Figure 6.10* shows, you will have a table of the top 10 customers, the number of orders they've placed, and other attributes about these users coming from the **Users** table, such as their city, email, credit card provider, and state. Note that while the **Sort** and **Row limit** steps made it so that our question only returns the top 10 rows by **Count**, the table is no longer sorted by **Count**. This is a result of the joint operation. If we want it sorted, we could always add another **Sort** section to the bottom of the notebook editor:

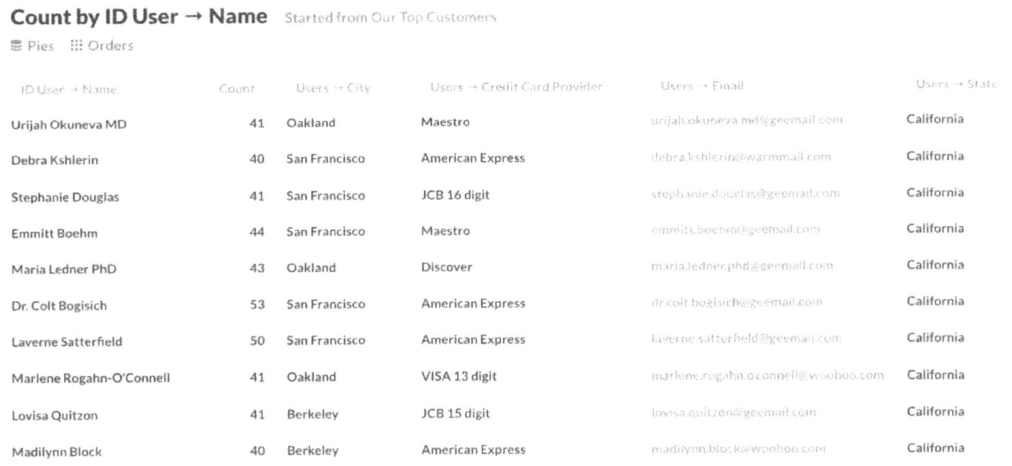
Count by ID User → Name Started from Our Top Customers
Pies Orders

ID User → Name	Count	Users → City	Users → Credit Card Provider	Users → Email	Users → State
Urijah Okuneva MD	41	Oakland	Maestro	urijah.okuneva.md@geemail.com	California
Debra Kshlerin	40	San Francisco	American Express	debra.kshlerin@warmmail.com	California
Stephanie Douglas	41	San Francisco	JCB 16 digit	stephanie.douglas@geemail.com	California
Emmitt Boehm	44	San Francisco	Maestro	emmitt.boehm@geemail.com	California
Maria Ledner PhD	43	Oakland	Discover	maria.ledner.phd@geemail.com	California
Dr. Colt Bogisich	53	San Francisco	American Express	dr.colt.bogisich@geemail.com	California
Laverne Satterfield	50	San Francisco	American Express	laverne.satterfield@geemail.com	California
Marlene Rogahn-O'Connell	41	Oakland	VISA 13 digit	marlene.rogahn.oconnell@woohoo.com	California
Lovisa Quitzon	41	Berkeley	JCB 15 digit	lovisa.quitzon@geemail.com	California
Madilynn Block	40	Berkeley	American Express	madilynn.block@woohoo.com	California

Figure 6.10 – The "Our Top Customers" question after joining to the Users table for more columns

Let's look at the results. It looks like all of our top 10 customers live in either Oakland, San Francisco, or Berkeley. This makes sense because our business is located in San Francisco.

Now that we're happy with this question, let's save it. Give it a name such as `Our Top Customers - Enhanced`. We'll want to save it as a new question, rather than overwriting the original. Also, because we are saving this for the marketing team, let's add it to the **Marketing** collection, which we just created.

Types of joins

You might have noticed, in the last section, that the join step was represented with a Venn diagram, with the circle on the left fully shaded and only the overlapping part of the circle on the right shaded. This was to indicate that the default join is what is called a **left outer join**. Clicking on that Venn diagram will show you the four types of joins you can do in Metabase, as pictured in *Figure 6.11*:

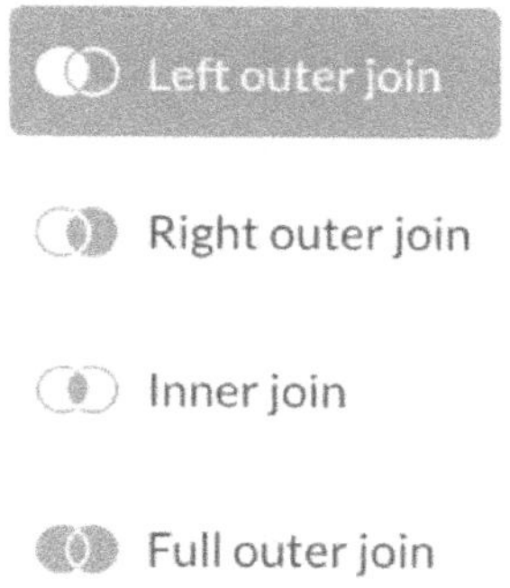

Figure 6.11 – The four types of joins in Metabase

A **left outer join** will keep all values from the table on the left and only the matching ones from the table on the right. An **inner join** will keep only the matches from the left and right tables. Most of the time, you'll want to use a left outer join or an inner join. A **right outer join** will keep all values from the table on the right and only the matches on the left. A **full outer join** will keep values from the left and right table, regardless of whether there is a match.

Because all users are in the **Users** table, changing the join from a **left outer** to an **inner join** will not change the results. However, if you used a **right outer join** (or a **full outer join**), it would return every column in the **Users** table, but only show the **Name** and **Order** counts for the top 10. Feel free to try it out to build more intuition if you are new to joins.

Building on a custom question

Based on these results, our marketing team is now curious about who our top 10 "non-local" customers are. Specifically, they are worried that these customers might be getting frustrated with our delivery costs. If delivery costs make up a significant portion of the "pie" of total spending, they could be deterring some of our top customers from hitting the order button. They've asked whether we can help them come up with a list of our top 10 non-local customers, and include how much of the money that they've spent has gone toward delivery costs. Finally, they want to contact these users, greeting them by their first name. So, their request is to have a table that includes the following:

- The first name of the customer
- The percentage of their total spend that has gone toward delivery costs
- The table sorted and filtered to show only the top 10 "non-local" users

Luckily, we've already created most of this question. We already have the logic built into the notebook editor to return the top 10 customers based on order count. So, instead of creating a new question from scratch, we can just work off of the question we already created.

Let's go through all their requirements one by one. As we go through them, we'll learn about **custom columns** and **custom expressions**, two powerful features in the notebook editor. We'll also learn how to start a new question from a saved question as if it were a database table.

Creating simple custom columns

Let's start with the first task: only showing the customers' first names. This is new for us since it involves taking the column with the customers' full names and *transforming* it to only return the first names. To calculate this, we need to use what are called **custom columns**. If you've used formulas in spreadsheet software, then custom columns will feel familiar to you.

Since extracting the first name from the full name is actually a bit complicated, let's warm up with something easier to illustrate the notion of custom columns:

1. If you aren't there already, open the editor to edit the **Our Top Customers – Enhanced** question.
2. Toward the top of the notebook editor, just below the **Data** section with the **Orders** table populated in it, click the **Custom Column** icon. It looks like a table with a + sign, just as in *Figure 6.12*.

3. A new custom column section will appear in your editor, along with a modal. In the modal is an empty text box for you to write your formula. Click inside the text box.
4. A dropdown will appear with all the fields you can use, as well as all the functions you can apply to the fields. In this case, fields are columns in your table, or columns referenced by a foreign key. **Functions** are transformations you can apply to your fields. Again, if you are familiar with spreadsheets, many of these formulas will be familiar to you.
5. We will do something very simple here since we are just trying to familiarize ourselves with what this does. Scroll down and click `sqrt` from **Functions**. This will populate `= sqrt()` in the field formula. Next, click **[Order Total]** from the list of fields. Your function should look like `= sqrt([Order Total])`.
6. In the **Give it a Name** text field, write `Square Root of Order Total` and click **Done**.
7. Now, let's see the data. Click the **Preview** button to the right. You will see a new column added to your **Orders** table. Verify that it is, indeed, calculating the square root of the order total:

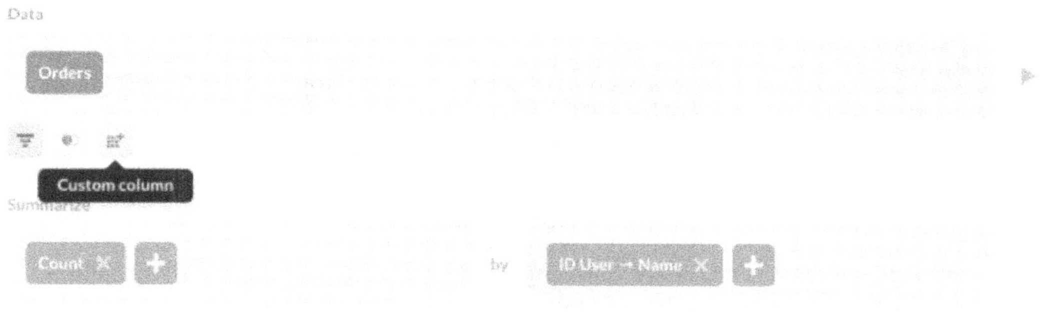

Figure 6.12 – Adding a custom column

To remove the custom column you just created (since knowing the square root of the order total is not a very valuable thing to know), click the **x** next to the column's name. Now that we've learned the basics of custom columns, let's move on and try a more advanced example.

Creating advanced custom columns

Recall that we want to extract the first name only from the customer's full name using a custom column. Let's see whether there is a function that looks appropriate for this in the **Custom Column** builder.

To get started, repeat the first four steps from the last section on *Creating simple custom columns*. Remember to add the custom column immediately after the first step, as in *Figure 6.12*. Have a look at all the functions available. Will any of them easily return the first name from a full name? If you are familiar with **regular expressions**, you may have gravitated toward the `regexextract` function. Regular expressions are used to extract patterns of text from a string. They are quite useful in analytics and data science, but are also complicated to learn. Learning them is beyond the scope of this book. It turns out that the regular expression to return the first word from a string is `"([\\w]+)"`. Let's apply the function and see how our **custom column** looks:

1. Choose the **regexextract** function.
2. The function takes two arguments. The first argument is the string you want to apply your regular expression to. Use **ID User + Name** for this argument.
3. The next argument is the regular expression. Use `"([\\w]+)"` for this second argument. The full formula should look as follows:

```
regexextract([ID User → Name], "([\\w]+)")
```

4. In the **Give it a Name** text box, write `First Name`.
5. Click **Done**.

Now, preview the data to see the first names of the customers. Note that since we're only looking at the **Orders** table, the name of the customer will not be displayed, since that column lives in the **Users** table. If you want to see the full name alongside the first name to verify that it's working, you can just create another custom column. In this case, the custom column would just be **ID User + Name**, with no formula to modify it.

As we have seen, custom columns are powerful ways to transform columns in our tables to fit better into our use cases. Next, we'll take what we learned from custom columns and apply them to summarizations. In Metabase, this is called a **custom expression**.

Creating custom expressions

The final data point the marketing team wants to know is the percentage of total spending that has gone toward delivery costs. That is, for each customer, they want the sum of their **delivery costs** divided by the sum of their **order totals**. Let's learn how to create a **custom expression** to create this ratio metric. We'll be building on the work we did in the last section, so make sure you've finished that section and still have the notebook editor open:

1. Find the green **Summarize** section, just below where we created the **First Name** custom column. Right now, it should only have **Count** in it. Click the + button to add another summarization.
2. From the dropdown, select **Custom Expression**. It's at the bottom of the dropdown, with a Greek sigma letter next to it.
3. A custom expression requires an **Aggregation** function, and optionally, a column transformation function such as those we saw in the last section. The only reason to use one of those column transformation functions would be if you need to transform your data first before aggregating it (for example, if you wanted to sum up the square roots). Since we want to sum up the delivery costs, click the **Sum** function under **Aggregations**.
4. In the **Sum** function, add `[Delivery Cost]` as the argument.
5. Next, tap the spacebar. A list of operators should appear in a dropdown. Select the / operator, since we want to divide the delivery cost by the order total.
6. Now, add an aggregation to sum up the order total. Type in `Sum([Order Total])`. Altogether, your custom expression should look as follows:

```
Sum([Delivery Cost]) / Sum([Order Total])
```

7. Give your custom expression a name – for example, `Delivery Cost over Total Spend`.
8. Click **Done**.
9. In the **Grouping** section, to the right of the **Summarize** section, click the + button.
10. Add the **First Name** custom column from the dropdown.
11. For now, since we haven't applied our filters for "non-local" users, let's remove the **Row Limit** section. Click the **x** button on that section.

To see our work so far, scroll to the bottom and click **Visualize**. We now have two of our three requirements in the question: the first name and the ratio of the delivery cost to the total spend. All that's left is filtering out the local users. We could jump back into the notebook editor here, but I want to use this opportunity to show you another very handy method of creating new questions. This method involves treating a saved question just like a database table. Before we start, have a look at *Figure 6.13* and make sure your notebook editor looks just like in the screenshot:

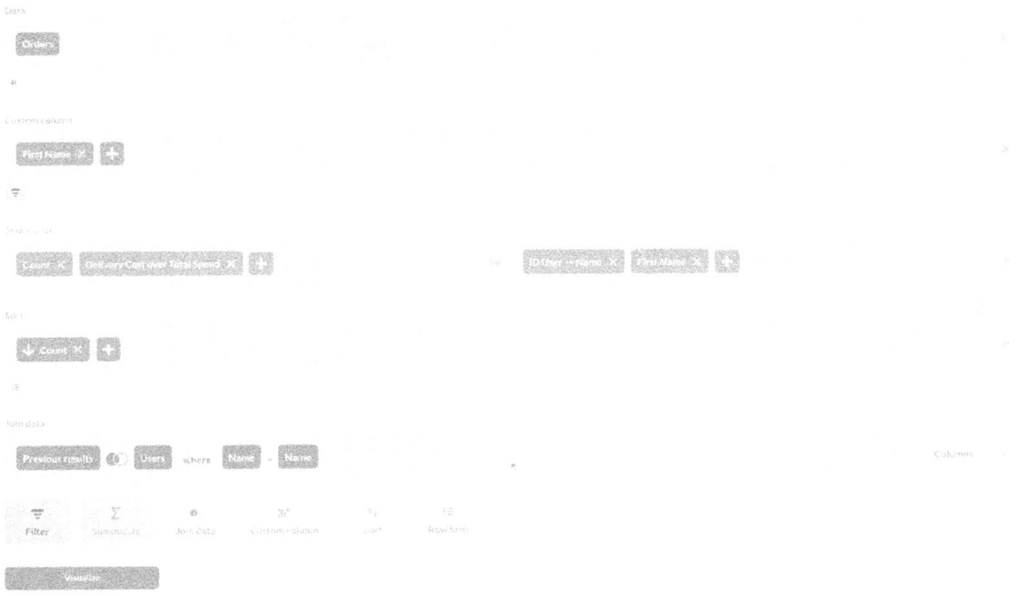

Figure 6.13 – The "Our Top Customers – Enhanced" question after adding a custom column and custom expression

Once your question matches the image, click **Save** and replace the original question with **Our Top Customers – Enhanced**.

Starting a question from a saved question

We will finish our question by filtering out local users. Since our business is located in the San Francisco Bay Area, we've determined that any user living in San Francisco, Oakland, or Berkeley is what we call a "local user."

To apply this filter, rather than opening back up the notebook editor, we'll act as if we are starting a brand-new question. However, instead of choosing a database table, we'll choose a saved question. Let's see how:

1. Click **Ask a question**.
2. From the three options, click **Custom question**.
3. Instead of choosing the `Pies` database, choose **Saved Questions**, as in *Figure 6.14*.
4. In saved questions, open the **Marketing** collection.
5. Click the **Our Top Customers – Enhanced** question:

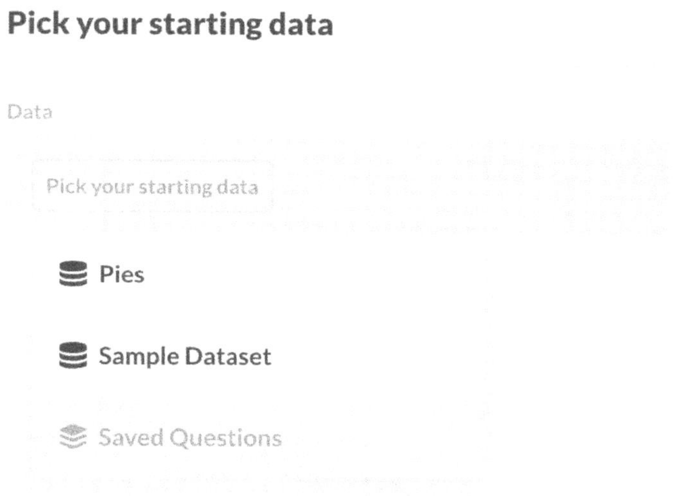

Figure 6.14 – Starting a question from a saved question rather than a database

By previewing the data, you can see how Metabase is treating this saved question just as it would a normal rectangular table. We can use this as a starting point to finish off our question:

1. In the **Filter** section, click **Add filters to narrow your answer**.
2. From the drop-down menu, select **Users | City**.
3. Change the dropdown from **Is** to **Is Not**. This is because we want to filter out our three local cities.

4. Next, type `San Francisco, Oakland, Berkeley,` all with a comma at the end so that Metabase is able to separate them out as separate strings, as in *Figure 6.15*:

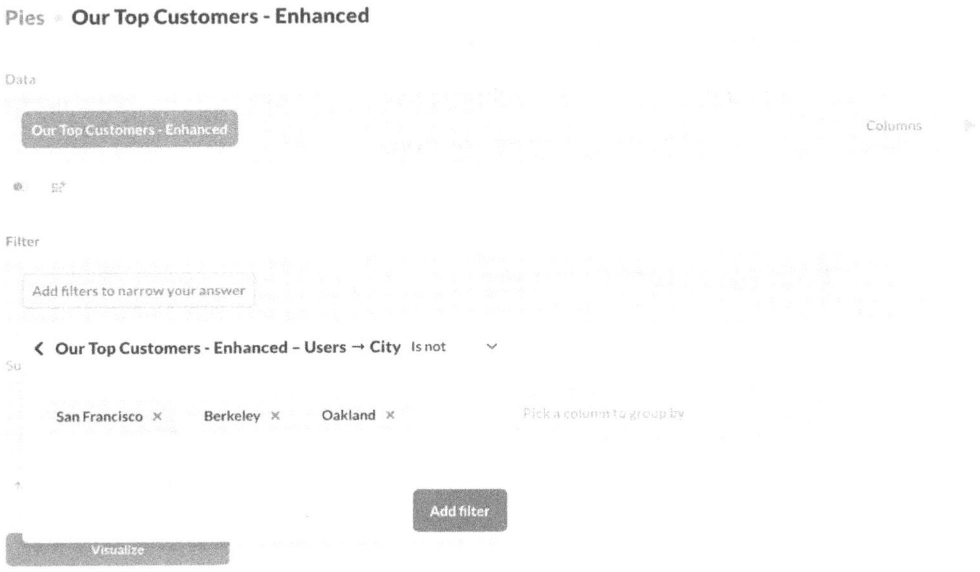

Figure 6.15 – Filtering out the users in our local cities

5. Once you've added all three cities, click **Add Filter**.
6. Now, add a section that will sort the rows by **Count** in descending order.
7. Finally, add back **Row Limit** so that we only return 10 rows.

In the end, your question should look just as in *Figure 6.16*:

Figure 6.16 – Asking a question based on a saved question rather than a database table

Let's visualize the results. A bar chart may no longer be the best way to visualize this data – a table is better. We could save this now, but why stop here? There are a few more actions we can take to make the results clearer to the marketing team. For example, the **Count** column is vague. It might not be clear what it is counting. Also, **Delivery Cost over Total Spend** might look better as a percentage, rather than a decimal value. It isn't necessary to be so detailed, but the more explicit you are with your questions, the better. In the next section, we'll learn how to make these final refinements to our question.

Formatting columns in questions

In *Chapter 5*, *Building Your Data Model*, we learned how to format columns in our tables via the Admin Panel. Now we are working with columns derived from a question, so formatting needs to take the context of the question into account. Unlike formatting table columns in the Admin Panel, anyone can format columns in a question. Let's format the data in this table so that it will look a bit nicer:

1. Click the **Count** column in the table.
2. Click on **Formatting** from the list of options in the box that pops up.

3. A side tray will appear on the left. In the **Column title** box, rename the column to **Total Orders**.
4. Click **Done**.
5. Now, let's do the same for **Delivery Cost over Total Spend**. Click it and open **Formatting**.
6. Under **Style**, change the value from **Normal** to **Percent**.
7. Click **Done**.

We're now finished and ready to save the question. Click **Save** and save it as a new question. Give it a name, such as `Top 10 Non-Local Customers`, and specify in the description what we mean by *non-local* and what we mean by *top*. Add it to the marketing collection.

As you can see, the notebook editor gives us the ability to build very powerful questions in a layered fashion. Now, let's learn about the final option for creating questions: writing a **native query**.

Creating a native query

In the last section, we learned how to create custom questions using Metabase's notebook editor. As we saw, the editor is quite powerful. With it, you can do all of the standard analytical database operations, such as filtering, summarizing, grouping, transforming, and joining – all by clicking. This is incredibly useful, both for a seasoned data analyst and for someone new to data. I find that it's also useful as an educational tool for those new to analytics and curious to learn more. It's easy to open a saved question and flip to the editor to see the "recipe" and learn how it was created.

Of course, as powerful as the editor is, there will always be some questions that it can't answer. The Metabase team is constantly adding features to cover more and more use cases, but addressing every single function for every supported database is a tall order. But for every use case that the editor cannot address, Metabase offers the option to create a question using SQL or another native query language. Let's learn how to use it. Note that we will be using SQL here, but even if you are unfamiliar with SQL, you should be able to follow along just fine.

Why use a native query?

One of the questions we wanted to answer at the beginning of this chapter was what our top-selling items are. This seems like a very basic business question that must be answered. However, you may have noticed that the way our data is organized is not exactly conducive to answer this. While it's simple for us to count orders, since each order is a row in the **Orders** table, an order can contain one or more items.

If you take a look at a single order, the problem will become clearer. Click **Browse Data | Pies | Orders** and click on the first order in the table. Under **Order Description**, we can see exactly what was ordered:

```
[
  {
    "id_menu": 7,
    "count": 1
  }
]
```

In the table, that data is represented as a **JSON** array. **JSON** stands for **JavaScript Object Notation**. As data analysts, we love data that lives nicely in rows and columns. Software engineers, on the other hand, love working with JSON. This is especially true for software engineers that work on web-based projects. This is because the JavaScript language is core to web browsers. As such, it is not at all uncommon to encounter a lot of JSON data in an application database. Some databases, such as MongoDB and other NoSQL databases, store everything as JSON!

JSON objects consist of key/value pairs. In the JSON in our **Order Description** column, the keys are `id_menu` and `count`, and the values are the actual ID and the numerical count. For example, the preceding JSON represents one order of `id_menu 7`. In the **Menu** table, we can look that up and see that it is **Garlic Pickles**.

As of the time of writing, Metabase's custom editor does not have any tools to work with JSON data. But because JSON is such a common data type in relational databases such as PostgreSQL, most SQL dialects have good libraries of functions to properly analyze JSON. Specifically, PostgreSQL has dozens of JSON-related functions that you can learn about at `https://www.postgresql.org/docs/9.5/functions-json.html`.

Generally, to do analytics, we like our data represented as rectangularly as possible. Take a JSON object, such as the one in *Figure 6.17*, as an example:

```
[
  {
    "id_menu": 1,
    "count": 1
  },
  {
    "id_menu": 5,
    "count": 1
  },
  {
    "id_menu": 7,
    "count": 1
  }
]
```

Figure 6.17 – The contents of a single order in a JSON array

It is much easier to work with this data when it is flattened out into simple rows and columns as in *Figure 6.18*, where we can apply standard database operations, such as aggregating rows and grouping:

id_menu	count
1	1
5	1
7	1

Figure 6.18 – The same data in Figure 6.17 represented in a rectangular format

Because transforming the data from *Figure 6.17* into *Figure 6.18* is not something Metabase's notebook editor is able to perform, we will have to use the native query option. Let's try it out.

Writing a native query

To write a native query, click **Ask a question** in the top bar and then click the **Native query** option and choose the **Pies** database.

You'll be presented with a blank console that you can write SQL in. Although we won't be covering how to write SQL in this book, let's see step by step how our SQL query works. SQL is an expressive language, so even if you have never learned it, you may still be able to understand what is going on.

To get started, let's look at our **Orders** table. Enter the following query:

```
SELECT * FROM orders
```

This just gives us the entire output of the table. Make note of `id_order 4`. We can see that this order contained one of three different items on the menu. Now run this query, which utilizes the `json_array_elements` function to expand the JSON arrays to sets of JSON values, putting each JSON object on its own line:

```
SELECT
id_order
, json_array_elements(order_description) as single_item_orders
FROM
    orders
```

Can you see what this query is doing? Now we have three rows for `id_order 4`. Each row now has a JSON object with a single `id_menu` item and a count. Now, we want to represent `id_menu` and the count in their own columns. To do so, run this query, which builds upon the last one:

```
SELECT
id_order
, single_item_orders->>'id_menu' as id_menu
, single_item_orders->>'count' as item_count
FROM
(
    SELECT
    id_order
    , json_array_elements(order_description) as single_item_
orders
    FROM
```

```
        orders
) each_order
```

Now we have a rectangular table that we can answer our question with. Each row contains a menu ID and the number of times that menu ID was added to a particular order.

> **Important Note**
> Unlike many other programming languages, there is no settled-upon style guide for how to write SQL. It's completely a matter of preference. Feel free to write SQL any way you like.

Because we're working in the SQL console, we lose all the metadata about our table that we curated in *Chapter 5, Building Your Data Model*. For example, the column names are in snake case (meaning words are separated by underscores instead of spaces). The foreign key relationships are also lost. This is a problem because ideally, we would be using the name of `id_menu` instead of its integer value. To bring in the name from the menu table, we'll need to write a SQL **JOIN**. To do that, run the following query. Again, we're building on the query we've already written:

```
SELECT
menu.name
, id_order
, item_count::INT
FROM
(
    SELECT
    id_order
    , single_item_orders->>'id_menu' as id_menu
    , single_item_orders->>'count' as item_count
    FROM
    (
        SELECT
        id_order
        , created_at
        , json_array_elements(order_description) as single_
item_orders
        FROM
            orders
```

```
    ) each_order
) each_order_flat
JOIN
menu
ON each_order_flat.id_menu::INT = menu.id_menu
```

Finally, we have our data represented in a way that can properly answer our question. The unfriendly JSON array from *Figure 6.17* is now laid out in three rows. We can see that order included one pumpkin pie, one order of dill pickles, and one order of garlic pickles. We can now modify our query to answer our question of how many of each item has been ordered. The results should look as follows:

```
SELECT
menu.name
, SUM(item_count::INT) as order_count
FROM
(
    SELECT
    id_order
    , single_item_orders->>'id_menu' as id_menu
    , single_item_orders->>'count' as item_count
    FROM
    (
        SELECT
        id_order
        , json_array_elements(order_description) as single_
item_orders
        FROM
            orders
    ) each_order
) each_order_flat
JOIN
menu
ON each_order_flat.id_menu::INT = menu.id_menu
GROUP BY
menu.name
ORDER BY
SUM(item_count::INT) DESC
```

It turns out that spicy pickles and garlic pickles are our top-selling items, and that blueberry pie is the lowest. Let's save this question and give it a name such as `Items Ordered`:

name	order_count
Spicy Pickles 🌶	43,151
Garlic Pickles 🧄	38,733
Banana Cream Pie 🍌	34,927
Dill Pickles 🌿	31,546
Chicken Pot Pie 🐔	30,108
Pumpkin Pie 🎃	25,062
Blueberry Pie 🫐	22,553

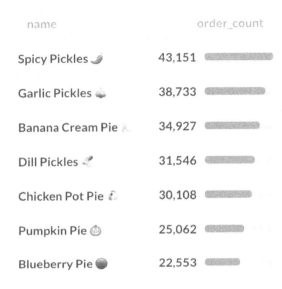

Figure 16.19 – The results from our question written entirely in SQL

The SQL query we had to write here is a relatively advanced one. Simple SQL queries are generally not necessary to write in Metabase since the notebook editor can easily capture the same business logic in a friendlier way. Many data analysts and scientists are so comfortable with writing SQL that they can actually express their questions *faster* by writing out SQL code compared to using the custom question editor. I would certainly put myself in that camp since I spend a lot of my professional days writing SQL (and even some of my leisure days). Even if you can write a SQL question faster than you can build one in the editor, I recommend using the custom question editor whenever possible. This is because using the editor leaves behind a blueprint that a less technical user that doesn't know SQL can easily follow and edit. We'll go much deeper into this topic in *Chapter 9, Using the SQL Console.*

In summary, SQL is the only option for any use case that can't be solved with a simple question or a custom question. Over time, the Metabase team will be adding more and more functionality to their custom question editor to bring it closer to parity with SQL. However, with so many databases and so many SQL dialects out there, there are likely always going to be a few use cases where SQL makes the most sense. There are other ways that using the SQL console can be quite useful in Metabase, and we'll learn more about them in *Chapter 9, Using the SQL Console.*

Summary

In this chapter, we learned how to create questions in several different ways. We learned about the importance of questions and how they are the fundamental building blocks for all the analytics we do in Metabase. We learned how to use Metabase's notebook-style editor to create custom questions and do complex operations, such as joins and creating custom columns and expressions. We learned how to save our finished questions and put them into collections for better organization. We also saw a few different ways that questions can be represented visually.

In the next chapter, we'll learn more about the various ways we can visualize data in Metabase. We'll cover all the different visualizations offered and learn about what types of visualizations are appropriate for different types of data.

7
Creating Visualizations

At this point, we have learned how to create questions, the fundamental building block in Metabase. Questions, as you may have gathered by now, are really more like answers. A saved question such as *How many orders have been placed?* tells us the answer to that question.

So far, we've mostly ignored considerations around how to present the data returned from a question. Up to this point, we've been letting Metabase make its best guess about what the output data should look like – that is, whether it should be displayed as a table of data, such as a spreadsheet, or rendered as a line or bar plot.

Visualizing data is an important tenant of analytics. Just as a picture can be worth a thousand words, a good visualization can communicate far more than the sum of its parts. In this chapter, we will learn about all the visualization options Metabase offers, including how to use them to create goals. Specifically, we will cover the following main topics:

- Customizing plots
- Creating bar plots, histograms, and row plots
- Exploring more visualizations in Metabase
- Setting up alerts
- Creating maps

Technical requirements

You will only need your instance of Metabase running with a connection to the `pies` database to work through the examples in this chapter.

Customizing plots

Without it being our explicit goal, we created a line plot in *Chapter 6, Creating Questions*. When we took our **Orders** table and counted the rows by **Created Date**, Metabase guessed that we would want the data to be displayed as a **line plot**. In analytics, especially business analytics, line plots tend to be the most popular type of data visualization. That is because line plots are used to show time series data where data is summarized over intervals of time, such as days, weeks, months, quarters, or years.

When we came across this line plot in the last chapter, we simply saved it as a question and moved on. Let's now create another one and explore all the ways Metabase will let us customize our visualization. Let's get started.

In the last chapter, we looked at order growth over time. Now let's look at user growth over time. Since this involves a single table (**Users**), a single aggregation (**Count of rows**), and a single grouping (**Created Date**), we can use the **Simple Question** feature:

1. Click **Ask a Question** from the top bar.
2. Click on **Simple Question**.
3. Under **Pick your data**, select **Pies** | **Users**.

4. Click the green **Summarize** button to open the summarize tray on the right-hand side.
5. Keep **Count of Rows** as the default **Summarize By** option.
6. Under **Group By**, select **Created Date.**
7. Click **by month**, and change the time grain option to **Day**.
8. Click **Done**.

You should see a time series plot, showing user growth over time, as in *Figure 7.1*:

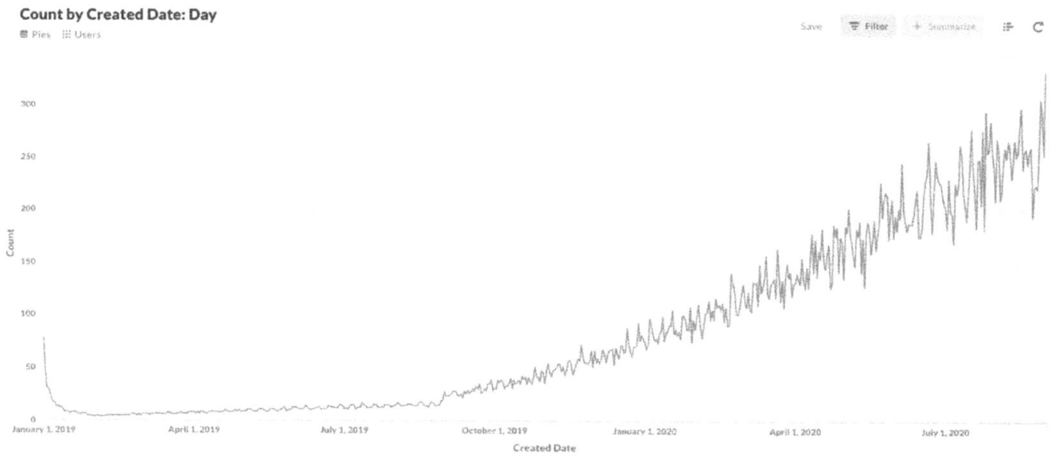

Figure 7.1 – A line plot of user growth over time

Let's take a moment to examine this plot. It seems to have a bit of a curious shape to it. Unlike our time series of order growth, which started very low and grew over time, this plot suggests that we had an initial spike of users when our business first opened that quickly dropped. Then it looks like we had a period of very slow growth from around February 2019 to September 2019, and then things started picking up. It would be great to understand the factors behind this, as it might give us some insight into our business. Let's make a mental note to return to this later since it looks interesting. For now, though, we have a nice looking plot showing user growth over time. But this is yet another blue line plot with generic names on the axes. Let's learn how we can polish the plot, making it look better and conveying more information.

Choosing a visualization

We've already seen our data visualized in a few different ways in Metabase. In the last chapter, we encountered line plots and bar plots. We also saw our data displayed simply as a single number or as a table (Metabase considers these visualizations as well). Metabase has more visualization options than these. Let's see them all. In the bottom left-hand corner of the page, find the **Visualization** button and click it. A tray of 14 visualization options, as in *Figure 7.2*, will appear. Although there are 14 options, 4 of those are grayed out. This is because Metabase has already determined that our data is not in the right shape for these. However, in this chapter, we will learn how and when to use each of the 14 visualizations:

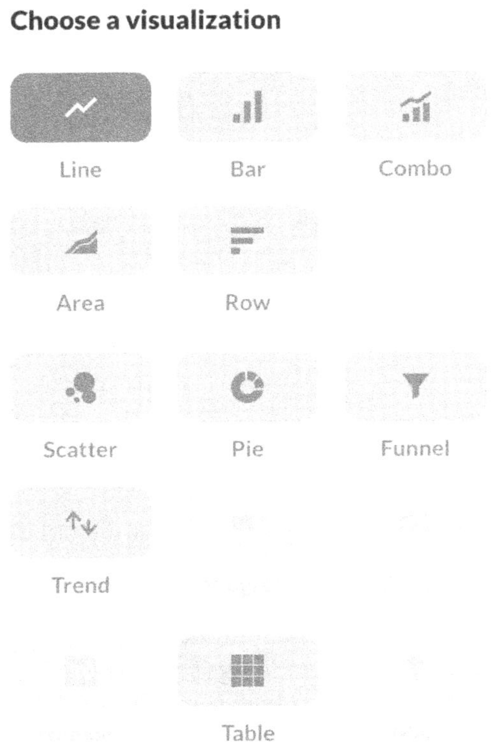

Figure 7.2 – Visualization options for our data. Metabase only makes visualizations available that make sense with the result set

Feel free to click on all the visualization options that aren't in gray, just to get a feel for what they do. For example, clicking on the **Bar** icon will simply change the plot from having the count of users by day represented by a point on a line to the height of a rectangle. To return to the set of visualization options, click the back arrow next to the words **Bar options**. Clicking **Area** will render the plot just like a line plot, but with the area between the line and the *X* axis shaded in. Go through as many as you like, although we will find a use case for each one in this chapter. With some visualization options, such as **Scatter**, you will notice it returns nonsensical results with this particular type of data.

We'll return to these visualization options later in the chapter. For now, let's stick with the **Line** plot and learn how to customize it.

Customizing a simple line plot

If you have not already, click **Line** from the visualization options. Below the **Line** options, you will see four pills (called a pill because it's shaped like a pill): **Data**, **Display**, **Axes**, and **Labels**. Let's learn about each one.

Customizing the Data option for your plot

The **Data** pill should be highlighted by default. If not, click it. When clicked, it will show dropdowns for both the *X* axis and the *Y* axis. Because our question only has a single grouping variable and a single summarization, there will be only one option for the *X* axis and only one for the *Y* axis. However, if we had multiple grouping variables or aggregations, we could pick the ones we want on the line plot here.

Clicking the gear icon next to **X-axis** or **Y-axis** will open up formatting options. Let's click the gear option next to the *X* axis. Because our *X* axis is a date, the options will be around how we want to format our dates in the plot. Depending on how you or your organization prefers to see dates rendered, you can choose this here.

Clicking the gear next to the *Y* axis will give us the formatting options for the *Y* axis. Let's learn about them one by one:

- **Style**: Since our *Y* axis displays a numeric value, this option allows us to style it either as a normal number, a percentage, a currency, or if it's a really large (or small) number, in scientific notation. For our purposes, leaving it as **Normal** is fine.

- **Separator Style**: Different countries have different conventions around how to separate numbers to make them more readable. For example, in the US, a million is represented by 1,000,000. In Europe, a dot is used instead of the comma, so a million would be 1.000.000. We learned how to set this at a global level in *Chapter 5, Building Your Data Model*, but if there are specific questions where you want to override that value, you can do so at the question level here. We will leave this as is.
- **Minimum number of decimal places**: Since we are counting only whole orders, we have no use for decimal places here, but you can imagine other questions might involve decimal places (such as average order value in dollars). To pick how many decimals you want to round up or down to, use the up and down arrows here.
- **Multiply by a number**: Should you need to scale your number up or down by a given factor, you can do so here.
- **Add a prefix**: Should you want to add context to the names on your axes, you can do so here. For example, adding `Users Signed up -` in this box will change the value on the *Y* axis from **1,000** to **Users Signed up – 1,000**.
- **Add a suffix**: Just like the **Add a prefix** option, except it will add the string to the end.

There are additional options that you will find under the **Data** pill for different plot types. We will cover those later in the chapter when we learn about the different plot types themselves. Now that we have an understanding of what the options under **Data** do, let's learn about the **Display** pill.

Customizing the display for your plot

To open the **Display** options, click the **Display** pill next to the **Data** pill. Let's learn about all the options one by one:

- **Add a Goal Line**: Optionally, you can toggle **Add a Goal Line** on to add a horizontal line to your plot representing some goal or target you would like to reach. For example, imagine we have given ourselves the goal of getting to 400 new users per day by the end of the year. To set that, toggle on **Add a Goal Line**, and type `400` into the **Goal value** text box. Optionally, you can change the text on the plot from **Goal** to something else, such as `New User Goal`, by typing that into the **Goal label** text box.

- **Add a Trend Line**: Adding a trend line works well for noisy data like ours. Toggling the **Add a Trend Line** option will either add a linear or polynomial-based trend line to best fit the data points in our plot.

Show values on data points: This will give you numerical labels on all or some of your data points. If you turn this on, you'll notice that there are many ways to customize this option. Metabase, as it often does, will make its best guess on how to format the values to leave enough space for them to be visually legible, but that can be overridden.

- **Choosing a color for your plot**: Click the blue square to see eight other colors you can apply to your plot. Variety is the spice of life, so I try to not make every plot of mine render in blue.
- **Naming your Y-axis**: Next to the color picker is a text field with the word **Count** in it. This corresponds to the name on the *Y* axis. As long as you save your question with a proper, descriptive name, such as `User Signups by Day`, there is no need to change the value here but it never hurts to be a little redundant. A good option for this field could be `Count of User accounts created`.
- **Picking a visualization**: Next to the text field are three icons that allow you to quickly change the type of visualization to an area or bar plot. We could also have taken these same actions in the **Choose a visualization** part of the flow we saw earlier.
- **Line Style**: If you've kept your plot as a line or area plot, this option allows you to pick the type of line you want. The default is a line plot made of straight-line segments from one data point to the next. The other options are to connect your data points with a wavy line or a horizontal and vertical line creating a step function. This is mostly a matter of personal taste and aesthetics. A straight line works well for our plot, so let's keep that.

- **Show dots on lines**: Based on the spacing of your data points, Metabase will guess whether you want dots on your line plot corresponding to your actual data points. This is what the **Auto** option is, which is selected by default. You may override that and explicitly turn them **On** or **Off**. Again, this is mostly a matter of personal taste. The purpose of having dots is to communicate the granularity of the *X* axis. For example, if we were looking at the count of users by month, dots would help us better see where the month breaks are, as in *Figure 7.3*:

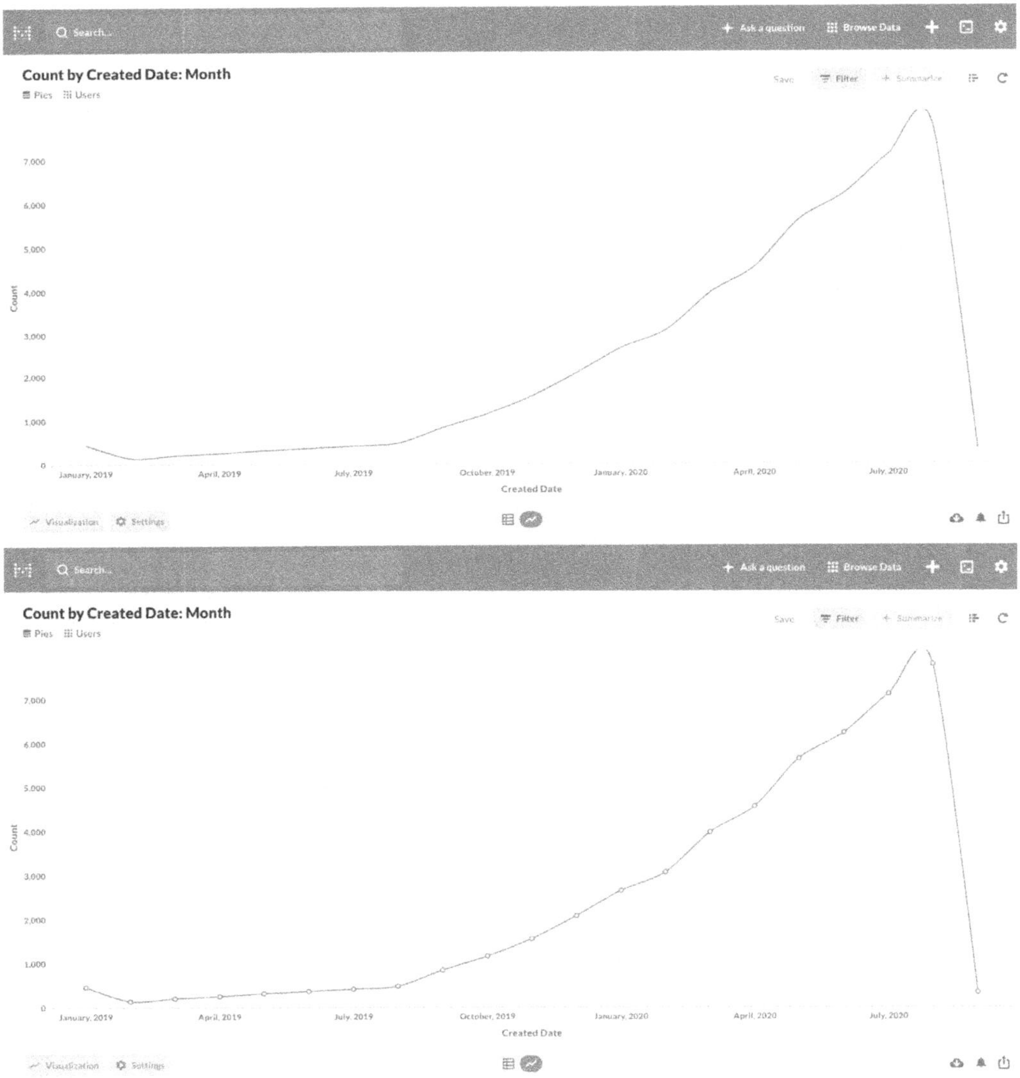

Figure 7.3 – Dots on a line plot offer visual clues about the granularity of the X axis

- **Replace Missing Values with**: This option allows us to specify what to do with dates in our time series that have no records. We happen to not have any missing values, but *Figure 7.4* shows what a subset of our plot would look like with missing values for the first week of April 1, 2019. The options, as seen in *Figure 7.4*, are either to show **Nothing** (top plot), **Zero** (bottom left), or **Linear Interpolated** (bottom right), which means a straight line is drawn between the missing data points. Since we have no missing data, all the options will look the same. In general, I think it's best to use **Nothing** or **Zero**, as **Linear Interpolated** may lead to missing a potential problem in the data:

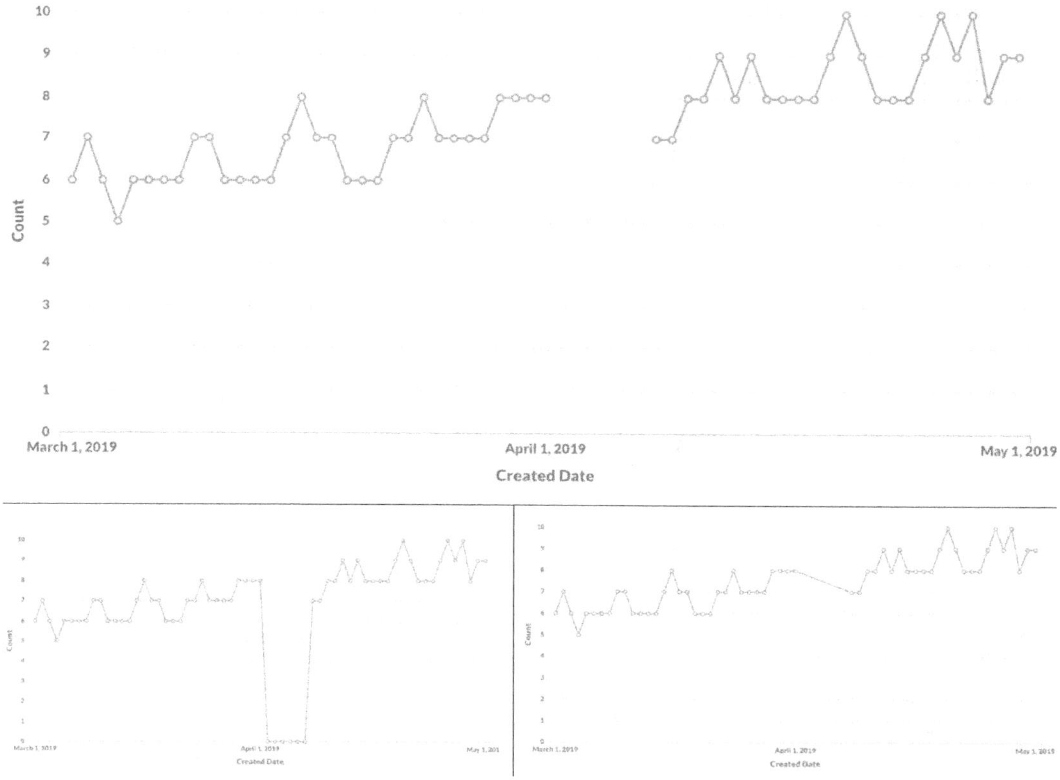

Figure 7.4 – Three ways to represent missing values on a line plot

Let's move on to the **Axes** option.

Customizing the Axes option for your plot

The next option for formatting our plot is the **Axes** option. Click the **Axes** pill to open up the options. Let's learn about them:

- **X-axis scale**: We are given the option to use a **Timeseries** or **Ordinal** scale for our plot. These behave similarly, but since we are looking at our data across time, **Timeseries** is the appropriate one. Had we used a categorical variable on our *X* axis, such as **Credit Card Provider**, **Ordinal** would be appropriate.
- **Y-axis scale**: The default scale in **Linear**, which means that the *Y* axis is based on evenly spaced numbers. You can also change this to a **Power** or **Log** scale. These scales can be helpful if the metric you are measuring grows exponentially, as they will stretch out the *Y* axis.
- **Show X-axis line and marks**: This option lets you format the labels on the ticks of your *X* axis. In our example, the *X* axis has dates printed out, such as **January 1, 2020**. You can choose to hide these, abbreviate them, or rotate them 45 or 90 degrees.
- **Auto y-axis range**: By default, Metabase automatically will start the *Y* axis at 0 and range upward to fit your maximum value in the plot. For some line plots, it may be visually confusing to have the *Y* axis start at `0`. For example, if your values are all quite large, having your axis start at `0` can compress the variation in the data and make it hard to see. To override that, turn off the **Auto** *Y* axis range toggle. You can then specify your own **Min** and **Max** values. For our plot, keeping the **Auto** *Y* axis range option on makes the most sense.

The last pill option to customize our line plot is **Labels**. Let's click on that and learn about it.

Customizing the Labels option for your plot

We are almost finished exploring all the ways to customize our plot. The **Labels** pill allows you to customize the names of your *X* and *Y* axis labels, or to hide them. Since we've already named our *Y* axis in the **Display** step, the only thing we can do here is name our *X* axis. **Created Date** is fine, but to be more explicit, let's change it to `Signup Date`. Click **Done** at the bottom of the screen, save the question, and add it to the **Our Analytics** collection.

We've now explored all the ways we can customize our line plot. You obviously don't have to go through them all each time you create a plot, but it's good to learn them once really well so that you know what your options are. Now that we've done that, let's learn about the other types of visualizations Metabase offers and when to use them.

Creating bar plots, histograms, and row plots

In the last section, we customized a line plot. While we were customizing it, we saw that we could have easily changed it to a **bar or area plot**, without sacrificing much of the visualization's fidelity. This is because the three types of plots – line, bar, and area – are all very similar and share code architecture. They all put one dimension on the *X* axis and one or more dimensions on the *Y* axis. The most common dimension on the *X* axis for line and area plots is a time-based dimension, such as a date. That's not always the case for bar plots. Let's learn about them, and what kind of data works best for them. We'll also learn about row plots, which are simply just bar plots rotated 90 degrees.

When to use bar plots

You can always use a bar plot instead of a line plot. However, when you have a lot of data points on your *X* axis, it will result in a lot of bars. To see what I mean, try changing the plot from the last section, which measured user accounts created by day, from a line plot to a bar plot. Notice that the bar plot is harder to read than the line plot. With data like this, where there are many data points to plot, I don't recommend a bar plot. Conversely, when you only have a few data points, such as when they represent a dimension with low cardinality, a bar plot tends to be far more legible than a line plot. Let's see an example.

Creating a bar plot

Before we create a bar plot, let's create a new question that will be well-suited for the example. Let's look at the average star rating for each menu item. To create this question, start off by clicking **Ask a question**:

1. Chose the **Custom question** option.
2. Click to choose the **Pies** database and then click the **Reviews** table.
3. Under **Summarize**, select **Average of**. Next, click **Star Rating**.
4. Click **Pick a column to group by**.
5. Find the **ID Menu** foreign key symbol and expand it. Alternatively, you could make a left outer or inner join to the **Menu** table on **ID Menu**.
6. Choose **Name** from the **Menu** table as the grouping variable.
7. Now, click **Sort** and choose **Average of Star rating** as the value to sort by.

8. Finally, click **Visualize**. Your notebook editor should look as in *Figure 7.5*:

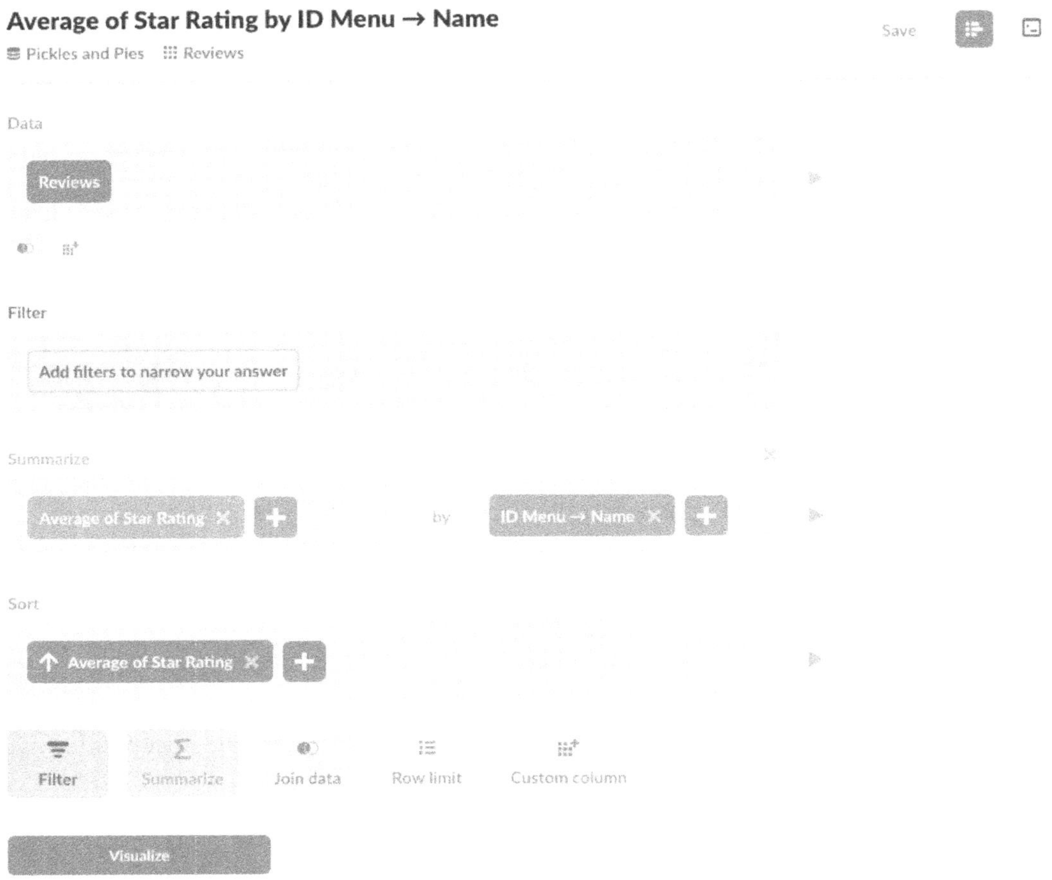

Figure 7.5 – Creating Average of Star Rating in the notebook editor

Metabase chooses, by default, to represent this as a bar plot. Let's change it to a line plot just to compare the readability of the two. Click **Visualization** and from the grid, click **Line**. The two plots are shown in *Figure 7.6*. It's a lot easier to see how the average ratings compare in the bar plot:

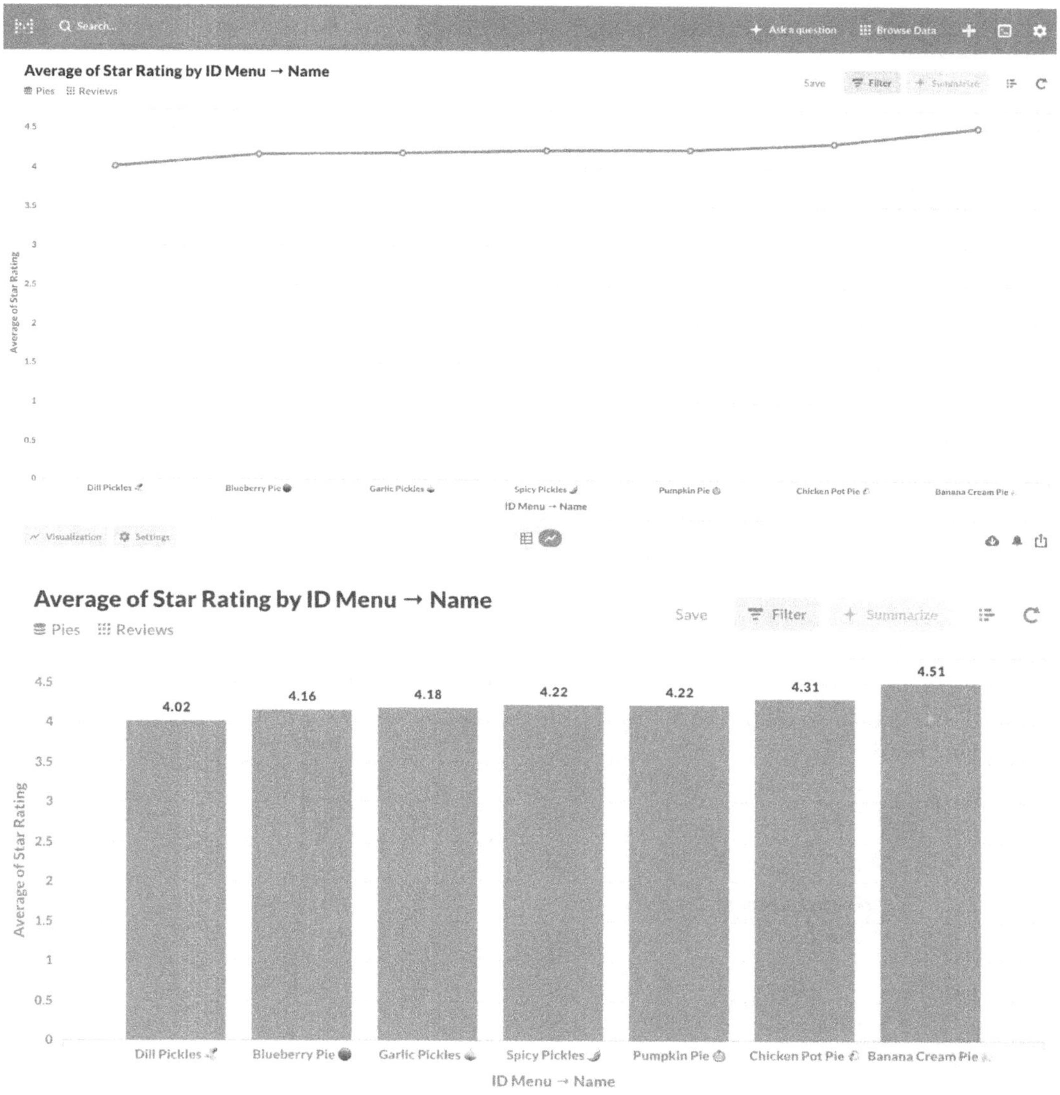

Figure 7.6 – Comparing a line plot to a bar plot. When the X axis has low cardinality, a bar plot is often easier to interpret

Let's save this question since we'll return to it in a moment. Call it `Average Star Rating by Menu Item`.

Notice how, in the bar plot we created, our variable on the *X* axis is a **discrete** variable. When we create a bar plot using a **continuous** variable, such as **Order Total**, we call it a **histogram**. Let's learn more about them.

Creating a histogram

Consider a variable such as **Order Total**, which captures the dollar value of a given order. This is a continuous variable since it can take on any value. For example, one order could total to $10.00, while another one could total to $10.01. With taxes, discounts, and everything else, an order could theoretically total to some irrational number. When visualizing continuous variables, the goal is to see the *distribution* of the data rather than each individual point. This is generally accomplished by creating a histogram, which is a bar plot where the bars span over a range of values. Let's ask another question to build more intuition:

1. Chose the **Custom question** option.
2. Click to choose the **Pies** database and then click the **Orders** table.
3. Under **Summarize**, select **Count of rows**.
4. Next, in the grouping section, click **Order Total**.
5. Click **Visualize**.

Instead of creating a bar for each unique **Order Total** value, which would lead to a noisy and difficult-to-interpret plot, Metabase smartly bins them based on *ranges* of **Order Total**. This helps us get a sense of the distribution of **Order Total**. As can be seen in *Figure 7.7*, most orders tend to be in the $7 to $22 range, and in rare instances, an order comes in totaling over $60:

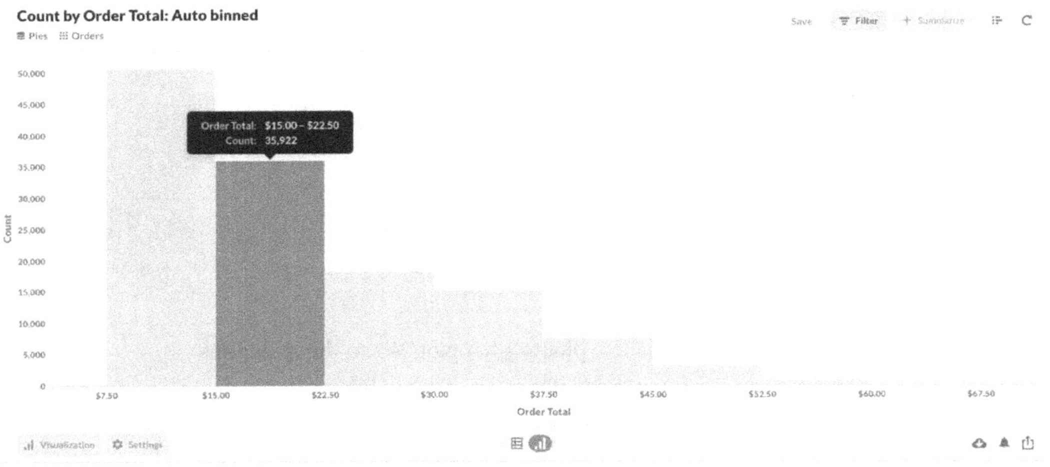

Figure 7.7 – A histogram showing the distribution of Order Total

Note that Metabase has automatically chosen the number of bins for the histogram, and even called it out in the title of the visualization: **Count by Order Total: Auto Binned**. If you would like to choose a different number of bins, you can do so by opening back up the notebook editor. In the grouping section, which should be populated with **Order Total: Auto Binned**, you can click on it and change the number of bins to **10**, **50**, **100**, or choose to not bin the data at all.

Similar to the bar plot and histogram is the row plot, which is just a bar plot rotated 90 degrees. They can often be easier to read than a bar plot. Let's quickly learn how to transform our bar plot into a row plot.

Creating a row plot

At this point, you have probably gotten the hang of changing the visualization, so this one will be easy. Transforming a bar plot to a row plot is as easy as clicking **Visualization** and choosing **Row** from the grid of options. Let's see an example. Open up the question we saved earlier, **Average Star Rating by Menu Item**:

1. Click **Visualization**.
2. Click **Row**.

This rotates the bar plot by 90 degrees. Some people think this is easier to read. If you like this better, you can save it and replace the original bar plot.

We have now explored the most common ways of visualizing a single metric and a single grouping variable. This will handle a lot of our plotting needs, but often we'll want to plot multiple metrics or one metric broken down by several dimensions on a single plot. We'll learn how to make plots like these next.

Plots with multiple dimensions or metrics

In *Chapter 6, Creating Questions*, we created the **Orders per Day** question and saved it as a line plot. We learned that our business has been steadily growing over time, which is great! Now we would like to learn a little more about this growth in orders. In particular, we want to understand how much of this growth can be attributed to **Pick-Up** orders versus **Delivery**. In this case, we're still interested in the same metric: **Orders per Day**. However, we want to see the metric broken down by two dimensions. Let's learn how we can create this question.

Creating a plot with two dimensions

Let's create our plot of **Orders by Day**, broken down by **Pick-Up** and **Delivery**:

1. Click **Ask a question**.
2. Choose **Custom question**.
3. In the **Data** section, choose **Pies** and **Orders**.
4. Choose **Count of Rows** in the **Summarize** section.
5. For the grouping variables, use both **Created Date** and **Order Type**. You can keep the time granularity of **Created Date** to its default value, **Week**.
6. Click **Visualize**.

The visualization shows us the growth over time of both types of orders – **Pick-Up** and **Delivery** – by using a line for each type. It looks like **Pick-Up** orders were the majority until October 2019, when **Delivery** orders started to take off. Now, **Delivery** orders are much higher than **Pick-Up**. By how much? It turns out, we can answer that by changing the plot to an area plot:

> **Important Note**
> You may have noticed that there appears to be a sharp drop in orders for the most recent week. Does that mean our business is in trouble? Fortunately, it does not. Our data only goes up to September 1, 2020, so imagine today is September 1. Because we're looking at orders per week, Metabase is defining the most recent week as August 30 to September 5. So, the reason our orders look lower is simply that we're at the start of the week!

1. From the grid of visualizations, choose **Area**.
2. Note that all this does is shade the area below the lines. For the parts of the area plot that overlap, the shading blends slightly.
3. Click **Display**.
4. Under **Stacking**, click the **Stack** radio button.

   Doing this *stacks* the areas on top of each other. This lets us see the total orders measured on the *Y* axis, but broken down by order type. This might be a better option if our main goal is to show total orders, where the breakdown by order type is a secondary goal. However, this hasn't properly answered our question "By how much?". Let's make one more change.
5. Click the **Stack – 100%** radio button.

This forces each value on the *X* axis to total up to 100% on the *Y* axis. The shaded areas correspond to how much of the total orders were either pick-up or delivery. This shows us that at the beginning, we were doing about 55% pick-ups and 45% delivery. More recently, even though pick-up orders have grown, they have been so far outpaced by delivery that they now only make up 21% of orders.

Note that we didn't have to change our question to represent our data differently here. Creating a question to show the percentage of **Pick-Up** versus **Delivery** orders would actually be quite difficult. Fortunately, Metabase's visualization library allows this to be done in just a few clicks. Let's save this question. Give it a name such as `Percentage of Pick Up and Delivery Orders by Week`, and add it to the **Our Analytics** collection.

Now that we've learned how to plot a single metric, broken down by two dimensions, let's learn how to plot two metrics.

Creating a plot with two metrics

Let's now imagine that we want to see our standard view of order count over time but we also want to add a line to track revenue over time. Just because orders are going up, doesn't necessarily mean that revenue is, too, although you would assume so. To take any ambiguity away, let's visualize it. Plotting two metrics is slightly different from what we were looking at before with order count broken down by two dimensions (**Delivery** or **Pick-Up**). For that question, both values represented counts of orders, so our *Y* axis was just representing order count. Now, we want to look at two metrics: orders *and* revenue. It's not possible to represent them both on the same *Y* axis, so instead, we'll create a plot with two *Y* axes. Here's how we'll do it:

1. Click **Ask a question**.
2. Choose **Custom question**.
3. In the **Data** section, choose **Pies** and **Orders**.
4. Under **Summarize**, scroll down to **Common Metrics** and expand it. You should see **Order Revenue**, provided you created that as a metric back in *Chapter 5*, *Building Your Data Model*. If you didn't create it as a metric in *Chapter 5*, choose **Sum of** and **Order Total** in the **Basic Metrics** section.
5. Now, still in the **Summarize** section, select **Count of Rows** from **Basic Metrics**.
6. Group it by **Created Date**, with **Week** as the time grain.
7. Click **Visualize**.

The plot we get from this question has two lines, just like in our last section. However, this one also has two *Y* axes. The one on the left is scaled to measure **Order Revenue**, in dollars, and the one on the right is scaled to measure the count of orders. As you would expect, they are very tightly correlated. Let's save this. Name it `Orders and Revenue by Week` and add it to the **Our Analytics** collection.

Creating a plot with many dimensions or metrics

In the last two sections, we learned how to create plots with two metrics, or a single metric broken down by two dimensions. This is easily extendible to as many metrics or dimensions as you like. Let's work through an example, showing the number of reviews by menu item over time:

1. Click **Ask a question**.
2. Choose **Custom question**.
3. In the **Data** section, choose **Pies** and **Reviews**.
4. Under **Summarize**, choose **Count of Rows**.
5. In the grouping section, expand the **ID Order** foreign key and choose **Created Date**. For the time grain, keep the default **by week** option.
6. Still in the grouping section, expand the **ID Menu** foreign key and choose **Name**.
7. Click **Visualize**.

   Metabase will return a multi-line plot, where each menu item has its own line on the plot. It's a bit messy to look at, so let's change it to a stacked bar plot.

8. Click the **Visualization** button.
9. From the grid of options, click **Bar**.
10. Click the **Display** pill, and under **Stacking**, click the **Stack** radio button.

This is much easier to interpret. If you like, you can also change the colors to more closely match the colors of the emojis. That can certainly improve the readability of the plot. When you are done customizing your plot, save it and call it `Reviews of Menu items over time`. Add it to the **Our Analytics** collection.

We've now covered the most used types of plots. There's still a lot more in Metabase's visualization library, though, so let's move on to the other ones.

Exploring more visualizations in Metabase

In this section, we'll learn about some of the other visualizations we can do in Metabase. We'll start with **scatter plots**.

Creating scatter plots

In the last section, we learned how to create plots with multiple dimensions and metrics. In our plot of order count and order revenue, we noticed the two values had a lot of **correlation**, or co-movement. A big part of analytics and data science involves looking at correlations, understanding how one metric moves when another one does as well. The type of plot most commonly used to visualize how two metrics correlate is the scatter plot. Let's learn how to make one.

First, let's think of two metrics that we'd like to examine the relationship of. Let's choose to examine how the average review score correlates with the number of reviews for a given menu item. We'd expect that the more reviews a menu item has the higher its average review score. Let's see whether there's any truth to that:

1. Click **Ask a question**.
2. Choose **Custom question**.
3. In the **Data** section, choose **Pies** and **Reviews**.
4. In the **Summarize** section, we will create two metrics. The first will be **Average of Star Rating**, and the second will be **Count of Rows**, representing the number of reviews.
5. In the grouping section, choose **ID Menu | Name**.
6. Click **Visualize**.

   Metabase will return a bar plot, with the menu items on the *X* axis and the average rating on the *Y* axis.
7. Click the **Visualization** button.
8. Change the visualization to **Scatter**. The plot returned will be blank.
9. Under the **Scatter** options, the **Data** pill should be highlighted. Under the **X-axis** section, select **Average of Star Rating** from the dropdown.
10. Under **Y-axis**, select **Count**.

You should see a plot appear with 7 points. By hovering your mouse over the points, you can tell that each point is a menu item. The *X* axis corresponds to that menu items average rating, and the *Y* axis corresponds to the total number of reviews. Is there a correlation between the two? It doesn't seem like it. However, if you hover over the points, you might notice that there are two linear relationships, depending on whether the menu item is a pickle or a pie. It appears that we've unlocked a key insight in our data: pickles tend to get rated lower than pies, but for the two categories, highly rated items tend to have more reviews associated with them! Let's factor this insight into our scatter plot. Open the question editor back up, by clicking the **Show Editor** icon in the upper right-hand corner. Let's create a custom column to separate pies from pickles:

1. Toward the top of the notebook editor, click the **Custom column** icon.
2. We will need to write a somewhat complex formula to create a column indicating whether the menu item is in the `Pickles` category or `Pies`. We did something similar to this in *Chapter 5, Building Your Data Model*, when we defined `Pickles` as a segment in our data. In this case, we'll use the following formula to say an item belongs to `Pickles` or `Pies`:

```
= coalesce(regexextract([ID Menu → Name], "Pickles"),
"Pies")
```

3. Give this formula a name, such as `Item Category`, and click **Done**.
4. In the grouping section, click the + button and add **Item Category** as a grouping variable. At this point, your notebook editor should look as in *Figure 7.8*:

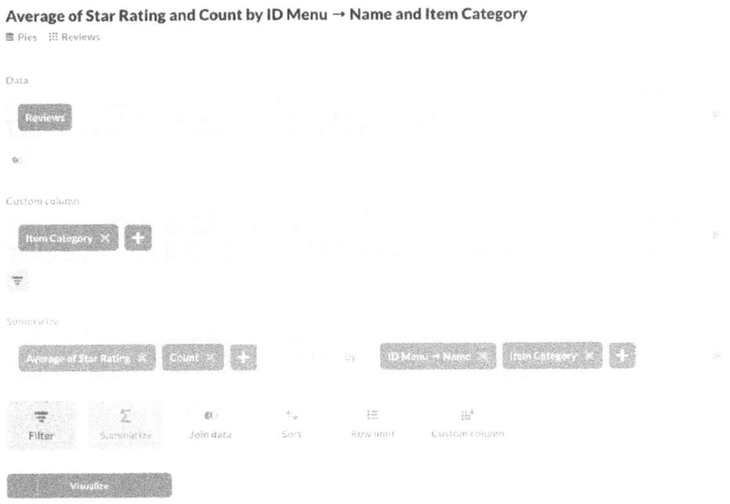

Figure 7.8 – Notebook editor view for our scatterplot

5. Now, return to the scatter visualization.
6. Under the **Data** pill option, add a series breakout to the *X* axis.
7. In the dropdown, select **Item Category**.

You should see the points in the scatter plot change color to represent whether the menu item is in the `Pickles` or `Pies` category. Now, the linear relationship between average star rating and reviews is clear – items with higher scores are reviewed more, and although the relationship appears linear, whether it's a pickled item or a pie has implications on both the review count and the average review. *Figure 7.9* shows the relationship. I've added my own trend lines to call out the two linear relationships. Let's save this. Call it `Review score and Reviews for Pickles and Pies`. Add it to **Our Analytics**:

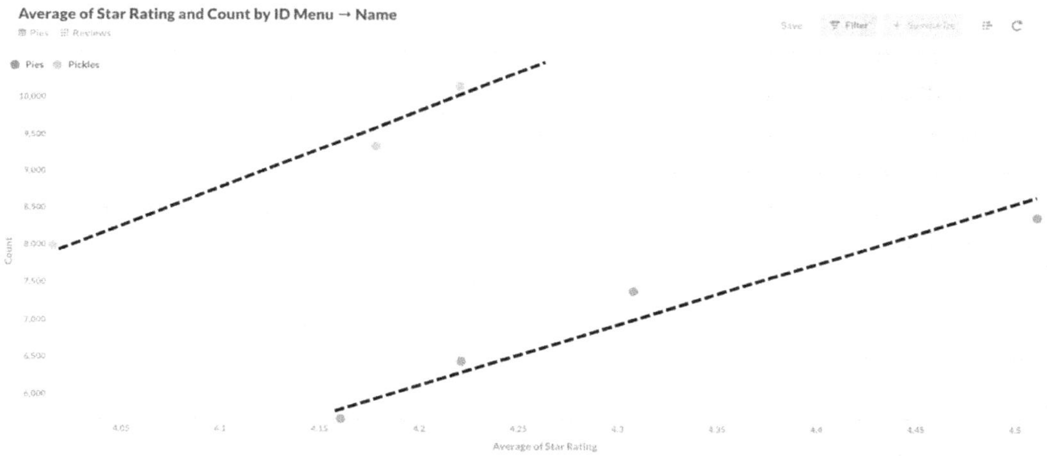

Figure 7.9 – The linear relationship between ratings and reviews for Pickles and Pies

Scatter plots like these will be useful anytime you want to explore the relationship between two metrics. Next up, we'll learn about pie plots.

Creating pie plots

Pie plots, like stacked area and stacked bar plots, are used to show what percentage of a metric belongs to a given dimension.

Many people in the analytics and data science community over the last decade have been vocal about the inefficacy of pie plots, crusading to remove them from the standard visualization libraries. This is because humans are not as great at differentiating the sizes of segments in a circle as they are at differentiating, say, the sizes of rectangles next to each other. To see what I mean, let's look at our bar plot showing the count of reviews by item in *Figure 7.10*:

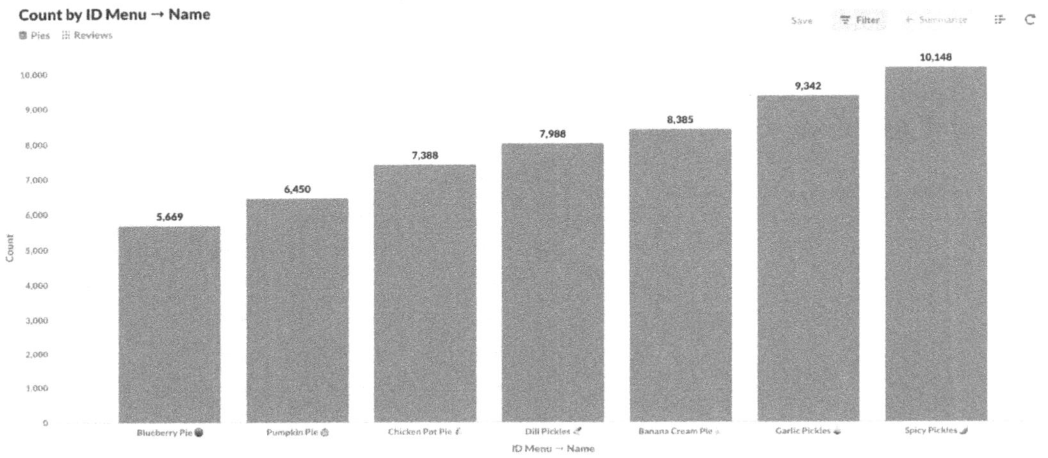

Figure 7.10 – Reviews by menu items rendered as a bar plot

Now let's look at that same data represented in a pie plot in *Figure 7.11*:

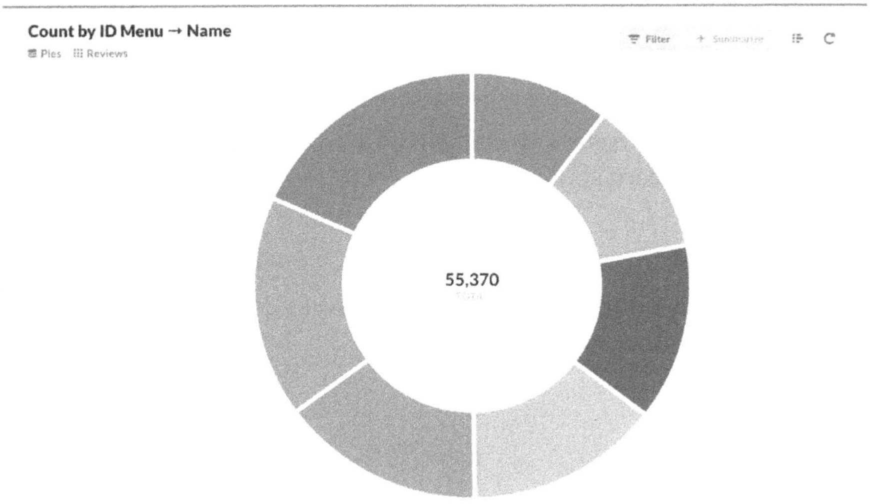

Figure 7.11 – The same data as Figure 7.10, but rendered as a pie plot

In the bar plot, it's easy to tell whether one bar is higher than another. In the pie plot, however, it's harder to compare segments. It's even harder to tell how much larger one segment is from another. We're just not as good at telling these segments apart as we are with rectangles.

At the same time, I'm of the opinion that a pie plot has its place in data visualization, provided it's used properly. We're good at recognizing when a quarter, a third, or half of a pie is gone, so when the breakdown of a given metric is something like that, a pie plot is appropriate. Let's not forget, after all, that our fictional business was founded on pies. Metabase shouldn't be the only thing that is "meta." Let's see how many of our reviews are for pickles versus pies. To do that, we'll borrow the same formula we used for our scatter plot:

1. Click **Ask a question**.
2. Choose **Custom question**.
3. In the **Data** section, choose **Pies** and **Reviews**.
4. Create a custom column with the following formula:

```
= coalesce(regexextract([ID Menu → Name], "Pickles"),
"Pies")
```

5. Give this formula a name, such as `Item Category`, and click **Done**.
6. In the **Summarize** section, choose **Count of Rows**.
7. In the **Grouping** section, choose **Item Category**, or whatever you named your custom column.
8. Click **Visualize**. This should return a table.
9. Click the **Visualization** button and choose **Pie**.

You can clearly see that the number of reviews is almost 50% pies and 50% pickles, but is slightly tipped in favor of pies. Also, note that the legend clearly breaks down the percentages in numerical form. This is completely appropriate for a pie chart since the information is legible. Let's save it and call it `Total Reviews of Pies and Pickles`. Save it, again, to **Our Analytics**. Next, we'll learn how to create funnel plots.

Creating funnel plots

Funnel plots are particularly useful when understanding how users move through the steps of some flow you've designed for them. A classic example is visualizing how many users come to your website's landing page, and of those, how many click the **Sign-up** button, and then of those, how many actually create accounts.

Another good use case for a funnel plot is to visualize how users interact with our product. For example, it could be interesting to see how many of our users have placed one order, how many have placed two, how many have placed three, and so on. This can give us a good understanding of how satisfied our users are with our product. For example, if a user only ordered once, it could be that they found the pickles or pies to not be delicious enough to order again.

Let's create a question to capture this notion of **user retention**:

1. Click **Ask a question**.
2. Choose **Custom question**.
3. In the **Data** section, choose **Pies** and **Orders**.
4. In the **Summarize** section, choose **Count of rows**.
5. In the grouping section, click **ID User**.

   If we were to stop here, Metabase would return each user and the number of orders that the user has made. However, we want to go one layer of summarization deeper.
6. Click the green **Summarize** button.
7. In the **Summarize** section, choose **Count of rows**.
8. In the **Grouping** section, click **# Count**.
9. Click **Visualize**. Your editor should look as in *Figure 7.12*:

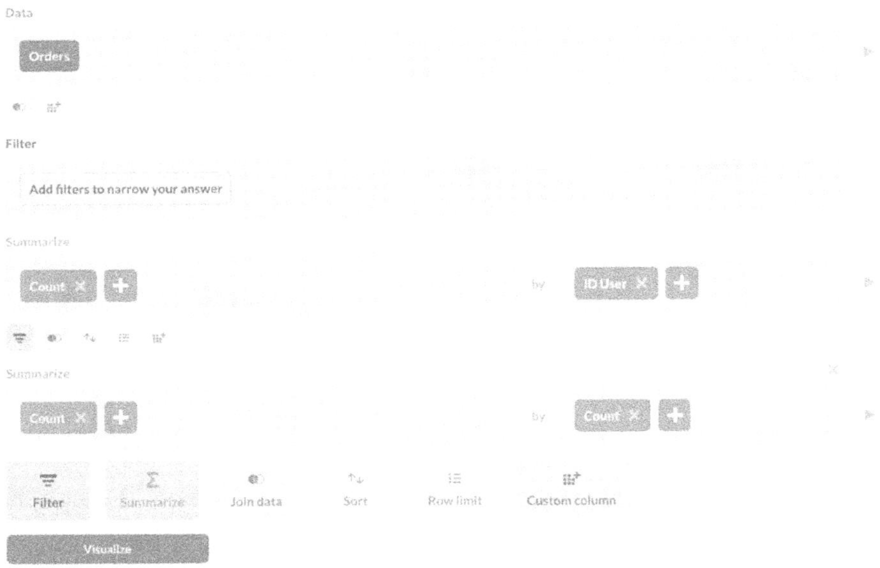

Figure 7.12 – Creating a question with two levels of summarization

This returns the count of the number of orders per user. You can see that most users have just a few orders, while there are other very loyal users who have placed 30, 40, and even 50 orders. Wow! It's nice to see that our product resonates with some of our users so much. For our purposes, let's imagine that we only want to see users who have placed between 1 and 10 orders. We'll want to add a **Limit** to our question:

1. Open back up the notebook editor by clicking the **Show editor** icon.
2. At the bottom of the editor, click **Row limit**.
3. In the **Row limit** field, enter `10`.
4. Again, click **Visualize**.
5. Next, click the **Visualization** button and change the plot to **Funnel**.

The plot, which we can see in *Figure 7.13*, shows how many users had 1, 2, and so on, all the way up to 10 orders:

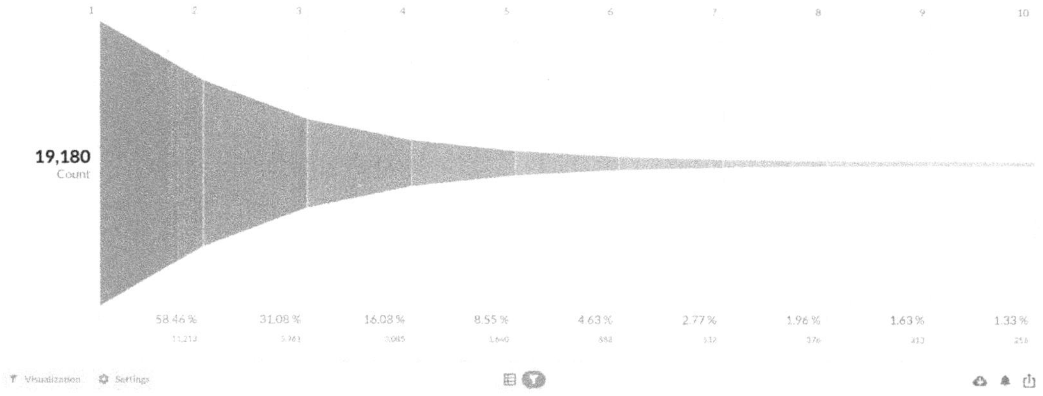

Figure 7.13 – A funnel plot showing orders per user

Before moving on, let's save this plot and give it a good name, such as `Orders per User (up to 10 orders)`. Next, we'll look at some simple visualization options based on single numbers.

Creating plots based on single numbers

Metabase has several useful ways to represent single numbers. While these types of visualizations are not very valuable on their own, they tend to be extremely useful when added to dashboards, as we will see in the next chapter. Let's learn how to make them.

Creating number, progress, gauge, and trend plots

In *Chapter 6*, *Creating Questions*, we created our first question, **Total Items placed**. Let's open it back up, by going to the **Our Analytics** collection and clicking on the **Total Items placed** question. You should see a single number.

Imagine that everyone in our organization is interested in this number. Perhaps the CEO has challenged the company to get to 200,000 orders by the end of the year, and so every day, employees ritually check this number. There tends to be one or two key metrics like this in every organization. Everyone is anchored to the number and doesn't need much context around it. For these types of metrics, using a single number visualization in Metabase is a good option. However, Metabase offers a few other ways to visualize a single number to give it more context. You can also set up **alerts** so that once a certain milestone is reached, you'll receive a notification. Let's learn about these, starting with **progress plots**.

Progress plots

Progress plots show a single number relative to a manually inputted goal. These are great for tracking an important metric that is aimed toward a specific number. For example, our goal might be 200,000 orders. Let's learn how to add that goal in a progress plot:

1. From the grid of visualization options, click **Progress**.
2. Next, under the **Display** pill, enter `200,000` in the text field under **Goal**.
3. Now, click the **Formatting** pill, and add `Orders` as a suffix (with a space in the beginning as padding).
4. Let's save this question, as we'll use it in the next section when we learn how to create **alerts**. Call it **Total Orders Placed (with Goal)**.

This visualization is helpful because it shows us how close we are to our goal. Another type of plot that is similar to a progress plot is a gauge plot. Let's learn about it next.

Gauge plots

A gauge plot is just like a progress plot, except instead of showing progress on a linear scale, it shows it on a circular scale. To change our progress plot to a gauge plot, click the **Gauge** visualization in the grid of options. You will see an animation appear, looking something like a speedometer in a car.

By default, the gauge is split into three sections: red, yellow, and green. Red will range from 0 to half of your metric's value. Yellow will range from half your metric's value to its value. Green will range from your metric's value to twice your metric's value. You can keep these as is, or change them to anything you like. You can add additional segments by clicking **+ Add a range** under the **Display** pill. Since our goal is 200,000, let's change the **Max** value for the green segment to that.

Depending on which one you prefer, save either the gauge or the progress plot. Call it `Total Orders versus Goal` and put it in the **Our Analytics** collection.

Trend plots

Trend plots are slightly different from number, progress, and gauge plots. They are based on time series data, not single numbers, but they display a single number with some information about how that number compares to itself in a previous range of time. Let's see an example:

1. From your Metabase home page, click **Browse all items** from **Our Analytics**.
2. Click the **Orders per Day** question.
3. Click on **Visualization** and choose **Trend**.

The visualization will present a single number, `678`, indicating the final number of our time series. Underneath, it will compare that number to the same number one day before. Depending on the time grain of our question, the comparison period will change. For example, if our question were showing us orders per month, the trend plot would compare our current monthly total to last month's.

Plots with trends, gauges, and goal lines are great ways to add context to your questions. It turns out that in addition to creating these goal-based annotations on your plots, you can also set up alerts in Metabase to be notified when goals are reached. Let's take a brief detour from our exploration of Metabase's visualization library to learn about alerts.

Setting up alerts

With Metabase, you can create **alerts** for any question. Alerts are trigger-based and will notify you either in Slack or via email. I find them to be most helpful for telling you when you've reached a goal, or when some special event happens. Let's learn about both types.

Goal-based alerts

To create a goal-based alert, start by opening the **Total Orders Placed (with Goal)** question we created in the last section. In the bottom-right corner of the page, find the bell symbol. Hovering over it reveals the text **Get alerts**. Click the bell. You'll be taken to the page pictured in *Figure 7.14*:

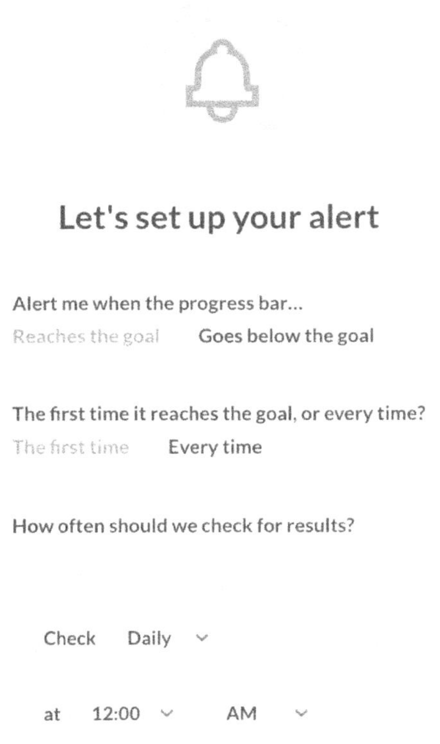

Figure 7.14 – Setting up an alert for our goal-based question

On the **Let's set up your alert** page, we can configure exactly how we want our alert to be configured. For our needs, the default options are perfect. With these options, we'll get an alert when the progress bar **reaches the goal** of 200,000. We could also get an alert for when the progress bar goes below the goal, but that doesn't make sense for this particular use case. We'll also get an alert **the first time** the goal is reached, as opposed to every time. For our use case, either option leads to the same result, since total orders can only go up.

In the next section, we can tell Metabase how often we want it to check for the results. The options are **Hourly**, **Daily**, or **Weekly**.

Finally, at the bottom of the page (shown in *Figure 7.15*), you can choose how you'd like to be alerted. The options are **Email** and/or **Slack**:

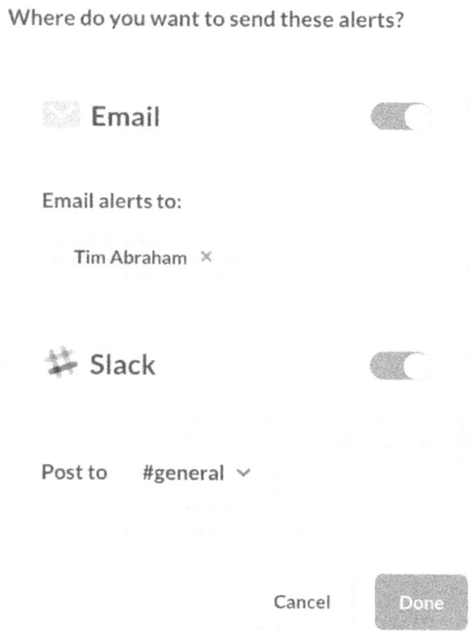

Figure 7.15 – Specifying the communication channels to send alerts to

Once you've configured everything for your alert, you can click **Done** to create it. Setting alerts based on reaching goals is one of the more useful ways to use alerts. Another powerful use case for alerts involves rare events. In the next section, we'll see an example.

Setting up event-based alerts

Imagine that our organization is building a VIP program and would like to reach out personally to any customer with an order of over $50. Since these high-value orders are rare, it would be cumbersome to manually check each day to see whether a new $50+ order has been placed. This is where alerts can be helpful. You can configure an alert to notify *only when* your question returns data; otherwise, it will just silently run in the background. Let's set this up. First, we'll need to create a new question:

1. Click **Ask a Question**.
2. Choose **Custom Question** from the three options.
3. Pick **Pies** as the database, and **Orders** as the table.
4. Now we'll add two filters. The first filter will check only for orders that were made yesterday, so add a filter based on **Created Date** being within the previous `1` day.

5. Add another filter based on **Order Total** being greater than `50`. Your notebook editor should look just as in *Figure 7.16*.
6. Now, click **Visualize**:

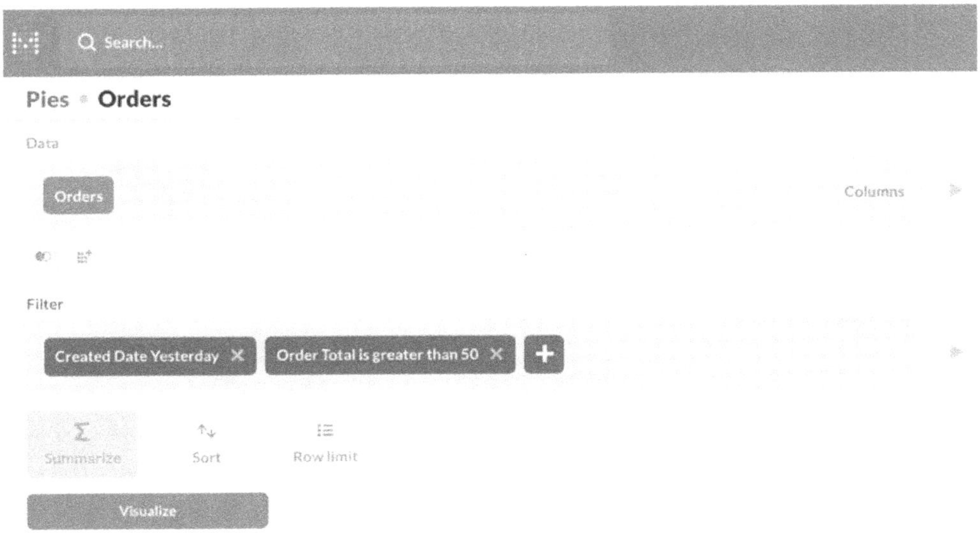

Figure 7.16 – A question to find new orders over $50, which we'll create an alert for

This should return a message saying **No results!**. That's fine since we don't expect to get an order above $50 often (never mind the fact that our example order data stops at September 1, 2020, and doesn't update. You'll have to imagine how this would work with live data).

7. Now click the alert bell in the lower right-hand corner.
8. You'll be prompted to save the question. Call it `High Value Orders in the last day`.

On the **Let's set up your alert** page, just as in the last section, you can choose how often you want Metabase to check this question. Since we've configured the question to look at yesterday's data only, it makes sense to check it **Daily** at **12:00 AM**, which is the default option. Next, choose whether you want the alerts to go out via email or Slack (or both), and click **Done** to create the alert. Now, whenever a day goes by with one or more orders totaling over $50, you'll know about it and can reach out to the customer personally.

We have now learned how to create alerts and covered nearly all the visualizations Metabase offers. There is one visualization that we haven't covered, and that's **maps**. Maps are probably the most impressive visualization Metabase offers, so I've been saving it for last. Let's learn about them.

Creating maps

Representing geospatial data on a map is surprisingly simple in Metabase. Most of the time, it "just works." To see what I mean, let's try a quick example.

Creating a region map of users by US state

Let's look at the steps to create a region map of users by US state:

1. Click **Ask a Question**.
2. Click **Custom question**.
3. In the **Data** section, choose **Pies** and **Users**.
4. In **Summarize**, choose **Count of Rows**.
5. In the **Grouping** section, choose **State**.
6. Click **Visualize**.

This will return an attractive map of the US filled in with a blue gradient mapped to display the count of users in each state, just as in *Figure 7.17*. We can see that most of our users are in California, which makes sense because that is where we are headquartered! It's also the most populous state in the US. However, our plot shows that almost 4 times as many users are in California compared to Texas. We can see Wikipedia that California only has about 37% larger of a population, so the high user count appears to be related to the location of our headquarters more than the baseline population being large (`https://en.wikipedia.org/wiki/List_of_states_and_territories_of_the_United_States_by_population`):

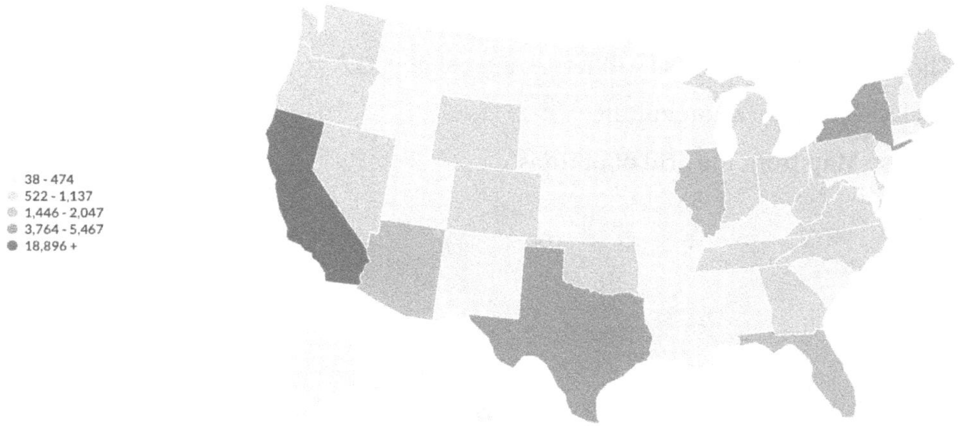

Figure 7.17 – Locations of our users by state

Metabase offers three types of maps. Let's learn about them:

- **Region Maps**: This is what we saw in the preceding example. At the time of writing this book, Metabase includes a regional map of the US, where each state is a region, and a map of the world, where each country is a region.
- **Pin Maps**: Pins are placed on the map by their latitude and longitude coordinates.
- **Grid Maps**: Similar to pin maps, but instead of having individual pins, the pins are binned into boxes and displayed like a heatmap.

We've already created a region map. Let's now create a **pin** and a **grid** map.

Creating a pin map

A pin map will render one dot, or pin, per subject on the map. As such, it works best when the number of subjects we want to plot is not too large. Having too many pins on a map is both hard to read and time-consuming to plot. To see what I mean, let's look at the location of our first 500 users:

1. Click **Ask a Question**.
2. Click **Custom Question**.
3. In the **Data** section, choose **Pies** and **Users**.
4. At the bottom of the editor, click the sort icon (it has an upward and downward arrow).
5. Sort it by **ID User**.
6. Now, click the **Row limit** icon at the bottom of the editor and limit the data to 500 rows.
7. Click **Visualize**. Metabase will return a table of data.
8. Click the **Visualization** button.
9. Choose **Map** from the grid of options.

You should see a map of the US with a pin for each of our first 500 users. Hovering over a pin will tell you information about the user. You can zoom in and out on the map as well. Zoom in on the great state of California. You will notice that because so many of our first 500 users are from California, it results in a lot of **over-plotting** (where it's hard to see how many pins there are because they are all on top of each other). When you encounter over-plotting like this, it's best to reduce the number of points in your plot to see it better.

To reduce the number of points in the plot, simply go back to the editor and change the limit from 500 to, say, 10. Now we can easily identify the location of our first 10 users.

Let's now learn how to make a grid plot.

Creating a grid plot

In the last two sections, we noticed that a disproportionate number of our users are in California, specifically the San Francisco Bay Area. When we tried to visualize the first 500 users using a pin map, it resulted in a lot of over-plotting, making it hard to compare different regions of high density. A grid map helps solves that. Let's learn how to make one:

1. Click **Ask a Question**.
2. Click **Custom Question**.
3. In the **Data** section, choose **Pies** and **Users**.
4. Add a filter. Have it filter records where the **State** column is **California**.
5. In the **Summarize** section, choose **Count of rows**.
6. In the **Group by** section, choose **Lat** and **Lon**. Note that Metabase has chosen to auto-bin them. Let's change that.
7. On each grouping variable, **Lat** and **Lon**, change it to **Bin every 1 degree**.
8. Now, click **Visualize**.

We get a lovely map of California with transparent squares overlaid on top, as in *Figure 7.18*. Each square represents a 1-by-1 degree area, and the colors range from green to red to determine how dense each square is. This makes it clear that most of our California users are located in the San Francisco Bay Area, which of course makes sense because that's where we are headquartered:

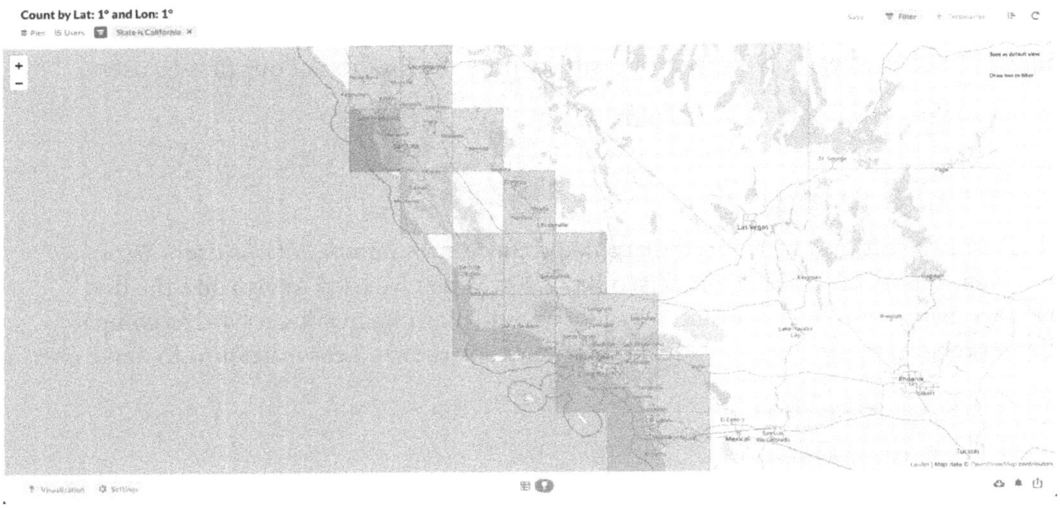

Figure 7.18 – A grid map of our California users

Pin and grid maps can be used all over the world, but region maps are restricted to US states and world countries. Fortunately, Metabase allows you to create your own region maps where the regions can be literally anything you like. Let's learn how to add a custom region map.

Adding custom maps with GeoJSON

In the last section, we saw several different ways to plot the location of our users. They all indicated that we have a heavy density of users in California, specifically the San Francisco Bay Area. However, they all leave something to be desired. The region and grid maps tell us that we have a lot of users in California and the Bay Area, respectively. The pin map tells us where our users in the Bay Area are, but the over-plotting makes it hard to compare one city to the next. None of them, however, tell us how many users we have in each city in the San Francisco Bay Area.

As of the time of writing, Metabase includes two region maps: one of the US states and one of the countries of the world. This covers a lot of use cases, but naturally, needs will arise that go beyond these two. For that, Metabase allows you to add your own **GeoJSON** files to create new, custom maps. While learning how to create your own GeoJSON map is beyond the scope of this book, there are many handy references online to guide you. For our purposes, I've created a GeoJSON file we can use that returns a map of the San Francisco Bay Area partitioned by city. Let's learn how to add this map to Metabase:

1. Open up the Admin Panel.
2. From the **Settings** menu, click **Maps**.
3. Click the blue **Add a map** button. A modal will pop up.
4. For the map's name, type `Cities in the San Francisco Bay Area`.
5. For the URL, input `https://github.com/PacktPublishing/Metabase-Up-and-Running/blob/master/map.geojson`.
6. Click **Load**. You should see a preview of the map.
7. Select **name** as the region's identifier.
8. Select **name** as the region's display name, as well.
9. Click **Add map**.

Now that we have our custom map, let's create a question so that we can leverage it in our visualization. Exit the **Admin Panel** and click **Ask a question**:

1. Click **Custom Question**.
2. In the **Data** section, choose **Pies** and **Users**.
3. Add a filter. Have it filter records where the **State** column is **California**.
4. In the **Summarize** section, click **Count of Rows**.
5. In the **Grouping** section, use **City**.
6. Click **Visualize**. Metabase will return a bar plot.
7. Click the **Visualization** button and pick **Map** from the grid of options.
8. Under **Map options**, find the dropdown under **Region map**. In this dropdown, select **Cities in the San Francisco Bay Area**, which is the map we just created.

Your map should look exactly as in *Figure 7.19*. Hovering over the darkest regions, you can see that San Francisco, Oakland, and Berkeley are the three cities with the most customers, respectively. Let's save this and call it `Map of Local Customers`. Save it to **Our Analytics**:

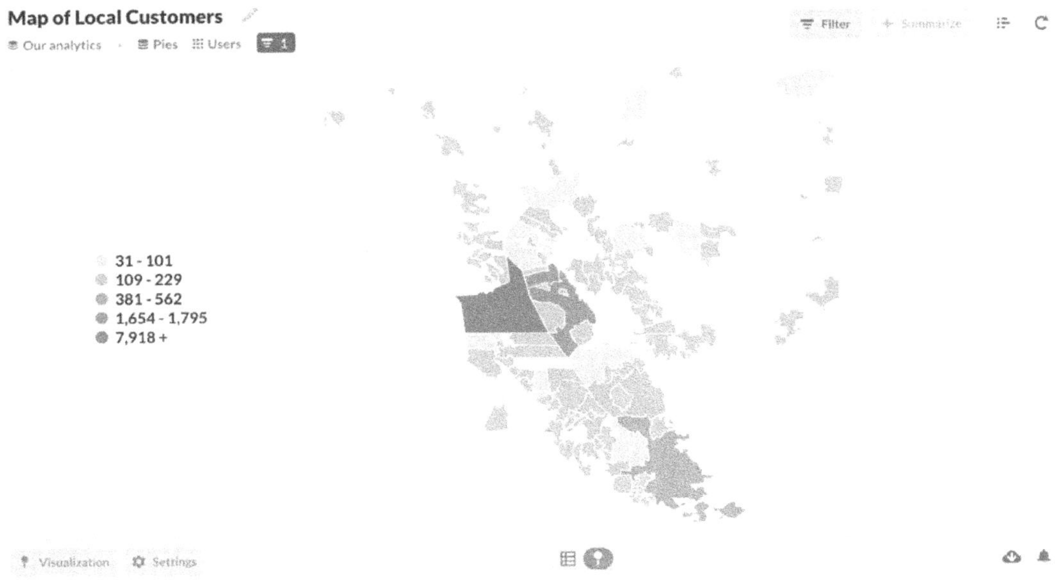

Figure 7.19 – A map of local customers using our custom map

As you can see, maps in Metabase are extremely powerful and fairly easy to use. As long as your data has a country field, a US state field, or latitude/longitude coordinates, a map is very simple to make. For special region maps, Metabase allows you to upload your own GeoJSON files.

Summary

In this chapter, we learned all about visualizations. We started with simple bar and line plots, then learned about other less common plot types, such as scatterplots and funnel plots. We learned how to make visualizations that focus on single important numbers, put them in context with goals, and created alerts that notify us when those goals are reached. Finally, we learned how to make impressive maps using geo-related data.

Just as a picture is worth a thousand words, a good visualization can instantly communicate a complex idea from a saved question. After working through this chapter, you should have a good understanding of what types of visualizations work best for certain questions.

At this point, we have quite a few saved questions and visualizations in the **Our Analytics** collection. In the next chapter, we'll learn how to put these on **dashboards**. A dashboard is just an organized set of visualizations, often used to convey a holistic understanding of something. Dashboards are one of the most used features in Metabase. We'll also learn more about collections and a feature in Metabase called a pulse, which lets you send out brief reports via email or Slack in a scheduled manner.

8
Creating Dashboards, Pulses, and Collections

So far, we've learned how to create questions and choose the right visualization for them. We've also amassed a solid amount of saved questions. Each question on its own explains something of interest about our business, such as how many orders we have fulfilled, how many users are using our product, or how many reviews each menu item has received. While these are all valuable on their own, they can be even more valuable when presented in one holistic view. For this use case, Metabase offers the ability for users to create **dashboards**, which are curated groupings of interactive questions arranged on a single screen.

Dashboards are fantastic when it comes to displaying a lot of valuable information, and we'll be learning how to make them in this chapter. Additionally, we'll learn how to make **pulses**. Pulses are short, high-level reports that can be sent out via email or Slack on a scheduled basis.

Having covered questions, dashboards, and pulses, we'll then return to collections and learn how to apply permissions to them.

In this chapter, we'll cover the following topics:

- Creating a simple dashboard
- Adding filters to a dashboard
- Adding Markdown to a dashboard
- Creating pulses
- Using MetaBot in Slack
- Organizing questions, pulses, and dashboards in collections

Technical requirements

To follow the examples in this chapter, you'll need an instance of Metabase with a connection to the `pies` database. You'll also need to have the email and Slack capabilities configured, which we learned how to do back in *Chapter 3, Setting Up Metabase*.

Creating a simple dashboard

As mentioned in the introduction to this chapter, a dashboard is simply a curated collection of interactive questions arranged on a single screen. Once you know what questions you'd like to curate for a dashboard, the process of actually creating one is very simple. Let's learn how, using some of the questions we have already created. Let's imagine that this dashboard is intended to give its viewers the most high-level understanding of the health of the business – a sort of **executive summary**. Some questions that might work well for this dashboard are related to the following:

- Order growth
- User growth
- Revenue growth

To create this dashboard, click the large + button in the top blue bar and select **New dashboard** from the menu, as in *Figure 8.1*:

Figure 8.1 – Creating a new dashboard

A modal will pop up, asking for a **name** and **description**:

1. Under **Name**, write `Executive Summary`.
2. Under **Description**, write `A high level overview of our key business metrics`.
3. Dashboards, in addition to questions, can be kept in collections. Let's keep this one in the **Our analytics** collection.
4. Click **Create**.

Once you click **Create**, you'll be brought to your dashboard. At this point, it's nothing but a blank canvas, as can be seen in *Figure 8.2*. We'll need to add questions to it, so let's get started:

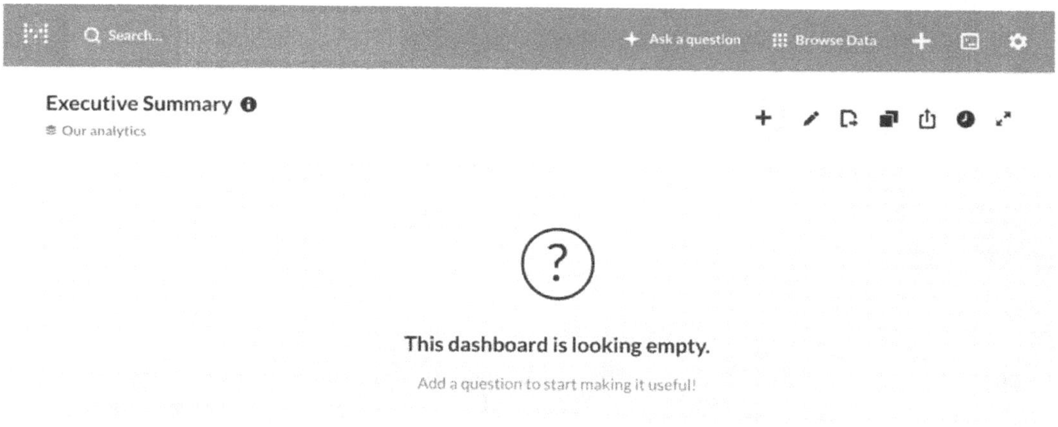

Figure 8.2 – Our blank Executive Summary dashboard before adding questions to it

In the upper right-hand corner of the dashboard, you'll see a set of icons. We'll learn what each of these icons does soon, but for now, draw your attention to the + icon, as that's what we use to add questions to our dashboard. Go ahead and click it.

Another modal will pop up, with all the questions we've saved so far. Our list is not too long, but there is also a search option to help narrow down results, so feel free to use it if that's easier. Find the **Orders per Day** question and click on it. This will place the question onto our dashboard, as in *Figure 8.3*:

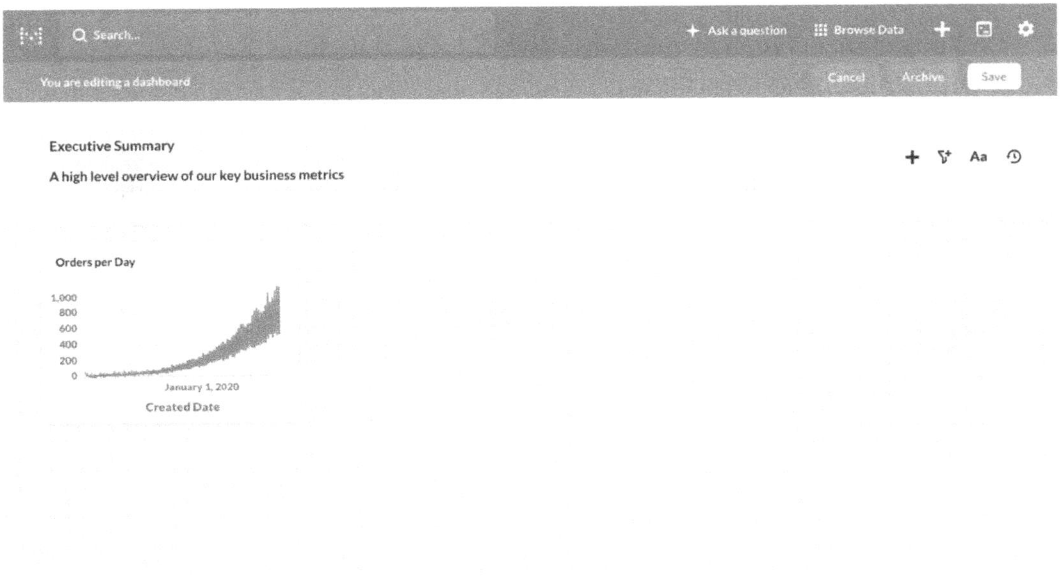

Figure 8.3 – Our first dashboard, with a single question on it

This should give you a sense of how dashboards work in Metabase. Notice that the canvas for the dashboard is covered with a grid of rectangles. You can resize the **Orders per day** question to cover a larger area of the grid by clicking and dragging its corner. You can also reposition the question by clicking anywhere else on it and dragging it to a new position. The grid of rectangles acts as a guide to help you understand how much space you're taking up and how much space you have left for other questions. Choosing the right size for your questions is a mixture of an art and a science, and in the next section, I'll give some tips to help you think through your approach.

Resizing questions in a dashboard

If you play around with resizing the question in your dashboard, you'll notice that a small image may compress the time series too much and make it hard to read. Determining the right size is actually tricky, and largely depends on how you imagine the dashboard might get used and what kind of screen you are using at the moment. For example, if you imagine that this dashboard will live on a 60-inch screen mounted somewhere in an office, it will be able to hold many small plots and still offer good readability. On the other hand, if you imagine the dashboard will mostly be viewed by individuals loading it up on a small laptop, or even a mobile phone, small plots will be hard to read and cause the dashboard to look overly crowded. Use your best artistic judgment, but also don't overthink it – after all, it's easy to make quick iterations of dashboards in Metabase.

Once you feel good about the size of your question and its placement on the dashboard, you can save it by clicking the **Save** button in the upper right-hand corner. The grid will disappear. The saved version is what your dashboard will look like to others.

Just like questions, dashboards can be saved to collections. Let's add this one to the **Our Analytics** collection. We'll revisit collections again later in this chapter.

Now that we've added our first question to the dashboard, let's add a few more.

Adding more questions to a dashboard

A dashboard with a single question really isn't any different than a saved question. The whole point of a dashboard is to unite multiple questions, all of which are somewhat related, to give you and your users a holistic understanding of your data. In that spirit, let's add the other questions for signup and revenue growth to our dashboard, starting with signup growth. Both of these questions were covered in *Chapter 7, Creating Visualizations*, but if you skipped them, just add anything you like.

Click the + button in the upper right-hand corner. Search for the **New Signups** question and add it to the dashboard (see *Figure 8.4*). Now, click the + button again and add the **Orders and Revenue by Week** question:

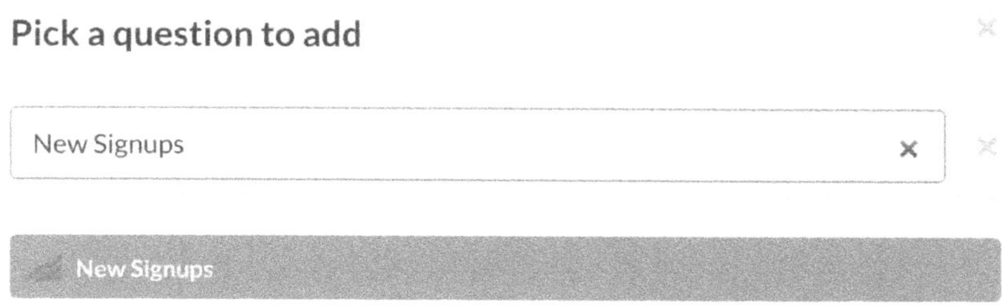

Figure 8.4 – Adding the New Signups question to our dashboard

I often like to have the most important chart take up the entire width of the screen, and then put two secondary charts underneath, as in *Figure 8.5*. Remember that you can always use the chart editing options we covered in *Chapter 7*, *Creating Visualizations*, to make the charts inside your dashboard more attractive. Having a variety of colors, alternating between line, area, and bar charts, and picking a unified naming convention for your chart's axes are three simple ways to make your dashboard more eye-catching.

Once you are happy with the look of your dashboard, save it again. You can always do further editing by clicking the **Pencil** icon:

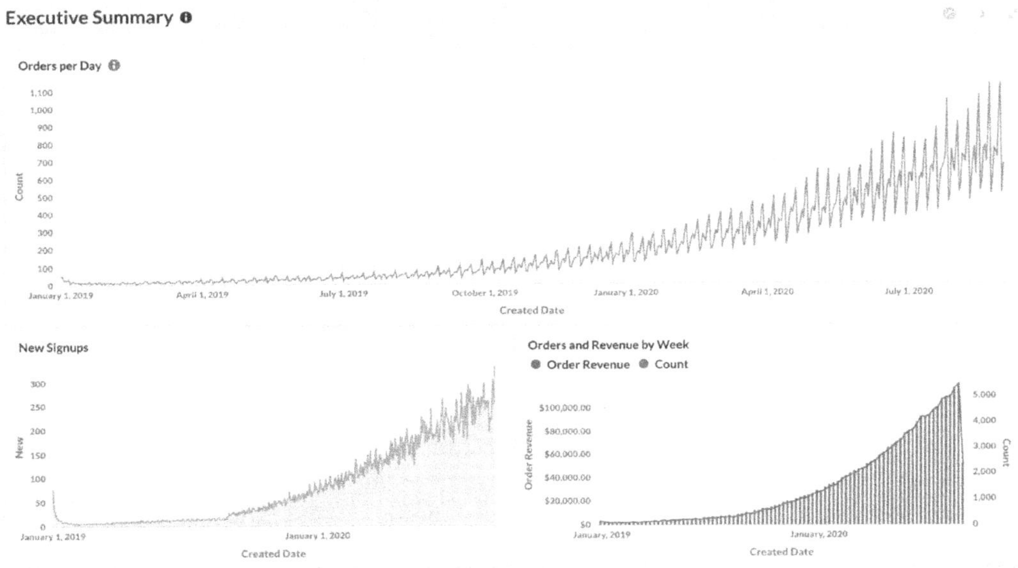

Figure 8.5 – Our first dashboard with multiple questions

Now that we've learned how easy it is to create a dashboard, let's build upon that foundation and learn about other dashboard features in Metabase, starting by adding filters.

Adding filters to a dashboard

Let's reflect on the **Executive Summary** dashboard we built in the last section. It provides a great high-level view of our business, showing the up-and-to-the-right growth across all our key metrics that so many organizations covet.

I can imagine this dashboard looking impressive on a large monitor in the office. The dashboard does a good job of telling the story of the business since its inception. What it doesn't do well is tell the story of how the business is doing *right now*. Nor does it do a good job of telling how segments of this business are doing – for example, the delivery business, or the growth of business in the state of California. These questions are more niche, so they don't all need their own dashboards. At the same time, there are people in our organization that certainly care about them! Just like we were able to apply filters to our individual questions, Metabase also allows **global filters** at the dashboard level. Applying one of these filters can affect multiple charts in the dashboard, instead of just one. Let's see how they work with a simple example. To add filters to our dashboard created in the previous section, we'll proceed as follows:

1. Open up the **Executive Summary** dashboard we just created.
2. Click the **Pencil** icon to go into edit mode.
3. Now, click the **Add a filter** icon in the upper right-hand corner. Note the options in the list that we could use for a filter: **Time**, **Location**, **ID**, or **Other Categories**. Let's use **Time**.
4. Under **What kind of Filter**, select **All Options**.

This will take you back to the dashboard. Each question has been replaced with a dropdown, as in *Figure 8.6*, where you can select the column you want the time filter to be applied to:

1. For the first question, **Orders per Day**, choose the **Created Date** column from the **Orders** table.
2. For the **New Signups** question, choose the **Created Date** column from the **Users** table.
3. For the **Orders and Revenue by Week** table, choose the **Created Date** column from the **Orders** table.

4. Once you've done that, click **Done** at the top of the screen.
5. After that, click **Save**:

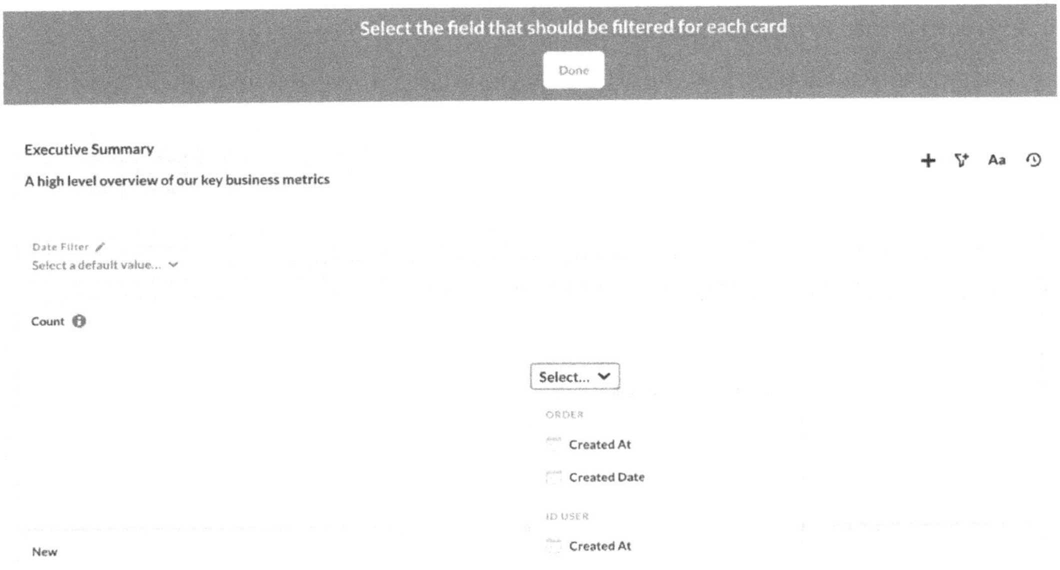

Figure 8.6 – Choosing which column to apply to the date filter

Now, changing the date filter on the dashboard will apply that filtering logic to all of the plots. Give it a try – for example, looking at dates between **July 1** and **July 31, 2020**. Now anyone who uses this dashboard can zoom in to specific time periods.

Let's apply another filter so that we can understand the growth of our business in specific US states:

1. Make sure you still have the **Executive Summary** dashboard open.
2. Click the **Pencil** icon to go into edit mode.
3. Click the **Add a filter** icon in the upper right-hand corner.
4. Under **What do you want to filter?**, select **Location**.
5. Now, select **State**.
6. One by one, select **State** for each chart. We only have one **State** column in our database, and it's in the **Users** table. Since we already called out the foreign key relationship from the **Orders** table to the **Users** table in *Chapter 5, Building Your Data Model*, Metabase is able to apply a **User** filter to a question about **Orders**.
7. Now, click **Done** at the top of the screen and save the dashboard.

We now have a filter where we can enter any US state and see how our business is growing there. *Figure 8.7* shows what the dashboard looks like when it is filtered to show California only. Testing out a few states, you may notice that business outside of California didn't start picking up until late 2019:

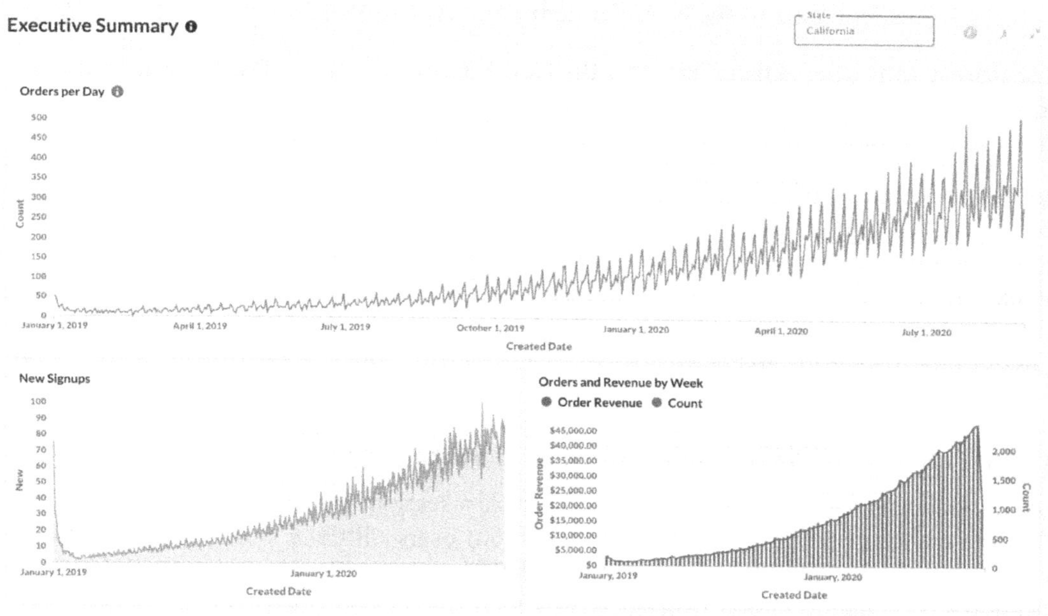

Figure 8.7 – The Executive Summary dashboard filtered to show only California data

Let's now apply one last filter to our dashboard so that we can understand the growth of **delivery orders** better:

1. Make sure you still have the **Executive Summary** dashboard open.
2. Click the **Pencil** icon to go into edit mode.
3. Click the **Add a filter** icon in the upper right-hand corner.
4. Under **What do you want to filter?**, select **Other Categories**.
5. For the first question, **Orders per Day**, choose the **Order Type** column from the **Orders** table.

6. For the **Orders and Revenue by Week** question, choose the **Order Type** column from the **Orders** table.
7. Up to this point, we haven't given our filters specific names because the defaults have been adequate. For this one, we can do better than **Category** as a name. Click the pencil icon next to the word **Category** and type in `Delivery or Pick-Up`.

Note that we can't select **Order Type** for the **New Signups** question. That is because there is no notion of an order type for a new signup. That means that applying this filter will affect the two order-related plots but not the user-related ones.

This can present a bit of ambiguity to users who may not know the underlying data and tables as well as a power user, so be mindful of that here. In this case, I think it's okay to add this filter and assume that users will understand that **Order Type** has no relevant context toward the count of **New Signups**. However, it never hurts to be overly verbose, so in the next section, we'll learn how we can add text to our dashboard, just to make it clear what our filters can and can't do.

Adding Markdown to a dashboard

Our dashboard is coming along nicely, but in the last section, we decided it might be helpful to add some text to our dashboard to tell our users a little bit more about how to use it. Dashboards in Metabase have a feature that lets you add text boxes in **Markdown**. Markdown (`https://commonmark.org/help/`) is a popular and very attractive mark-up language that is easy to learn. In *Figure 8.8*, there is an example of Markdown on the left and what it renders to on the right. While we won't go deep into how to write Markdown in this book, here are a few key pointers that should help you master the basics:

- **Headings** start with one or two # symbols, such as `## Things to know about this Dashboard`.
- To make **bulleted lists**, start each line with a `*` symbol. To change to **numbered lists**, start each line with `1.`, `2.`, and so on.
- To put words in **bold**, surround them with double asterisks, such as `**asterisks**`.
- For **italics**, surround in single asterisks, such as `*italics*`.
- For **monospaced code**, surround in backticks, such as `` `backticks` ``.

- To add a **hyperlink**, put text in brackets and the link in parentheses, such as `[My Link to Metabase](www.metabase.com)`.
- Adding an **image or GIF** is just like adding a hyperlink, except you add an `!` to it, such as `![My Image](www.mylink.com)`.

You can add a text box to your dashboard in the same way that you'd add a question. Let's learn how:

1. Make sure you still have the **Executive Summary** dashboard open.
2. Click the **Pencil** icon to go into edit mode.
3. Click the **Aa** icon to add a text box.
4. To make room for the text box, let's make our **Orders by Day** chart smaller and place the text box on the right of it.
5. You can write whatever you like in the text box. In *Figure 8.8*, on the left, there is some example text written in **Markup**.
6. To preview your **Markup**, click the **eye** icon.
7. Once you are happy with your text box and its contents, click **Save**:

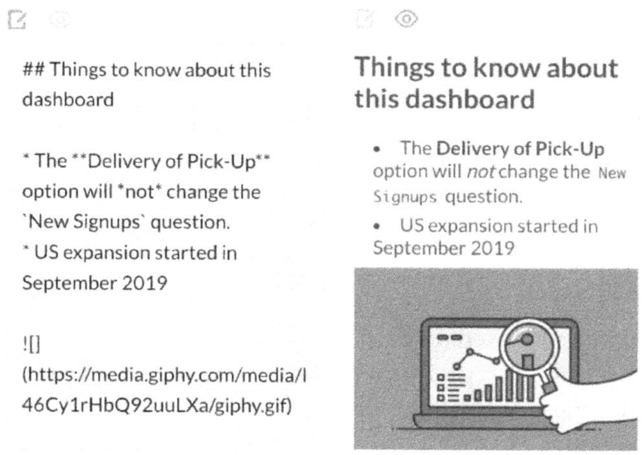

Figure 8.8 – An example of Markdown text on the left, and what it renders to on the right

Now that we've learned how to add questions, filters, and text to our dashboard, let's learn how to make it look good in full-screen mode.

Configuring your dashboard for full-screen viewing

In the last section, we learned how to add filters and text to a dashboard. Filters are very useful in making your dashboard interactive, and text boxes can help your user understand how the filters work. Some dashboards, on the other hand, are not designed to be interactive. If your dashboard is going to be mainly displayed on a large screen in the office, for example, it doesn't make as much sense for it to be interactive. For dashboards like these, Metabase offers a full-screen viewing mode with some helpful features. Let's learn about them, using our **Executive Summary** dashboard as an example:

- **Entering Fullscreen**: From your **Executive Summary** dashboard, click the **Enter Fullscreen** icon, which shows two diagonal arrows pointing in opposite directions.
- **Changing to Nighttime mode**: If you'd like to have your dashboard in **Nighttime** mode, click the **moon** icon. To switch back to **Daytime** mode, click the **sun** icon.
- **Setting up auto-refresh**: If you are using a read replica of an application database, your data will be constantly updating. You can set your dashboard to refresh at 1, 5, 10, 15, 30, or 60-minute intervals by clicking the **clock** icon. This will automatically rerun the queries for the dashboard at each interval and refresh the plots.

To exit **Fullscreen** mode, either hit the *Esc* key or click the **Exit Fullscreen** icon.

At this point, we've learned how to make a dashboard, save it to a collection, add text and interactive filters to it, and display it in **Fullscreen** mode. Now, let's learn about another way to organize sets of questions. This is what is referred to as a pulse in Metabase.

Creating pulses

So far in this chapter, we've focused on dashboards as the primary way to communicate high-level, business-critical findings. Dashboards are fantastic tools, and I've known a lot of people to find dashboards so useful that they make opening them up part of their morning routine – potentially having a glance even before their morning cup of coffee. This is especially true for people in executive roles who need to have easy and constant access to the data.

Perhaps even more convenient than a good dashboard, though, is a **daily email report**. In Metabase parlance, these would be called **pulses**. Pulses, like dashboards, are comprised of one or more questions. Unlike dashboards, which you need to go to Metabase to view, a pulse is composed and sent out via email or by Slack. Most pulses are sent daily, but you can create pulses to be sent hourly, weekly, or monthly as well. Let's learn how to make one:

1. To create a pulse, click the large + button in the top blue bar and select **New Pulse** from the menu, as in *Figure 8.9*.
2. Give your pulse a good name, such as `Daily Snapshot`.
3. Pick a collection for your pulse to live in. Let's choose the **Our Analytics** collection for this one.
4. Now, select some saved questions to include in your pulse. Let's pick **Orders by Day** and **New Signups**.

I find that the most useful questions to include in daily pulses are time-series questions with daily time grains. This is because Metabase formats these questions such that the most recent daily values are highlighted, as in *Figure 8.9*:

Figure 8.9 – How the New Signups question is shown in a pulse. The number for the most recent day is highlighted

You can add as many questions as you like to a pulse, but a concise pulse with just a few properly chosen questions tends to be better in my experience. Metabase is also opinionated about this, too. You'll get a reminder at your 11th question that the pulse is getting a bit long. I like to keep them to 4 or 5 questions.

Once you've picked your questions, you can choose how you'd like to send the pulse. The options are to send via email or Slack. We learned how to set up both in *Chapter 3, Setting Up Metabase*. Let's learn about the email option for now.

Sending a pulse by email

To schedule your pulse to be sent out over email, first click the **Email** toggle to the on position in the **Where should this data go?** section:

1. In the **To:** field, enter the users that you'd like to send the pulse to.

> **Important Note**
> In addition to sending pulses to users who have a Metabase account, you can also send them to email addresses belonging to users that *don't* have a Metabase account. This can be useful for sending metrics to vendors, investors, consultants, affiliates, or anyone that you would like to share some data with but not create an account for.

2. In the **Sent** field, choose either **Daily**, **Weekly**, or **Monthly**. **Weekly** and **Monthly** offer more options to choose the day of week and month. Let's make ours **Daily**.
3. In the **at** field, choose the time of day you'd like the email to go out. Remember that you can always change Metabase's default timezone in the Admin Panel.
4. I recommend sending yourself a test email first, to make sure the pulse matches your expectations.

As mentioned, you can send pulses over Slack as well. Choosing between email and Slack isn't an either-or decision; you can send them out on both channels if you like. In the next section, we'll learn how to send pulses via Slack.

Sending a pulse via Slack

To send a pulse over Slack, first click the **Slack** toggle to the on position, below the **Email** section we just looked at:

1. In the **Post to** section, choose a channel or user you want to send the pulse to.
2. In the **Sent** section, choose the cadence in which you'd like to send the pulse. With Slack, you can also send **Hourly**, which is not an option for email.
3. To test that it works, click **Send to Slack** now.

Since Slack can be a noisier channel than email, some people like to have a pulse sent to a Slack channel hourly and keep the email cadence to daily. I personally think that is a good setting for an organization, provided there are enough events happening throughout the day to justify an hourly report.

Our fictional business, for example, is likely to have orders placed each hour. However, there are also hours that go by where no orders are placed. We can configure our pulse so that it only sends out when there are results by toggling on the **Skip if no results** section at the bottom. This can be helpful for pulses that are based on rare events.

Finally, when you've tested your pulse and are happy with it, click **Create pulse**. This pulse will now automatically be sent to its audience at the cadence you specified. Of course, this assumes that you are running Metabase as a web app and not locally on your computer. You could send pulses out this way, too, but you'd have to keep your computer on at all times.

Using MetaBot in Slack

In the last section, we saw how we can use Slack to send out pulses. You may recall how, in *Chapter 3, Setting Up Metabase*, we set up MetaBot, our Metabase Slack bot. At the time, since we didn't have any saved questions, there was not much we could do with MetaBot. Now that we have a lot of saved questions, it's time to see some examples of what MetaBot can do.

You can interact with MetaBot either by chatting directly with it or by adding it to one of your channels. Chatting directly with MetaBot is a helpful way to fetch Metabase questions quickly, without needing to access Metabase. Having MetaBot in a channel is helpful in facilitating data-driven discussions. We'll see examples of both, but first, let's learn how MetaBot works.

Discovering MetaBot's features

To see what MetaBot can do, go to Slack, click on the Metabot app, and type `metabot help`. MetaBot will respond with **Here's what I can do: help, list, show**:

- `help` simply brings up the preceding message, which we've already seen.
- `list` will show you the 20 most recent questions created in your Metabase.
- `show` will show one of your questions in Slack, provided you add either the question number or name. For example, if you want to show the **Total Signups** question, you would type `metabot show Total Signups`.

Now, let's see how we might use these in practice.

Interacting directly with MetaBot

You can think of the MetaBot Slack app as a lightweight interface into viewing your Metabase questions. For example, imagine you're in a meeting and someone asks "how many signups did we have yesterday?". Since we've made a question about that in the past, we could go to Metabase and pull it up. Perhaps more convenient, though, is to just chat to MetaBot.

Even if we don't remember the name of the question verbatim, we can simply type `metabot show signups` to search all questions that have the word `signups` in them. Then you can either use the name of the question or the question's number to pull the question into Slack.

This is an easy way to quickly look up questions outside of Metabase. Another scenario where MetaBot can be helpful is in discussions on Slack channels. Let's learn how to utilize MetaBot in those next.

Using MetaBot in Slack channels

Imagine you are having a discussion on your **#random** Slack channel about how the business is doing. You, as the data champion in your organization, are always looking for opportunities to enhance these discussions with facts and figures. Instead of sending the members in the channel to Metabase to see the great saved questions about the growth of orders, you can take a lower friction route by adding MetaBot to the conversation. To add MetaBot to the channel, you can simply mention `@metabot`. Alternatively, you can use Slack's **Add an app** feature in the channel. Both will work.

Once MetaBot is in the channel, you can use the `metabot` commands just as before. To show everyone how orders are trending, simply type `metabot show trend in orders per day`, as in *Figure 8.10*:

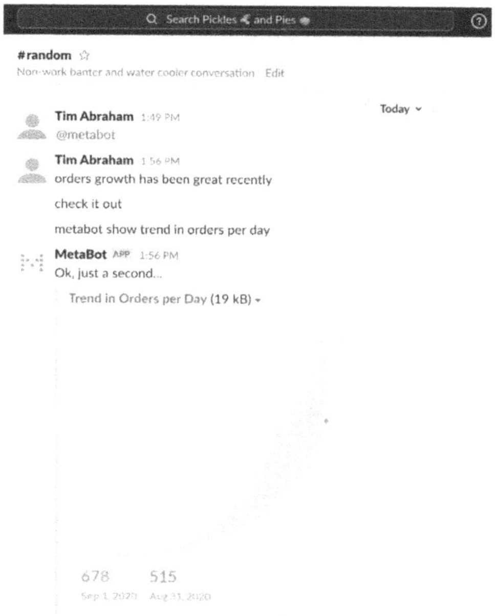

Figure 8.10 – Using MetaBot in a Slack channel

As you can see, using MetaBot in Slack is a convenient and lightweight way to give your Metabase questions a role in discussions on Slack.

Having covered Slack, let's return to Metabase and learn more about collections. Although we've interacted with collections throughout the last few chapters, we haven't taken the time to actually explore what they are, so let's get started.

Organizing everything in collections

Over the last several chapters, we've learned how to create questions, dashboards, pulses, and collections. Let's take a step back and reflect on how all these pieces fit together.

Questions are the fundamental building block of analysis in Metabase and are visualized as a plot, single number, or table of data. Dashboards and pulses both contain multiple questions, usually related to one another. Finally, collections are like the folders or directories on your computer. They contain questions, dashboards, pulses, and even other collections. Unlike dashboards and pulses, whose purpose is to display the information of several questions to a user, the purpose of a collection is simply to hold these assets and allow organization.

We've now saved quite a few questions to the **Our Analytics** collection. Remember that the **Our Analytics** collection comes as default with Metabase and is like the home directory on your computer. All other collections you create live in this collection.

The **Our Analytics** collection should also contain the dashboard and pulse we created in this chapter and the **Marketing** collection from *Chapter 6, Creating Questions*. Let's have a look at it. From your Metabase home page, find the **Our Analytics** section and click **Browse all items**. This will display all the various Metabase items we've saved so far, as in *Figure 8.11*:

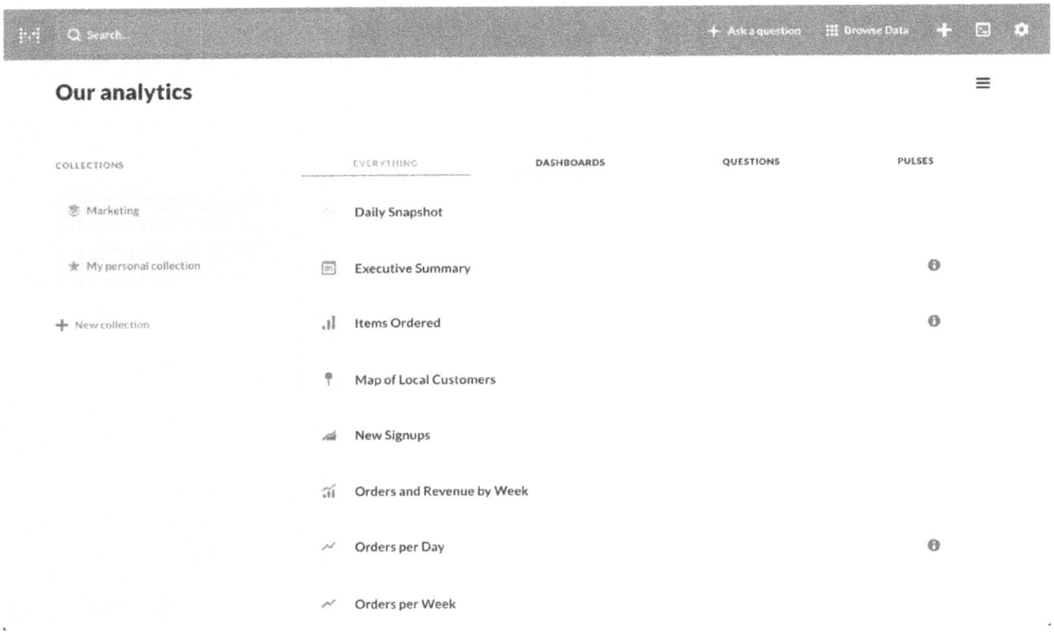

Figure 8.11 – The items we've saved in the Our Analytics collection

So far, we've essentially saved everything to the **Our Analytics** collection. You can see how this might get unwieldy over time. If a new user were to sign up for Metabase and open this up, they might feel a little lost or overwhelmed. Fortunately, there is a way we can highlight the top few items in this collection that users should pay attention to. Let's learn how to do that.

Pinning items in collections

Metabase allows you to **pin** items in your collections so that they always remain at the top of the page. Let's learn how to pin the three most relevant items in our collection:

1. From the **Our Analytics** collection, find the **Executive Summary** dashboard. This is the dashboard we built earlier in the chapter.
2. Hovering your mouse over **Executive Summary**, notice the ellipsis on the right side (the three dots). Click the ellipsis.
3. From the menu of options, choose **Pin this Item**.
4. Follow *steps 1–3* to pin the **Daily Snapshot** pulse and the **Pies on our Menu** question. At the end, your collection should look just as in *Figure 8.12*:

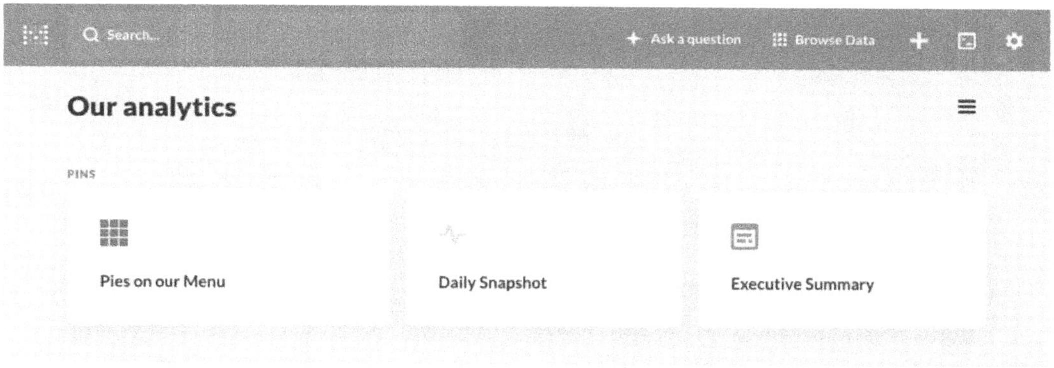

Figure 8.12 – Pinning the items we want everyone to easily find in the Our Analytics collection

You can continue to pin items to this area. After three items, a new row will be created. Just be mindful that the purpose of pinning items is to help your users find the most important items in a potentially long list of questions, dashboards, and pulses, so try to keep it to a few rows at most.

To rearrange pinned items, simply click and drag the items to a new position. To remove a pinned item, click the pushpin icon.

Any dashboard in the **Our Analytics** collection that gets pinned will also show up as a pinned item on your Metabase home page. If you were to go back to your Metabase home page now, it would look something as in *Figure 8.13*:

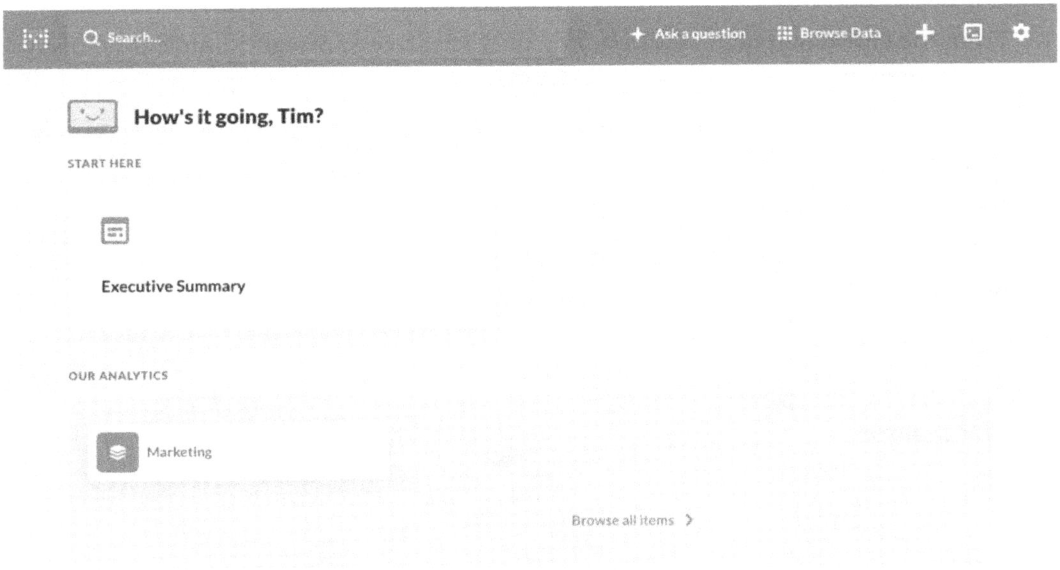

Figure 8.13 – The dashboard we pinned in Our Analytics now shows up as pinned on our home page

Pinning items is a helpful way to get the most important information in front of you and your users. Perhaps just as important is keeping sensitive information *away* from users who you do not want to give access to. In the next section, we'll learn how to do that using permissions.

Understanding permissions in collections

Back in *Chapter 5, Building Your Data Model*, we were introduced to permissions. In that chapter, we learned how to set permissions for databases, database tables, and even database table columns. This was largely to control what types of users can create questions on certain tables or databases. In addition to these data permissions, Metabase offers permissions at the collections level as well. Let's learn how to apply them.

Setting collection-level permissions

There are two ways to set collection-level permissions. Let's see them both.

The first way to set collection-level permissions is similar to the data-level permissions we learned about in *Chapter 5, Building Your Data Model*. To do this, start in the **Admin Panel**:

1. From the top bar, click **Permissions**.
2. Next to the **Data permissions** tab, find the **Collection permissions** tab and click it.

You'll see a grid that is 1 row by *N* columns, where *N* equals the number of groups you have set up in Metabase. If you followed along in *Chapter 5, Building Your Data Model*, when we learned about the vertical permissions framework, you should have five groups. Even if you have multiple collections, this page will only offer you the ability to set permissions for the **Our Analytics** collection. As we mentioned before, the **Our Analytics** collection is the root, or home, level collection, and all other collections are considered **sub-collections** of it.

The other way to set collection-level permissions is to navigate to the collection itself. Let's now do that:

1. From your Metabase home page, click **Browse all items** in the **Our Analytics** section.
2. Click the **Lock** icon in the upper right-hand corner.

Instead of a 1 row by *N* columns grid, you should see a transposed *N* row by 1 column grid, as on the right-hand side of *Figure 8.14*:

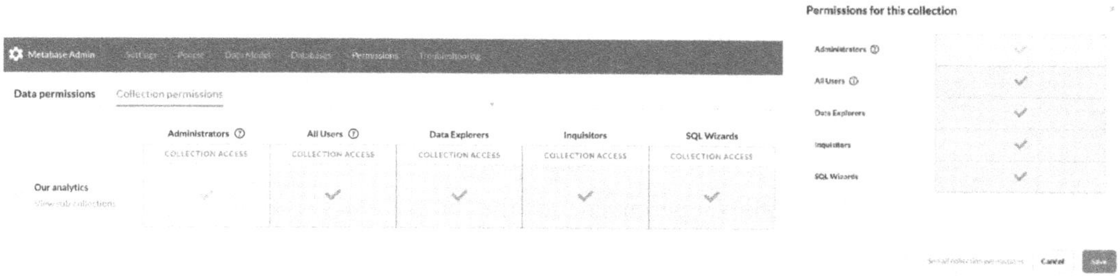

Figure 8.14 – Two views of collection-level permissions

Now that we know how to find the permission settings for collections, let's learn what collection-level permissions we can give our groups.

Choosing collection permissions

Recall how in *Chapter 5*, *Building Your Data Model*, we learned that Metabase's permission model is at the **group** level. There are three types of permissions a group can have for a collection. Let's learn about them:

- **No access**: Users in this group cannot view anything in the collection, or even the collection itself (unless it's the **Our Analytics** collection or the group has access to any of the collection's sub-collections).
- **View collection**: Users in this group can view all the questions, dashboards, pulses, and collections within the collection. They cannot, however, save new items to it, move items to and from it, delete items, or edit and delete the collection itself.
- **Curate collection**: Users in this group can do everything users with the **View collection** permission can do, as well as all the actions that **View collection** users cannot do.

In determining which permission to give to which group, it's helpful to think back to *Chapter 5*, *Building Your Data Model*, and what we learned about data-level permissions. For example, if you were to give a group the permission to explore and write queries against the **Orders** table, you would at the *very least* want to grant them **view permissions** on collections that focus on the **Orders** table. If, on the other hand, you restricted their access to the **Orders** table, you wouldn't want to give them **curate permissions**.

Using the vertical permissions framework we developed in *Chapter 5*, *Building Your Data Model*, *Figure 8.15* presents a good permissions setup for the **Our Analytics** collection:

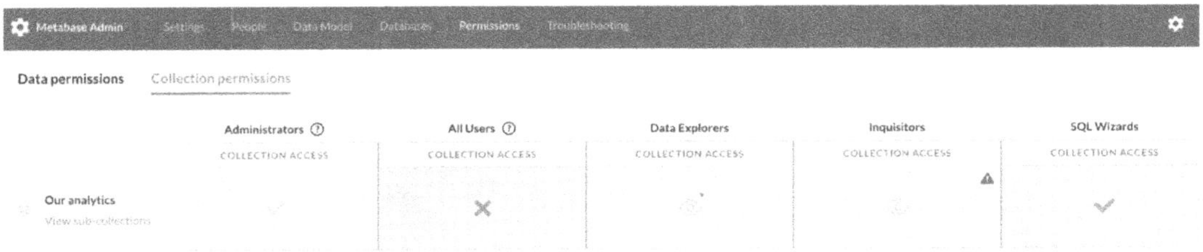

Figure 8.15 – A setup for permissions on the Our Analytics collection

According to *Figure 8.15*, anyone who is only in the **All Users** group will not be able to access any of the items in the **Our Analytics** collection. Anyone with membership to the **Data Explorers** or **Inquisitors** groups can view the items in the collection, but can't make any edits. Finally, the **SQL Wizards** and **Administrators** group users have full edit access.

> **Important Note**
>
> While a user with only group membership in the **All Users** group would not be able to access any items in the **Our Analytics** collection, they could still receive a pulse in the **Our Analytics** collection.

I like this setup because I like to think of the **Our Analytics** collection as the production-level space where a few trusted questions, dashboards, and pulses live. To maintain a high bar of quality, you would only want to allow edit access to the power users, who in our case are **Administrators** and **SQL Wizards**.

If you choose a setup like this, I also recommend relaxing the permissions for **sub-collections**. For example, if you have a **Marketing** sub-collection, you would probably want to allow the **Inquisitors**, and possibly **Data Explorers**, to have curate access, even though they only had **view access** for the **Our Analytics** collection. For any questions pertaining to marketing that you want to restrict access to, you can simply create another sub-collection within **Marketing**. For example, a sub-collection in your **Marketing** collection called **Market Budget Tracker** could have more sensitive data in it. For this sub-collection, you could use stricter permissions. For a visual example, see *Figure 8.16*:

Figure 8.16 – Permissions for the Marketing collection and the more sensitive Marketing Budget Tracker collection

Why use collection-level permissions?

You might be wondering why there are permissions at *both* the data and collection level. After all, collections are mainly comprised of questions, and questions are generally based on a single database table. The reason why we might want to allow a user to have access to a question but not the underlying table is that questions are generally *summarized* versions of a table. Summarizing data will often also anonymize it. For example, a question that shows you the average order revenue per day includes information about every user's orders but doesn't allow you to actually look at each user one by one.

Having access to the **Orders** table, on the other hand, allows you to look at each individual order and user, and also offers you the entire suite of summarization, filtering, and grouping options that databases tend to offer. In that sense, allowing a user access to a collection is a safer and stricter (from a security standpoint) option than allowing them access to the underlying data table. Of course, this means you have to be mindful of how you build your questions. After all, it's possible to create a question that returns just the raw output of a table! A question like that could defeat the whole purpose.

In summary, if you have sensitive data that you don't want certain users to have row-level access to, your best option is to restrict their data access, allow them collection access, and make sure all the items in the collection are summarized properly.

Summary

In this chapter, we learned how to put multiple questions to work on a dashboard. Dashboards are great at showing lots of related questions all together in one view. We also learned how to make a pulse and have it emailed out on a scheduled basis or sent via Slack. We explored the ways that we can use MetaBot, Metabase's Slack bot, to access our saved questions in a lightweight fashion. We then learned best practices on how to organize all these items in collections. Finally, we learned how to set up group-level permissions at the collection level.

Having learned about questions, dashboards, pulses, and collections, we have now covered all the main features in Metabase for analytics. In the next chapter, we'll step into a more advanced topic and learn how to leverage SQL queries in Metabase. We've already seen one example of this back in *Chapter 6, Creating Questions*, when we had a question that the editor could not answer. As the analytical needs of an organization increases, the need to turn to SQL queries for answers will grow. Fortunately, Metabase recognizes this. In the next chapter, we'll see how, by writing SQL queries, you can unlock a lot of powerful analytics in Metabase.

9
Using the SQL Console

Traditionally, data analysis on relational databases has always been performed using **SQL**, or **Structured Query Language**. While there are many tools and languages for data analysis, SQL is usually thought of as the starting point or the common denominator.

Over the last several chapters, we've learned that many of the routines you would usually resort to SQL for can be performed easily using Metabase's notebook editor. Indeed, this is one of the selling points of the product: by allowing anyone to carry out what would normally be relegated to SQL programmers, Metabase has democratized data analysis.

At the same time, there is certainly a time and place for using SQL in Metabase. Having proficiency in SQL can make Metabase better for everyone in many ways, and that's what we'll be covering in this chapter. Specifically, we'll cover the following topics:

- Introduction to SQL in Metabase
- Creating Questions-as-Tables using SQL
- Using variables in SQL queries
- Creating saved SQL snippets

Technical requirements

You will need a running instance of Metabase with a connection to the `pies` database. As we'll be writing a lot of SQL in this chapter, it's helpful to have some knowledge of the language. If you don't know SQL, you'll still be able to copy, paste, and run all the queries, but you will get more out of the chapter if you also understand what they do.

> **Important Note**
>
> NoSQL databases, as their name suggests, cannot be queried with SQL. They can still be queried with their own query languages, and these can be run inside Metabase, but they tend to look very different from SQL. In this chapter, we will only cover SQL, as most Metabase users tend to use relational databases.

Introduction to SQL in Metabase

After spending time learning Metabase's notebook data editor, you might be wondering what the pros and cons of using SQL instead are. If you are using a relational database with Metabase, all questions that can be created with the notebook editor can be expressed with SQL instead. The reverse of that statement is not true. Only *some* questions expressed with SQL can be created with the notebook editor. There are many functions and operations that can be carried out with SQL that don't exist in the notebook editor. This will likely change over time, as the Metabase team is constantly improving the notebook editor, but for the time being, having a solid background in SQL means you can ask questions that would not be possible to express in the notebook editor.

Just because any question created in the notebook can be written in SQL, does not mean that all questions *should* be written in SQL. There are benefits to using the notebook editor instead of SQL. Although this chapter is about using SQL in Metabase, it's equally important to understand when not to use SQL, so we'll start there.

Recall back to *Chapter 6*, *Creating Questions*, where one of the very first questions we created in that chapter was **Total Orders placed**. This question is about as simple as it gets, and its recipe in the notebook editor is reproduced in *Figure 9.1*:

Figure 9.1 – One of the first questions we made, Total Orders placed

We'll be examining the pros and cons of a question like this, expressed in the notebook editor, and one written in SQL. Before we do that, though, don't we need to write this question in SQL? It turns out that we don't, since Metabase offers the ability to see a notebook editor question in SQL. Let's see how.

Translating notebook editor questions into SQL

If you were to look under the hood of Metabase, you'd see that all operations in the notebook editor map to an operation in SQL (at least for relational databases that use SQL). That means that all computations built in the notebook editor are compiled to SQL and run as SQL queries. You may have realized this already, but if not, it's good to know.

Because all operations in the notebook editor get translated to SQL anyway, it's easy for Metabase to offer you a glimpse at the translated query. That means that any question written in the notebook editor can be translated into a SQL query (again, provided the database you are working with is a relational database). It turns out that this is a helpful feature for people learning SQL since they can just toggle back and forth. Let's see an example, using the **Total Orders** question we've been working with:

1. Have the **Total Orders** question open.
2. Click the **Show Editor** icon to open up the notebook editor.

3. In the upper right-hand corner, next to the **Show Editor** icon, find the **View the SQL** icon (as pictured in *Figure 9.2*). Click it:

Figure 9.2 – The icon to change notebook editor questions into SQL

A modal will pop up with the actual SQL that will run when this question is rendered:

```
SELECT count(*) AS "count"
FROM "public"."orders"
```

SQL is an expressive language, so even if you aren't familiar with programming in SQL, you'll likely be able to read and comprehend the query. It's simply counting the number of rows, represented by the wildcard asterisk, from the **Orders** table.

4. Click the **Convert this question to SQL** button.

   This will move the query into the **SQL console**.

You can do this for any question you create in the notebook editor, no matter how complex. Let's see one more example, using one of the more advanced questions we made in *Chapter 7, Creating Visualizations*. Let's try it with the **Review score and Reviews for Pickles and Pies** question:

1. Open the **Review score and Reviews for Pickles and Pies** question by either searching for it in the search bar or finding it in the **Our Analytics** collection.
2. Click the **Show Editor** icon to open up the notebook editor.
3. Now, click the **View the SQL** icon to see the question written in SQL.

This query is a lot more complex than the one for **Total Orders placed**. Those of you with a SQL background may also notice that the SQL produced by this feature is more verbose than a SQL programmer might normally write. For example, all tables and table aliases are wrapped in double quotes and table alias names are often longer than the names of the tables themselves. A SQL programmer might write the `INNER JOIN` part of the query as follows:

```
FROM
    reviews a
JOIN
    orders b
ON
a.id_order = b.id_order
```

However, Metabase writes it as follows:

```
FROM "public"."reviews" INNER JOIN "public"."orders" "ID Order"
ON "public"."reviews"."id_order" = "ID Order"."id_order"
```

Metabase's SQL is harder to read but that's because they're creating it programmatically. They aren't going to use the tips and shorthand that a SQL programmer might use.

> **Important Note**
>
> You may be wondering what the `"public"` part of the queries that Metabase generates is referring to. Databases in PostgreSQL have what are confusingly called schemas, which can be thought of as directories within a database that hold tables. It's confusing because we normally think of a schema as a description of the columns of a particular table. The default schema in a PostgreSQL database is called `public`.

I recommend using the **View the SQL** feature as a way to help others in your organization get more comfortable with SQL.

Now let's spend a little more time learning about the SQL console.

Learning about the SQL console

We just had a look at the **Total Orders placed** question we made in the notebook editor and saw how Metabase translated it to SQL. This question is about as simple as it gets: take the **Orders** table and count the rows. Now, let's write this same question using SQL directly from the console.

Before we begin, let's familiarize ourselves a bit more with the SQL console in Metabase. In *Chapter 6*, *Creating Questions*, we learned that we can reach the SQL console by clicking **Ask a Question | Native Query**. Another, perhaps more intuitive, way that requires fewer clicks is to find the icon of a **command-line prompt** next to the + button on the top blue bar. Hovering over it reveals the words **Write SQL**. Click that icon to bring up the SQL console, shown in *Figure 9.3*:

1. Click the **Select a database** dropdown and pick **Pies**.
2. Now, click on the dictionary icon on the right side of the console. This will open up the data dictionary that we created in *Chapter 5*, *Building Your Data Dictionary*.
3. In the data dictionary, click **Orders** to see the schema of the **Orders** table:

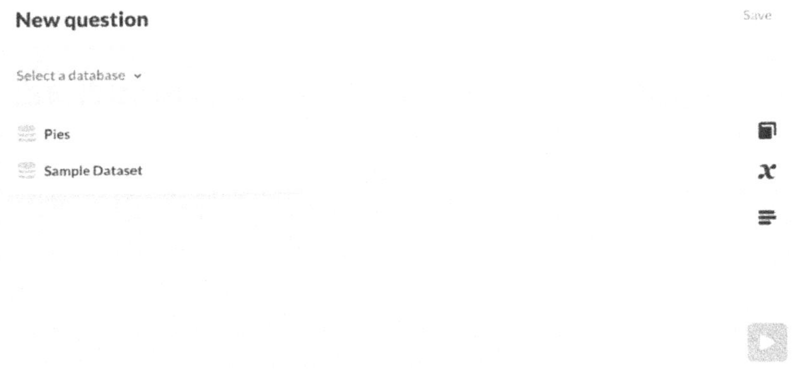

Figure 9.3 – The SQL console in Metabase

> **Important Note**
>
> The names are not transformed into the *friendly* versions we have gotten used to seeing in the GUI. They are represented just as they are in the database.

It's helpful to have the data dictionary close at hand since it's easy to forget what the schemas of our tables look like. Metabase also has a type-ahead feature in the SQL console that helps with this.

Now that we're familiar with the SQL console, let's write our query.

Writing a simple SQL query

Recall that each row in the **Orders** table represents one order. Therefore, the total number of orders is simply the count of rows of the table. To express this in a SQL query, type the following:

```
SELECT
COUNT(1) as total_orders
FROM
orders
```

Here, we are simply counting the rows of the **Orders** table, and calling the results `total_orders`. You could give the results a more friendly name if you like by wrapping the string in quotes, as follows:

```
COUNT(1) as "Total Orders"
```

However, I prefer using `snake_case` (where words are separated by underscore characters instead of spaces) in my SQL queries, so I'll be using that convention throughout the chapter.

You can almost read the query like a story (a poorly written one, albeit) and understand what it's going to do. There is no official "style guide" for writing SQL, but I prefer to use tabs to indent parts of my query that aren't commands. You could also write this query out in a single line, though, especially given its simplicity.

To run the query, either hit *Ctrl* + *Enter* on Windows or *Command* + *Enter* on Mac and Linux. You can also click the play button icon at the lower right. You should see the total number of orders, **131,639**, appear. Even though we already have a question with the same number saved, let's save this one anyway so that we can compare and contrast:

1. Click **Save**.
2. Name the question `Total Orders Placed (SQL)`.
3. Save it into your **personal collection**.

Now that we've learned how to write and run a simple SQL query in the console, let's compare it to the one we created in the notebook editor.

Comparing SQL questions to notebook editor questions

Depending on your fluency in SQL, it might have been faster and easier for you to write a query like the one we just wrote, rather than building it out using the notebook editor. That is clearly the case for me since I've been writing SQL for about 10 years and can write it almost at the speed of thought! However, there is a cost to writing everything in SQL, which we will now see.

In one tab of your browser, open up the **Total Orders placed** question (the one we created in *Chapter 6, Creating Questions*, using the notebook editor). In another tab, open the **Total Orders Placed (SQL)** question we just created.

Although both questions give the same answer, there is a difference in how they look and what you can do with them. The one built with the notebook editor offers a **Filter**, **Summarize**, and **Show Editor** option at the upper right, whereas the one built with SQL only offers an option to open back up the SQL console. This can be seen in *Figure 9.4*:

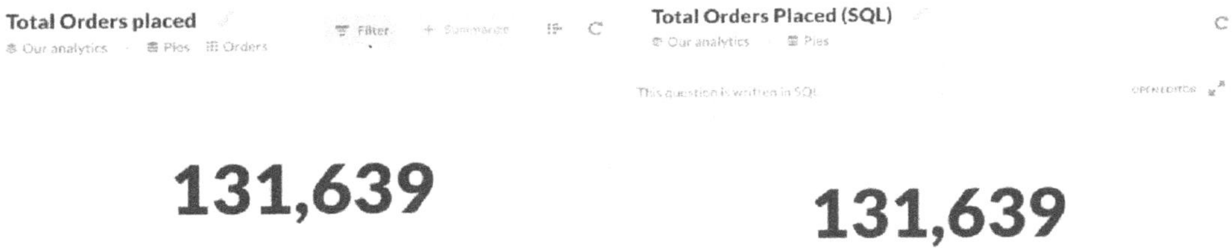

Figure 9.4 – The same question, but written in the notebook editor (left) versus the SQL editor (right)

That means if you were to share the notebook editor-built question with a user that doesn't know SQL, there's a good chance they'd be able to explore it by changing the filter, summarizing other values, drilling through step by step, or using it as a jumping-off point to make further edits in the notebook editor. None of those actions would be possible with the SQL-based question. So, even though it might be easier to write this question in SQL, it is going to be more valuable to others if it's done in the notebook editor.

As a rule of thumb, if a question can be easily created in the notebook editor, I think it's smart to do it there rather than write it in SQL. Even if you could easily write it in SQL, by creating it in the notebook editor, you open up a lot of paths for exploration by non-SQL users.

However, this doesn't mean that any question that can be done in the notebook editor should be done. There are cases where writing questions in SQL is clearly advantageous over the notebook editor. For example, a SQL query can often concisely answer a question that would be brittle and hacky in the notebook editor.

Choosing SQL over the notebook editor

In our fictional business, Pickles and Pies, customers can review items they order on a 1–5 star scale. These reviews are stored in the **Reviews** table. Because reviews are not mandatory, we might ask a series of questions around the **review rate**, defining it as the percentage of orders with a review associated with them. Imagine we want to find the review rate for our users' *first order only*. Let's see how to ask this question using the notebook editor. Get ready, because it's going to be a lot of work:

1. Click **Ask a Question**.
2. From the three options, choose **Custom Question**.
3. Pick **Pies** as your starting data.
4. Pick **Orders** as your table. Feel free to click **Visualize** if you want to refresh your memory of what this table looks like.

First off, we'll need to find the first order per user. There are a few ways we could do that in a SQL query. One obvious way is to group by **ID User** and find the minimum order ID. This works because, as you may have noticed, our order IDs are integers that increment by 1 each time a new order is created. If we were storing our order IDs using some other data type, such as a UUID, this wouldn't work.

However, in the notebook editor, it's not possible to summarize by taking the minimum of **ID Order**. This is because Metabase knows that **ID Order** is an **Entity** key and wants to prevent us from using it in a summarizing function. To get around this, we have to do something a little hacky, which is to create a custom column that returns the same value as **ID Order**. Let's see how:

1. Under the **Data** section, click to add a custom column.
2. In the **Formula** section of the custom column, we'll simply multiply the order ID by 1, like so:

```
= [ID Order] * 1
```

3. Give this custom column the name `ID Order Alternative`. If you like, preview the data to ensure it matches the original order ID.
4. Now, in the **Summarize** section, choose **Min of ID Order Alternative**. Group it by **ID User**.
5. Next, create a left outer join to the **Reviews** table, using **Min of ID Order Alternative** as the left-hand join key, and **ID Order** as the right-hand join key.

At this point, your notebook editor should look as in *Figure 9.5*:

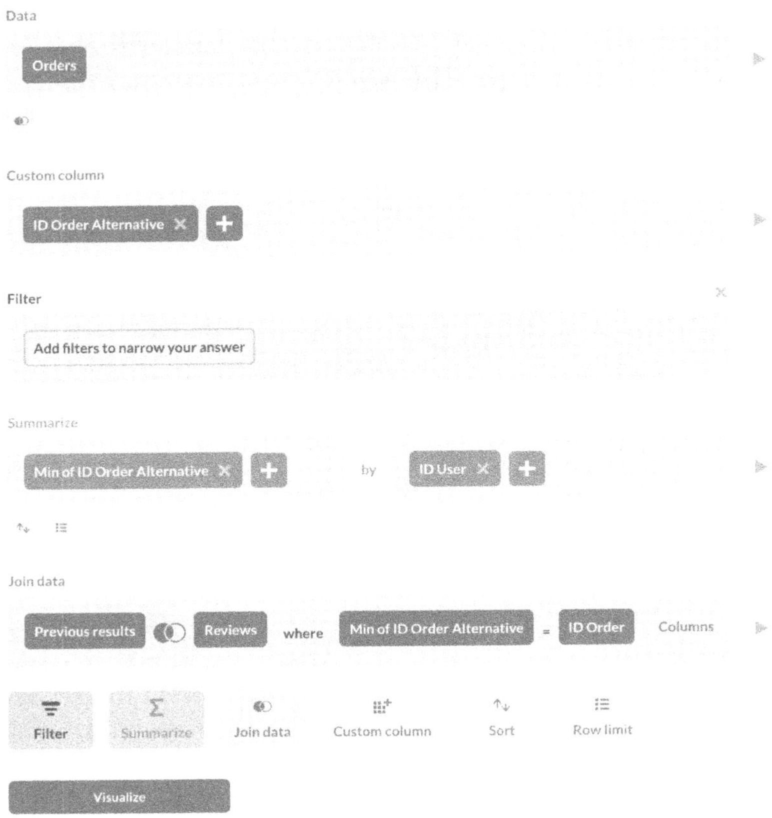

Figure 9.5 – A circuitous way of finding the first order per user and joining to the Reviews table

One thing we must be careful about is that although reviews have **ID Order** as a column, they are not necessarily one-to-one mapping with **Min of ID Order Alternative**. A review is for a specific item in an order, and as we've learned, an order can have multiple items. That means that an order can have multiple reviews associated with it. For example, I could order a banana cream pie and a pumpkin pie in a single order. Then, I could review the banana cream pie, giving it 5 stars, and review the pumpkin pie (also with 5 stars). This would create two rows in the **Reviews** table, but only one in the **Orders** table.

Therefore, to answer our question, instead of counting the number of rows as we usually do, we'll have to count the number of **distinct ID orders**. This will take care of duplicates from the one-to-many mapping. Since we want to return a ratio, we can turn this into a custom expression:

1. Click **Summarize** and create a custom expression.

2. In the **Formula** field, type the following:

```
Distinct([Reviews → ID Order]) / Distinct([Min of ID
Order Alternative])
```

3. Name this Custom Expression `Review Rate`.

4. Finally, click **Visualize**. At this point, your notebook editor should look as in *Figure 9.6*:

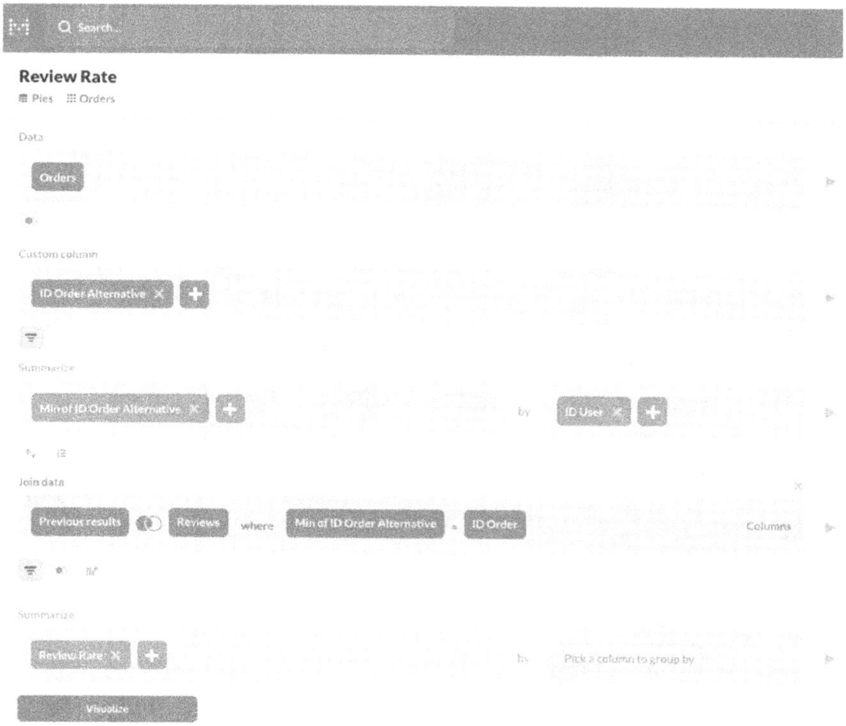

Figure 9.6 – The notebook editor should look like this as you finish step 4

Wow! That was a very involved custom question with many steps. The step where we returned the minimum of **ID Order Alternative** felt a little hacky, too. Although we got to a result, you could argue that this question is maxing out the capabilities of the notebook editor. You could also argue that the logic in the editor is too complex for a non-technical user to find any paths for further exploration. This feels like a question that might be better left as a SQL query. Let's see whether expressing it with SQL is any easier. Open up the SQL console and write the following query:

```
SELECT
    COUNT(DISTINCT b.id_order)/COUNT(DISTINCT a.id_
order)::FLOAT as first_order_review_rate
```

```
FROM
(
    SELECT
    *
    , ROW_NUMBER() OVER (PARTITION BY id_user ORDER BY id_
order) as user_order_rank
    FROM
    orders
) a
LEFT OUTER JOIN
    reviews b
ON
    a.id_order = b.id_order
WHERE
    user_order_rank = 1
```

Running the query gives the exact same results as our custom question. Given the complexity of the custom question, I think it's safe to say that the SQL route is preferable to implement and follow for this question. However, if a non-technical user were to open this up, they would have no paths to explore it any further. So, even though it might be easier to create this question in SQL versus the notebook editor, it's not entirely clear that this is the right route to choose.

Fortunately, there is a way we can create this in SQL and make all our users happy. This involves creating what I call **Questions-as-Tables**. Let's learn how to do it.

Creating Questions-as-Tables using SQL

In the last section, we learned that while SQL can often be an easier option, it has a major drawback: SQL questions are hard for non-SQL users to explore. This presents a clear problem for a product such as Metabase, since Metabase aims to democratize data and allow anyone, no matter how technical, to explore it and find answers to their questions. Their solution to this is the notebook editor, but we've already seen that the notebook editor either can't answer a question, such as **Items Ordered**, which we learned about back in *Chapter 6*, *Creating Questions*, or is too unwieldly, as we saw in the last section with the review rate.

Unfortunately, having messy or unwieldy data in your application database is more of a rule than an exception. It's often quoted that 80% of a data scientist's job is cleaning messy data. In my experience, that sounds about right, and a lot of that cleaning is done with SQL. Remember that application databases are designed to make an application (such as an online Pickles and Pies shop) run effectively. How easy or hard it will be to do analytics on them is generally not taken into consideration.

Fortunately, there is a solution to all of this. We saw in *Chapter 6*, *Creating Questions*, that in addition to starting a question from a database table, you can also start a question from a **saved question**. That means that you can create a question based on a SQL query, save it, and have others use that question as a starting-off point. This is what I call creating Questions-as-Tables. It sounds complicated, but it's actually very simple. It's also, in my opinion, the most valuable contribution a power user can make to Metabase. Let's learn how, using the review rate question we explored in the last section as our motivating example. Open up the SQL console.

Since we want to give our users as much freedom to explore this question as possible, we will change our query from the last section so that we have the following:

- The query is **unaggregated**, exposing as many rows as possible for filtering.
- The query projects as many columns as possible, too. This is not just for filtering, but also for grouping and summarizing.

With these two principles in mind, we'll write the following query:

```
SELECT
    a.*
    , COALESCE(order_reviewed, 0) as order_reviewed
    , avg_rating_of_order
    , unique_items_reviewed_in_order
FROM
    orders a
LEFT OUTER JOIN
(
    SELECT
        id_order
        , MAX(1) as order_reviewed
        , AVG(star_rating) as avg_rating_of_order
        , COUNT(1) as unique_items_reviewed_in_order
    FROM
        reviews
    GROUP BY
        id_order
```

```
) b
ON
    a.id_order = b.id_order
```

Go ahead and run this query. The query takes all the information from our **Orders** table and joins it to a summarized version of the **Reviews** table, giving us a result with all the columns from the **Orders** table and the following summarized values from the **Reviews** table:

- A column, `order_reviewed`, which is `1` if the order has a review associated with it and `0` otherwise.
- A column, `avg_rating_of_order`, which is the average of the review scores for items in an order. If there are no reviews associated with an order, the value in this column will be `NULL`.
- A column, `unique_items_reviewed_in_order`, which is the number of unique items that were reviewed in the order. If there are no reviews associated with an order, the value in this column will be `NULL`.

Metabase will return this data in a table format, as in *Figure 9.7*, which is great because we actually want to treat this as a table:

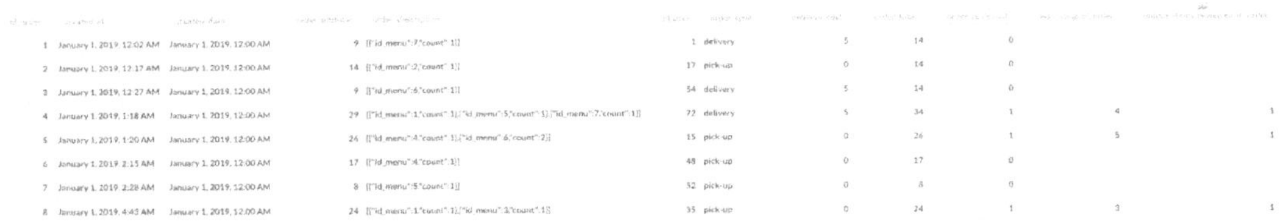

1	January 1, 2019, 12:02 AM	January 1, 2019, 12:00 AM	9	[{"id_menu":7,"count":1}]	1	delivery	5	14	0		
2	January 1, 2019, 12:17 AM	January 1, 2019, 12:00 AM	14	[{"id_menu":2,"count":1}]	17	pick-up	0	14	0		
3	January 1, 2019, 12:27 AM	January 1, 2019, 12:00 AM	9	[{"id_menu":6,"count":1}]	54	delivery	5	14	0		
4	January 1, 2019, 1:18 AM	January 1, 2019, 12:00 AM	29	[{"id_menu":1,"count":1},{"id_menu":5,"count":1},{"id_menu":7,"count":1}]	72	delivery	5	34	1	4	1
5	January 1, 2019, 1:20 AM	January 1, 2019, 12:00 AM	26	[{"id_menu":4,"count":1},{"id_menu":6,"count":2}]	15	pick-up	0	26	1	5	1
6	January 1, 2019, 2:15 AM	January 1, 2019, 12:00 AM	17	[{"id_menu":4,"count":1}]	48	pick-up	0	17	0		
7	January 1, 2019, 2:28 AM	January 1, 2019, 12:00 AM	8	[{"id_menu":5,"count":1}]	52	pick-up	0	8	0		
8	January 1, 2019, 4:43 AM	January 1, 2019, 12:00 AM	24	[{"id_menu":1,"count":1},{"id_menu":3,"count":1}]	35	pick-up	0	24	1	3	1

Figure 9.7 – The results of our "Orders and Reviews" query

Before we save this question, let's create a new collection that we can use for these Questions-as-Tables. Open a new browser tab and go to your Metabase instance. Open up the **Our Analytics** collection and add a new collection to it by clicking **+ New Collection**. For this new collection, do the following:

- Give it the name `SQL Derived Tables`.
- Give it a description such as `These are helpful views onto our tables that are ideal for exploration in the notebook editor.`
- Add it to **Our Analytics**.

Now, you can go back to the tab with your SQL query and save it. Give it the following name and description:

- **Name**: `Orders and Reviews (if applicable)`
- **Description**: `A query that joins the Orders table to a summarized Reviews table. You can use this to calculate Review Rate metrics.`

Finally, save it to the **SQL Derived Tables** collection.

Now that we've written a query that outputs something that looks like a database table, let's learn how we (and others) can use this as a starting-off point for further questions.

Using saved questions to ask more questions

One incredibly useful feature in Metabase is the ability to make questions based off of saved questions, rather than database tables. Let's see how, using the Questions-as-Tables saved question we created in the previous section:

1. Click **Ask a Question**.
2. From the three options, click **Custom Question**.
3. Now, instead of choosing the **Pies** database as your starting data, click **Saved Questions**.
4. Click into the **SQL Derived Tables** folder and select the question we just created, `Orders and Reviews (if applicable)`.

We're now able to use the results of our SQL query in the notebook editor as if it were a standalone table. Moreover, anyone else in our organization with the right permissions can explore and create questions off of this saved question, opening up a lot of new analysis that otherwise would not be possible because of the complex relationship between the two tables. Let's now see how easy it is to calculate **Review Rate** from here:

1. In the **Summarize** section, click **Average of** and choose **order_reviewed** as the column to summarize.
2. Click **Visualize**.

And that's it! We can see that 0.4 of our orders have a review associated with them. We can easily change this to a nice looking percentage by clicking **Visualization** and changing the style to **Percent**.

Now, let's imagine we want to look at this over time. By now, we've gone through this exercise many times. Usually, it's the time series that we want to see, rather than a single number. Let's edit our question to see the review rate over time:

1. Open back up the notebook editor by clicking the **Show editor** icon.
2. In the **Pick a column to group by** section, add **created_date**. Let's use **Month** as our granularity.
3. Now, click **Visualize** to see a time series plot of review rate by month. It should look just as in *Figure 9.8*:

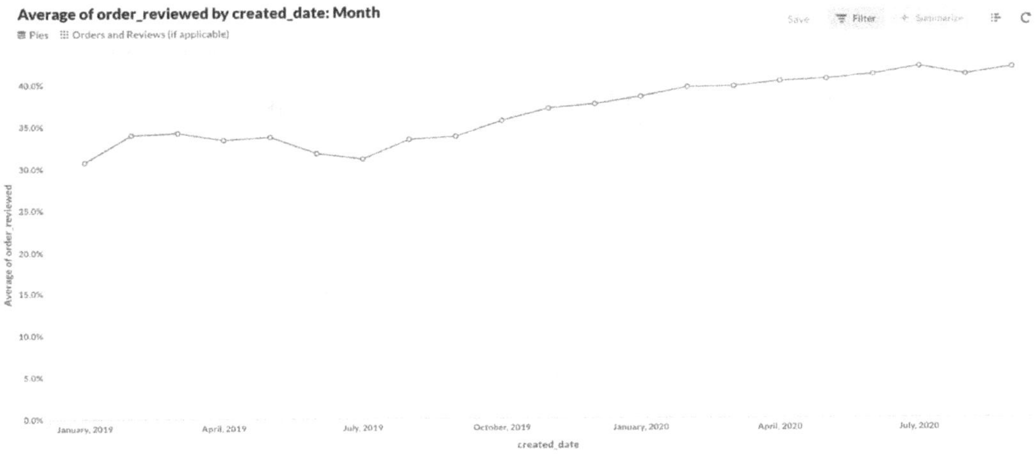

Figure 9.8 – Our review rate over time

As you can see, by using SQL to transform our **Orders** and **Reviews** tables, we've created a really convenient saved question that other users can play around with and easily use to answer various questions around **Review Rate**. To me, this paradigm is the most useful way a power user can unlock value to others in Metabase. Let's see another example.

Back in *Chapter 6, Creating Questions*, we used a SQL query to flatten our **Orders** table so that each row was an item ordered, rather than an order (which can contain many items). This allowed us to see how many of each item have been ordered. Our **Orders** table is a great example of how data that is designed to work well as the backend data store for an application is not always well designed for analytics. Knowing how many of each item has been ordered is an absolutely critical piece of analytics; in fact, you could argue that it's *the most important* thing we'd need to know about our business. But the schema of the table, in particular the way in which items in an order are represented in a JSON array, makes it impossible for users without knowledge of advanced SQL to do any sort of analysis on the topic.

The way we solved this in *Chapter 6, Creating Questions*, was by writing a SQL query that returned the count of orders of each item and presented it in a bar plot. Now, in the spirit of making this a Questions-as-Tables saved question that other users can do their own analysis on, let's rewrite the query so that it returns a table where each row is an item in an order:

1. Start off by opening up the **Items Ordered** question, which we created in *Chapter 6, Creating Questions*. If you skipped that section, you can just write out the following query.
2. Edit the query so it looks as follows:

```
SELECT
*
, CAST(single_item_orders->>'id_menu' AS INT) as id_menu
, CAST(single_item_orders->>'count' AS INT) as item_count
FROM
(
    SELECT
     *
     , json_array_elements(order_description) as single_
item_orders
    FROM
        orders
) a
```

Run the query. You may have to change the visualization to **Table**.

Here, we have changed the query so that instead of summarizing the item count for each menu item, we're instead leaving the results unaggregated. We're also projecting all columns from the **Orders** table, which will open up more paths for subsequent analysis.

3. Now, click **Save**. Let's replace the original question, which we named **Items Ordered**.

Now, let's see how simple it is to recreate the bar plot we made back in *Chapter 6, Creating Questions*, using this saved question as our "table." First, though, let's move this question to our **SQL Derived Questions** collection:

1. From your Metabase home page, open the **Our Analytics** collection.
2. Find the **Items Ordered** question and click and drag it to the **SQL Derived Questions** collection.
3. Now, click **Ask a Question**.
4. Choose **Custom Question**.
5. Pick **Saved Questions | SQL Derived Tables | Items Ordered** as your starting data.
6. In the **Summarize** section, choose **Sum of** and **item_count**.
7. In the **Grouping** section, choose **id_menu**.
8. Click **Visualize**.

Now we can see the total number of orders of each item, almost exactly as we saw in *Chapter 6, Creating Questions*. The only thing different about this question is that instead of having the proper menu item names, we just have the item IDs. That isn't great, so let's fix that. Open the notebook editor back up.

Unfortunately, because we're starting with a saved question and not a database table, we lose the foreign key relationship we called out in the **Data Model** part of the **Admin Panel** back in *Chapter 5, Building Your Data Model*. That means that even though our saved question has columns in it, such as `id_menu` and `id_user`, Metabase doesn't know that they match up with primary keys in our **Menu** and **Users** tables, so we have to call them out explicitly in a join. In the notebook editor, under the **Data** section, do the following:

1. Click the **Join Data** icon toward the top of the notebook editor.
2. Since we want to bring in the **Name** column from the **Menu** table, we'll join to the **Menu** table. Select it from the dropdown.
3. On the left side of the join, pick `id_menu` as the key.
4. On the right side, pick **ID Menu**.
5. You can leave the join as a left outer join, but an inner join will give the same result.
6. Now, change the grouping variable to **Menu | ID Name**.
7. Click **Visualize**.

Now, the results look exactly like what we got in *Chapter 6, Creating Questions*. The big difference is that these results were merely aided by a SQL query, rather than achieved solely by one. Of course, that means that any user in your organization can now easily create many different iterations of this question without ever knowing that your SQL query is powering a lot of the work. Let's save this question, calling it **Count of Menu Items Ordered**.

Imagine that at this point we want to put this question on our **Executive Summary** dashboard that we built in *Chapter 8, Creating Dashboards, Pulses, and Collections*. Remember how that dashboard had filters on it for dates, states, and whether the order was a delivery or pick-up? In the next section, we'll learn how we can add this chart to our dashboard in a way that is compatible with our filters.

Adding SQL-based saved questions to dashboards

Recall that we want to take the **Count of Menu Items Ordered** question we made in the last section and use it in our dashboard. Let's see what happens when we simply add it to the dashboard as is:

1. Open up the **Executive Summary** dashboard.
2. Click the **Pencil** icon to start editing the dashboard.
3. Click the + icon to add a question.
4. Find the **Count of Menu Items Ordered** question, and click it to add it to the dashboard. Optionally, resize it for visibility.
5. Now, let's connect our filters to our newly added question. Edit the date filter so that it filters the `created_date` column.
6. Edit the **Delivery or Pick-Up** column so that it filters the `order_type` column.
7. Now, click **State**. Note that there is no option to filter for **State**. We'll come back to this later. For now, click **Done** and save the dashboard.

We're now able to apply the **Date** and **Delivery or Pick-Up** filters to our new question. However, we have no option for **State**. That's because the **State** column comes from the **Users** table. We need to join the data in our question to the **Users** table to make any filters on its columns functional. Let's go ahead and do that:

1. Open the **Count of Menu Items Ordered** question.
2. Click the **Show Editor** icon to open up the notebook editor.
3. After the section where we joined **Items Ordered** to **Menu**, create another **Join data** section.
4. In that, join **Previous Results** to **Users**. You can use either a left outer join or an inner join.
5. On the left side of the join, pick **id_user**.
6. On the right side, pick **ID User**.
7. Save the question, replacing the original question.

   The results of the question haven't changed. All we've done is joined our data to the **Users** table to bring in additional columns. Now, return to the **Executive Summary** dashboard.
8. Click the **Pencil** icon to edit the dashboard.
9. Now, click **Edit** on the **State** filter. You're now able to filter the **Count of Menu Items Ordered** question by **State**.
10. Click **Done** and **Save**.

Because SQL-based saved questions lose their foreign key mappings, it's just a matter of adding them back via joins in the notebook editor to enable filtering on all the possible columns in the foreign tables. Those joins can be created in the SQL editor as well, but to get them to work with filters requires extra work. We'll learn about that in the next section, where we'll focus on using variables in SQL queries.

Using variables in SQL queries

In the last section, we learned how to connect filters to saved questions written in SQL. However, to do so, we needed to use the notebook editor as an intermediary step. It would not have worked had we written the question in pure SQL. Let's see for ourselves, by recreating the **Count of Menu Items Ordered** question in pure SQL:

1. Open up the **Items Ordered** question we saved earlier.
2. Click the diagonal arrows to expand the editor.

3. Edit the SQL as follows:

```
SELECT
    c.name
    , SUM(item_count) as items_ordered
FROM
(
SELECT
    *
    , CAST(single_item_orders->>'id_menu' AS INT) as id_menu
    , CAST(single_item_orders->>'count' AS INT) as item_count
FROM
    (
        SELECT
            *
          , json_array_elements(order_description) as single_
item_orders
        FROM
            orders
    ) a
) b
JOIN
    menu c
ON b.id_menu = c.id_menu
JOIN
    users d
ON b.id_user = d.id_user
GROUP BY
    c.name
```

This query does exactly the same thing as the edits we made in the last section via the notebook editor. Let's save it and add it to our **Executive Summary** dashboard. Give it the name `Count of Menu Items Ordered - SQL` to distinguish it from the same question finished in the notebook editor. Add it to the **Executive Summary** dashboard.

Now, open up the **Executive Summary** dashboard. Notice how connecting the dashboard filters to this new question is not possible. Metabase is unable to recognize the columns in our query as potential columns to filter on. Fortunately, this does not mean that queries written in pure SQL are ineligible for dashboards. The solution requires us to use something that Metabase calls **variables**, which we'll now learn about.

Adding variables to SQL queries

In Metabase, variables are values in SQL queries that allow you to add dynamic filters that anyone can use. It's easiest to learn with a motivating example, so let's get started.

Let's imagine we want to create a SQL-based question to find the count of users in a specific state. This would be easy to do in the notebook editor, but it's also pretty simple in SQL. Here's what it would look like to find users in California:

```
SELECT
    COUNT(1) as total_users
FROM
    users
WHERE
    state = 'California'
```

Running this query should return `18,896`. The query is simple enough that most users, regardless of their familiarity with SQL, should be able to edit it to a different US state. Still, there is an easier and more user-friendly way that doesn't require editing the SQL.

In the SQL editor, delete the word `'California'`, and instead type `{{state}}`. The double brackets indicate that you are adding a **variable**, and once you type this, a side tray on the right side of the SQL console will open up, as in *Figure 9.9*:

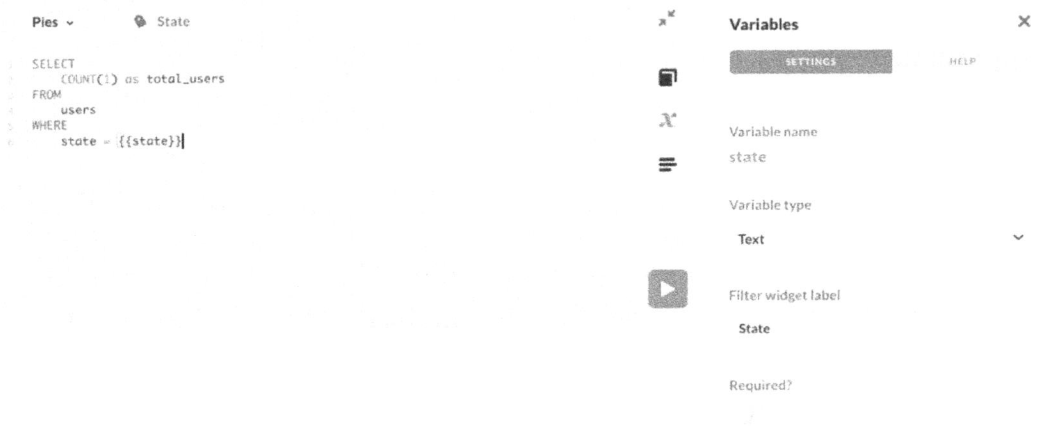

Figure 9.9 – A SQL query with a variable inserted

Since variables can be a little confusing to work with, Metabase includes a **Settings** and **Help** tab whenever it sees that you're working with one. The **Settings** tab has some options to configure your variable, but for our example we can leave everything as default. Note how a filter widget has appeared at the top of the SQL console and in *Figure 9.9*. Try typing `California` in this box and running the query. Now, change it to `Texas` and run again. Whatever value that is entered into the filter widget is assigned to the `{{state}}` variable.

> **Important Note**
>
> Variables in SQL queries are a Metabase feature. They would not work in `psql`, for example, or in most standard SQL prompts that come with a relational database.

As you can see, variables are a great way to make SQL queries more approachable to users who normally might be intimidated by computer code. Now that we've seen a simple example of a variable in a SQL query, let's learn more about what we can do with them.

Configuring variables

It just so happens that the default settings for our **State** variable in the last section were appropriate for our use case. That won't always be the case. Let's learn more about the configuration options we can choose when creating variables.

If it's not already open, open the **Variables** side tray by clicking the **X** icon on the right side of the SQL console. The default variable type is **Text**, but you can also have it be **Number**, **Date**, or what is called **Field Filter**. Changing it to **Number** or **Date** just means that the value the filter widget is expecting will be a number or date instead of text. For example, say you have the following line:

```
state = {{state}}
```

You could change that line to the following:

```
created_date >= {{date}}
```

Now, if you change the **Variable type** filter to **Date**, the filter widget will change to one with a calendar icon. Clicking inside it will offer a calendar widget to pick dates from.

In these examples, I have used `{{state}}` and `{{date}}` as my variable names, but you could literally type anything you want. They are just placeholders. Metabase will take whatever value you use for your variable, capitalize it, and use that value as the default label for the filter widget. You can also change that label to anything you like, by typing a new value in the **Filter widget label** text box.

We've now learned how to use text, date, and numeric variables to dynamically add user input to our queries. Let's see what happens if we add the `{{state}}` variable to our query, but run it with no value inside the filter box. Type the following query into the SQL console:

```
SELECT
    COUNT(1) as total_users
FROM
    users
WHERE
    state = {{state}}
```

Now, try running the query with nothing in the filter widget. You should get an error, with a message reading `Cannot run the query: missing required parameters: #{"state"}`. If you think about this for a moment, the reason should be clear. With no value to inject into the `{{state}}` variable, the query has no value to compare the `state` column to. While this might make perfect sense to someone who knows SQL, error messages are always confusing and scary to non-technical users. Fortunately, there is a way to avoid this by using **optional variables**. Let's learn how to use them.

Adding an optional variable

In the last section, we learned how to add variables to our queries, but also discovered that when they have no value, they can cause a query to throw an error. This can easily be mitigated by making a variable optional. It turns out that this is as easy as wrapping part of your query in double square brackets. Let's see an example, building on the query we've been working with. In the SQL console, edit your query as follows:

```
SELECT
    COUNT(1) as total_users
FROM
    users
[[WHERE state = {{state}}]]
```

By putting `WHERE state = {{state}}` in double brackets, we are making that piece of text optional. If no `{{state}}` variable is present, the entire content inside the brackets will be removed at runtime. If the `{{state}}` variable is present, the value will be injected into the variable and the rest of the content in the brackets will be rendered.

You can also use this technique in fancier ways. For example, imagine that we want to change this query so that if it's run with no value in the filter widget, it defaults to the count of users in California or Oregon:

```
SELECT
    COUNT(1) as total_users
FROM
    users
WHERE state [[= {{state}} --]] IN ('California', 'Oregon')
```

In this query, we're taking advantage of the `--` comment symbol in PostgreSQL. If the query were run with no value in the filter widget, the portion in square brackets would be removed and the line would render as follows:

```
WHERE state IN ('California', 'Oregon')
```

If the query were run with a value in the filter widget, such as `Texas`, the line would render like this instead:

```
WHERE state = 'Texas'-- IN ('California', 'Oregon')
```

The `IN ('California', 'Oregon')` part would not get removed, but the comment symbol in our optional variable would comment that part out. Of course, if you were to make this query a saved question, you would want to give a very verbose name and description to the question so that users know exactly what is going on under the hood.

Making variables optional is a clever way to make your queries with variables even more dynamic and user-friendly. They are especially useful with variables where the data type is text, date, or number. We have not yet learned about the fourth type of variable, **Field Filter**, so let's learn about it now.

Configuring Field Filter variables

Field Filter variables are more complicated than the variables we previously learned about, but far more powerful. Let's create one.

Change the query we've been working with, like so:

```
SELECT
    COUNT(1) as total_users
FROM
    users
WHERE
     {{state}}
```

Instead of projecting a column in our `WHERE` clause and using a comparison operator such as `state = {{state}}`, now we just have the `{{state}}` variable alone. If we were to keep the variable type as **Text** and type `California` in the filter widget, we'd get an error because the query would render as follows:

```
SELECT
    COUNT(1) as total_users
FROM
    users
WHERE
     'California'
```

This, of course, is not proper SQL, since we need a column after our `WHERE` clause. Now, let's change **Variable type** to **Field Filter**:

1. A new dropdown named **Field to map to** appears. This is where you pick the column or field that you want your variable to map to. Since we want to filter on **State**, pick the **Users** table and the **State** column from the dropdown.
2. Now, click into the filter widget. Because we explicitly specified the column we want to filter on in the last step, the filter widget is able to display the full cardinality of the **State** column for us and recognize the variable type.

This comes with several advantages over a variable of the **Text** type. For one, we don't have to worry about spelling mistakes. Although most Americans have the spelling of "Mississippi" burned into their minds since grade school, users outside the US might have trouble spelling it. This way, we can simply use **Type ahead** or pick the states we want from the dropdown. We can also pick multiple states, which is something that we could not do in the **Text** example.

Of course, **Field Filters** will only be as valuable as the metadata backing our data model that we created in *Chapter 5, Building Your Data Model*. This is why I continuously stress the importance of curating your data model.

As you can see by now, variables are easy ways to make your queries more dynamic and useful to non-technical users. Right before this section, I wrote about how variables can also be useful in dashboards. Let's see how.

Using variables in dashboards

Earlier in the chapter, we saw that while queries written in pure SQL can be added to a dashboard, the filters on the dashboard will not work with them. It turns out that the way to solve this is to use variables. Let's see an example by creating a question in SQL for total signups with an optional variable for `created_date` and `state`. In a new SQL console, type the following:

```
SELECT
    COUNT(1) as total_signups
FROM
users
WHERE
    {{created_date}} -- id_user <> 0
AND
    {{state}}
```

Note that both variables are optional by default. Because all SQL queries with filters need a `WHERE` clause, I have added one such that if I have no `created_date` value to inject into my variable, it will filter on `id_user <> 0`, which I know has an effect on the query.

Let's now configure our variables, starting with `created_date`:

1. The variable type should be **Field Filter**.
2. The field to map to should be **Created Date** from the **Users** table.
3. The filter widget type doesn't matter for the dashboard, but you should make it something that will make sense for the question when viewed by itself. I like **Date Filter**.
4. The filter widget label also doesn't matter for the dashboard, but it makes sense to give it a sensible name.

For the `state` variable, configure the following:

1. The variable type should be **Field Filter**.
2. The field to map to should be **State** from the **Users** table.
3. The filter widget type doesn't matter for the dashboard, but you should make it something that will make sense for the question when viewed by itself. I like **State**.
4. The filter widget label also doesn't matter for the dashboard, but it makes sense to give it a sensible name.

   We're almost done:

5. Change the visualization to **Number** so that it appears as one large number.
6. Save the question, giving it the name `Total Signups`.
7. When prompted about adding it to a dashboard, click **Yes**. Add it to the **Executive Summary** dashboard.

Now that we've built our question in SQL with optional variables and added it to our dashboard, let's configure the filters on the dashboard so that their values are mapped to our variables:

1. From the **Executive Summary** dashboard, click the **Pencil** icon to go into edit mode.
2. Click **Edit** on the **Date** filter.
3. Find the **Total Signups** question and choose **Created Date** from the dropdown menu.
4. Click **Edit** on the **State** filter.
5. Find the **Total Signups** question and choose **State** from the drop-down menu.
6. Click **Done** and **Save** on the dashboard.

Now you can change the values in the **Date** and **State** filters and see the newly created **Total Signups** question change to reflect the filtered values, as in *Figure 9.10*:

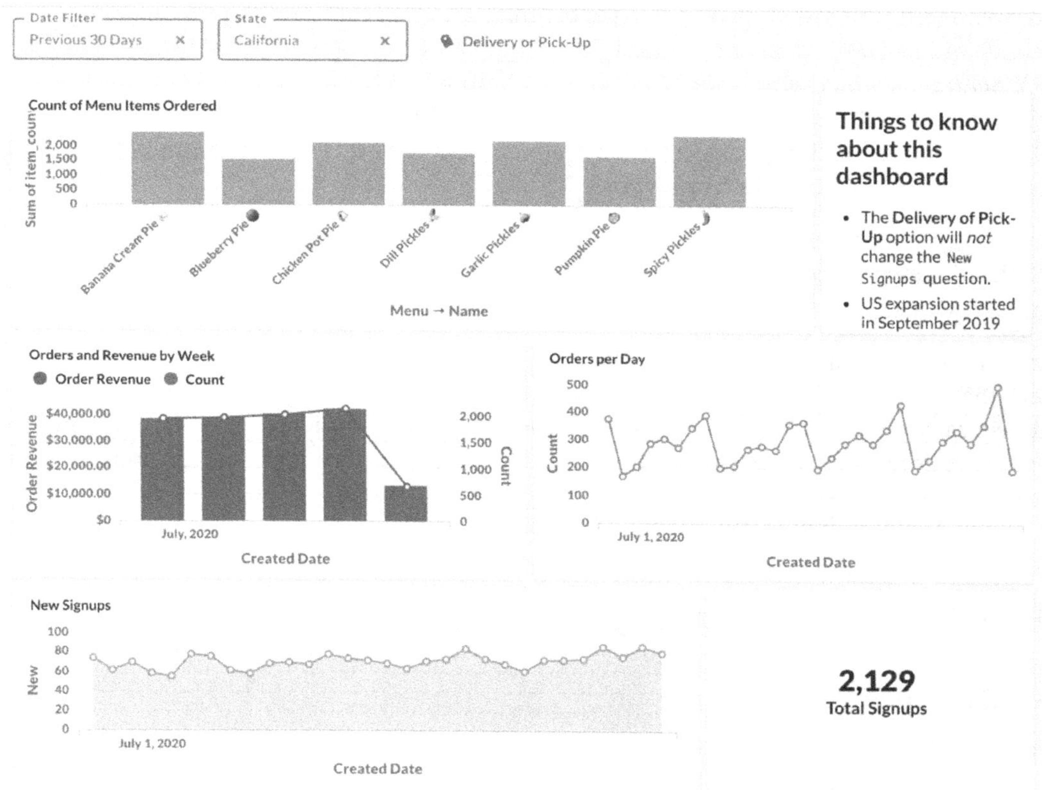

Figure 9.10 – Our Executive Summary dashboard in a filtered state. We now have a question written in pure SQL (Total Signups) and a question based on SQL (Count of Menu Items Ordered) that respects our filters

We've now learned how to take questions written in pure SQL, add them to a dashboard, and use variables to ensure that our dashboard filters are still functional. Next, let's learn about a feature in Metabase called SQL snippets.

Creating saved SQL snippets

It may feel like a lot of the SQL we've written has been copied, pasted, and reused over and over again from other queries. This is common in SQL, common in programming in general, and considered an anti-pattern. In fact, there's a principle in computing called the **DRY principle**, which stands for **Don't Repeat Yourself** (`https://en.wikipedia.org/wiki/Don%27t_repeat_yourself`). The principle is about how you should not rewrite the same line or lines of code again and again, as it is time-consuming and introduces more risk of bugs from typos.

Metabase has taken this principle to heart and has a feature called **Saved SQL Snippets**. A SQL snippet is a block of SQL that you can call upon in a single variable whenever you want to reuse it.

Throughout this chapter and book, we've been working with some iteration of the same query that takes the **Orders** table and flattens it out, such that every row becomes an item ordered, rather than an entire order. This seems like a good candidate for a SQL snippet since we've gone back to it so many times. Let's learn how to turn it into a SQL snippet:

1. Open up the **Items Ordered** saved question.
2. Expand the SQL editor.
3. Highlight the entire query and right-click. A menu of options will pop up, as in *Figure 9.11*.
4. Click **Save Snippet**.
5. Give the snippet a name, such as `Flattened Orders`.
6. Give a description, such as `Our Orders table, but flattened so that each row is an item ordered rather than an order.`

Unlike other saved items, SQL snippets don't get saved to collections. They are available to anyone with SQL editor permissions on at least one database. In Metabase's enterprise edition, there are SQL folders for organizing and creating permissions around snippets:

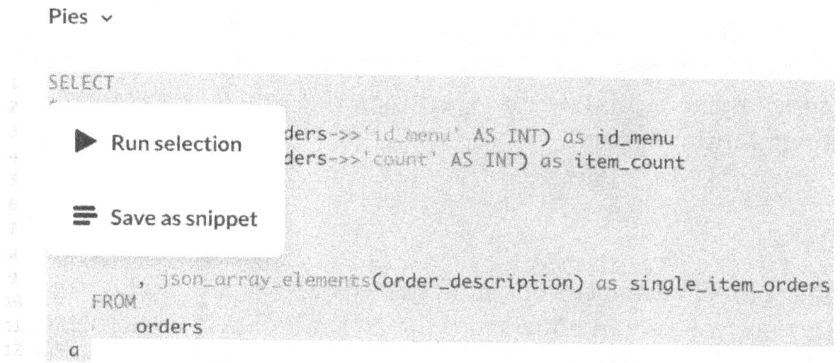

Figure 9.11 – Saving our Items Ordered query as a saved snippet

Now that we've learned how to save a snippet, let's see how we can use it in a new SQL query:

1. Open up the SQL editor.
2. On the right side of the editor, you'll see the same icon as in *Figure 9.11*. Click that to open up your saved snippets.
3. Click **Flattened Orders**.

Instead of the full query, you will only see the following:

```
{{snippet: Flattened Orders}}
```

You can run this as if it's a query. It will return the same results as the query backing it. The text in the brackets is merely a pointer to the saved SQL snippet. With that in mind, we can start new SQL queries that use this saved snippet as a base, just as we did earlier in the chapter with the notebook editor and our Questions-as-Tables saved question. For example, to get the number of items ordered by menu item name, we can simply write this and save ourselves 13 lines of complex SQL from needing to be written:

```
SELECT
    b.name
    , SUM(item_count) as items_ordered
FROM
( {{snippet: Flattened Orders}} ) a
JOIN
    menu b
ON a.id_menu = b.id_menu
GROUP BY
    b.name
```

SQL snippets are a great way to avoid the cardinal sin of repeating yourself. They are also great for storing a lot of complex SQL that you'd rather not expose to your users. Metabase only recently added them (as of the time of writing), so I would expect them to get more and more useful in future versions.

Summary

We covered quite a bit of advanced content in this chapter, all around how to best use SQL in Metabase. By now, you should understand that SQL absolutely has a role to play in a fully functioning Metabase environment. Moreover, you should understand the time and place where SQL is appropriate, and where it's better to stick with the notebook editor.

I've seen a lot of novice SQL programmers become very proficient at SQL after having the chance to play around with it in Metabase. SQL is an incredibly powerful language that has staying power. I believe we'll be using it for decades to come. It tends to be one of the easier languages to learn, too, so I encourage you to make it a part of your Metabase environment.

This chapter concludes our exploration of the core features of Metabase. In the next chapter, we'll learn about some advanced features of Metabase, find out where to go for additional help, and learn how we can contribute to Metabase's development.

Section 3: Advanced Functionality and Paid Features

This shorter section will go over advanced features and the premium features that are included in the Enterprise product, as well as where to go for additional help and how to contribute to the project.

This section contains the following chapter:

- *Chapter 10, Advanced Features, Getting Help, and Contributing*

10
Advanced Features, Getting Help, and Contributing

At this point, we've covered all of the core features of Metabase. We started our journey covering how to properly deploy and set up an instance of Metabase. We then learned how to connect to a database and enhance our data model's metadata. Finally, we learned how to create questions, both in the notebook editor and the SQL console, make them into interactive visualizations, and add them to dashboards and pulses. We're now equipped with everything we need to create a well-functioning analytics environment for an organization of any size.

Because this book is intended for power users, we won't simply stop at an overview of all the core features. Power users should know about everything Metabase has to offer, including where to get help. In the first half of this chapter, we will learn about some of the advanced features Metabase offers. Just because I use the word "advanced," does not mean that enabling or using these features is difficult. By "advanced," I mean that I only consider these features necessary for some use cases.

Then, in the second half of the chapter, we'll learn about all the ways you can get further help beyond the contents of this book. While this book and the official Metabase documentation will get you quite far, inevitably there will be times where some issue with Metabase stumps you and requires you to do some sleuthing on your own. Fortunately, there is a vibrant community of Metabase users and developers online who are happy to help. This chapter will introduce you to all the places on the internet where you can get help, file bugs, and even, if your passion drives you to it, contribute code to the Metabase project.

Specifically, in this chapter, we'll cover the following topics:

- Caching queries
- Embedding and sharing externally
- X-raying your data
- Troubleshooting in Metabase
- Getting help on Discourse
- Creating issues and filing bugs on GitHub
- Contributing on GitHub

Technical requirements

You'll need your instance of Metabase running with a connection to the `pies` database. If you'd like to try embedding Metabase questions and dashboards on external websites, you'll need write access to a website or blog to try it out on.

While not needed, it will be helpful to make yourself an account on Metabase's Discourse support forum (`https://discourse.metabase.com/`) and on GitHub (`https://github.com`).

Caching queries

The data that we've been working with in the `pies` database is relatively small. The number of rows per table is in the tens or hundreds of thousands. What's more, the queries we've been running have been relatively inexpensive. When I refer to them as inexpensive, I mean in terms of compute power. With relatively small data, a powerful PostgreSQL database, and a scalable Metabase environment all living in the same VPC, we have not had to deal with the most common pain point in analytics: slow-running queries.

Unfortunately, slow-running queries are unavoidable in the real world. This is especially true when you grant query privileges to everyone, or at least most, in your organization. The cost of opening up your data to everyone is that people are going to write some... how do you say it, creative queries. Fortunately, Metabase offers a **caching** feature to help minimize any pain points that crop up around waiting for poorly optimized or expensive queries to run. Let's learn more.

What is cache?

Cache tends to be one of those concepts that people think is more complicated than it actually is. The concept of cache in Metabase is really easy to understand.

When you execute a query, that query is sent to your database. The database computes the results and returns it. If that query is cached, its results are also saved in a temporary location. By saving them temporarily, if the same query is run again, the saved results in cache can be retrieved. This makes it so that the query doesn't actually get run again. There's no trip to the database, no database computation, and no return trip back to the client. Fetching it from cache skips all those steps.

Say you have a saved question where the underlying query takes 3 minutes to run, and once it runs, it returns a single number. By storing the result in cache, you only need to wait 3 minutes once. Any time you open the saved question after that, provided the cache hasn't been deleted, the results can be fetched immediately.

Now that we understand what cache is, let's learn how to configure it in Metabase.

Configuring cache

The cache configuration in Metabase lives in the **Admin Panel**, so to get started, open it up. Under the **Settings** menu, on the left side in the **Admin Panel**, find the caching option, as in *Figure 10.1*:

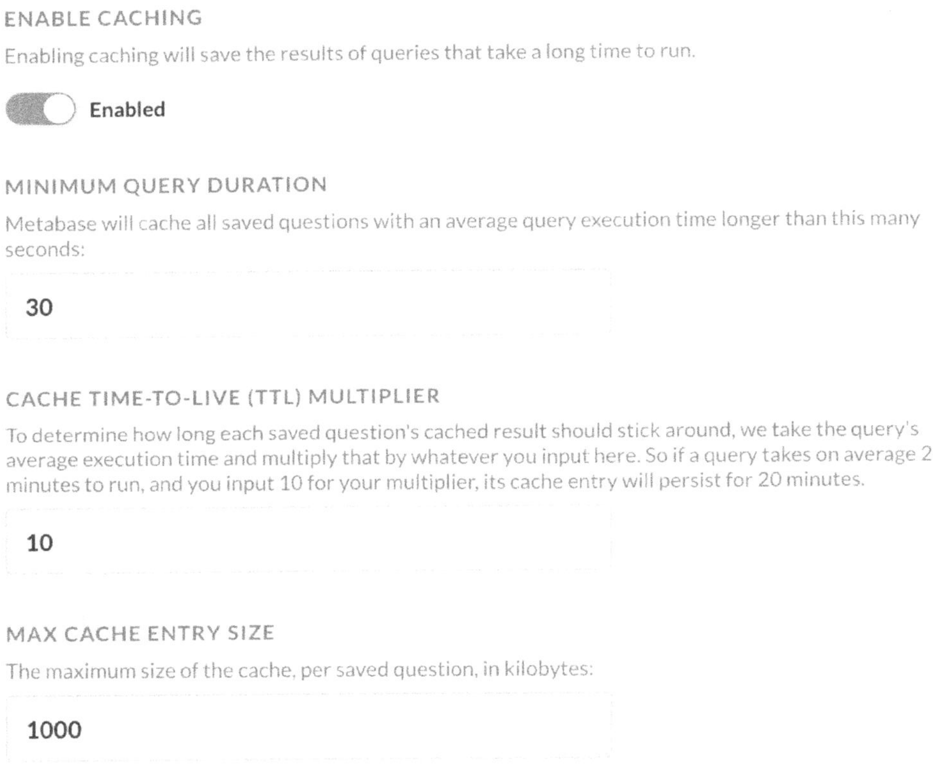

ENABLE CACHING
Enabling caching will save the results of queries that take a long time to run.
Enabled
MINIMUM QUERY DURATION
Metabase will cache all saved questions with an average query execution time longer than this many seconds:
30
CACHE TIME-TO-LIVE (TTL) MULTIPLIER
To determine how long each saved question's cached result should stick around, we take the query's average execution time and multiply that by whatever you input here. So if a query takes on average 2 minutes to run, and you input 10 for your multiplier, its cache entry will persist for 20 minutes.
10
MAX CACHE ENTRY SIZE
The maximum size of the cache, per saved question, in kilobytes:
1000

Figure 10.1 – Caching options in Metabase

There are four parameters in configuring cache, so let's learn about them one by one:

- **Enable Caching**: Toggle this option to turn caching on.
- **Minimum Query Duration**: This field takes a number in seconds. When a query takes more than the specified number of seconds, it will be cached. The default is **30**. As you learn more about the performance of your database and the type of queries your users run, you can adjust this.

- **Cache Time to Live Multiplier**: As I mentioned earlier, results in cache are stored temporarily. At some point, they get deleted. This parameter allows you to control when they get deleted. Metabase keeps track of the average execution time of all your queries. As it reads in *Figure 10.1*, if a query takes 2 minutes on average to run, and this parameter is set to `10`, the cached results will be deleted after 2 x 10, or 20, minutes.
- **Max Cache Entry Size**: Any saved questions with a file size larger than this value, in kilobytes, will not be cached. This prevents your cache from filling up with questions that return things such as entire tables and other large datasets.

You might be wondering why it's not best to just cache everything. That would certainly speed up everything. In the next section, we'll learn about the limitations and costs of using cache.

Limitations of cache

If saving a query in cache means it can be accessed instantly, why should we ever wait for a query to finish? Even if it only takes 3 seconds to run a query, if caching would mean we get the results in milliseconds, wouldn't that be better? Not necessarily. There are two reasons why setting a low minimum query duration and high time-to-live multiplier might backfire:

- **Cache storage is limited**: The amount of storage you have for cache is limited by the size of the server you are running Metabase on. Unlike databases, which are designed to store lots of data, servers are not architected to do that.
- **The cache can get stale**: Think about our **Total Orders** question. This query simply counts the number of rows in our **Orders** table and returns a single number. By using the cached value, Metabase returns that single number, rather than rerunning the query. However, what if the number of orders goes up between the time the query was cached and the time a user opens the saved question? If that happens, the user would see a stale number, which would give them an incorrect answer to their question. What's more, since cache is not something the average user needs to know about, they probably would have no idea that they are looking at a stale cache.

On that last point, there is a way to know whether a saved question you are viewing is coming from cache. If you look at the lower right-hand side of a question, you'll see a tag, as in *Figure 10.2*, if the results are coming from cache:

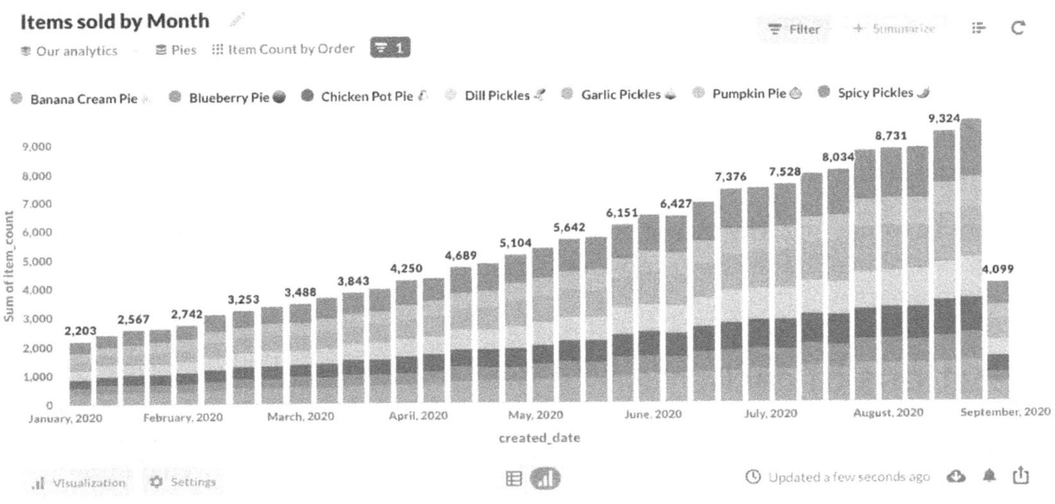

Figure 10.2 – A cached question will show when it was last updated in the lower right-hand corner

Using cache is not a panacea, but it is useful. Over time, as you use Metabase with your data, you'll get a feel for what role is right for cache.

Now that we've covered cache, let's move on and learn about a very handy set of features in Metabase that allow you to extend its usefulness to new audiences.

Embedding and sharing externally

Metabase offers the ability to make questions and dashboards publicly available, meaning they can be shared with anyone – not just users with Metabase accounts. The thing I like most about this feature is that it lets you use all of Metabase's functionality and their visualization library externally. If you've ever tried to create your own interactive data visualization from scratch on a website, you will know that it's not simple. That's why it's nice to know that we can stand on the shoulders of Metabase to make it easy.

There are two ways you can share Metabase questions and dashboards externally: via public URLs and by embedding them on external websites. We'll start off learning about the first method: sharing via public URLs.

Publicly sharing questions and dashboard

Let's imagine our marketing team is running a contest where our top customer earns free pickles and pies for life. They've announced the contest, but need an easy way to show the leaderboard. Because we've already created a saved question for them called **Our Top Customers** back in *Chapter 6, Creating Questions*, the marketing team can easily access this information themselves in Metabase.

However, even with Metabase's permission model in place, it's still a bad idea to create accounts for any customer that wants one. Managing permissions, adding these users to groups, and keeping track of everything is simply too cumbersome and fragile. Creating a public URL that points to this question enables us to let anyone view the leaderboard without worrying about them seeing anything else that they should not have access to.

To share a question or dashboard publicly, you need to first enable public sharing in the Admin Panel. Let's learn how. Start by opening up the Admin Panel:

1. Under the **Settings** menu, on the left side in the **Admin Panel**, find the **Public Sharing** option.
2. Slide the toggle on to enable public sharing.

Only users with admin access can create publicly available questions and dashboards. Also, any publicly shared dashboards or questions will get listed out here, so you can know exactly what is available to the public.

Now that we've enabled public sharing, let's go ahead and make the **Our Top Customers** question public:

1. Open the **Our Top Customers** question, either by searching for it or by finding it in the **Marketing** collection.
2. There will now be a share icon in the lower left-hand corner of the question. Click it to open up the **Sharing** modal, pictured in *Figure 10.3*.
3. Slide the toggle on to enable **Public Sharing** for this particular question.
4. Copy the **Public** link. Note that this link lives in the same domain your Metabase instance lives at but is under a `/public/` path in the URL.
5. Open the link in an incognito window, or sign out of Metabase and open it to ensure that it is publicly accessible.

Now, the marketing team can hand this link out as part of their marketing materials for the contest. Anyone with access to the link can see this saved question and download the results of it. There are no paths in it to the notebook editor, or any other part of your Metabase instance, so anyone viewing this is completely isolated to just this one question:

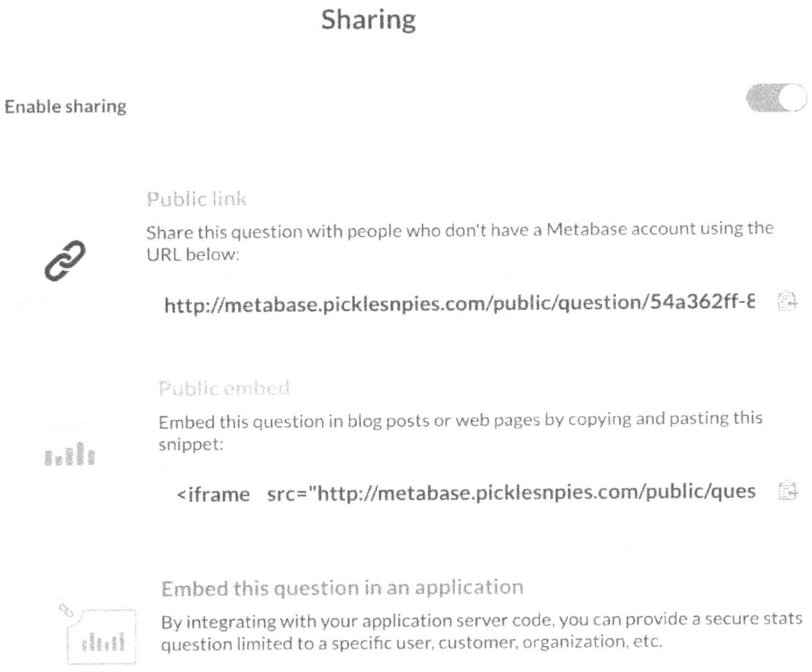

Sharing
Enable sharing
Public link
Share this question with people who don't have a Metabase account using the URL below:
http://metabase.picklesnpies.com/public/question/54a362ff-8
Public embed
Embed this question in blog posts or web pages by copying and pasting this snippet:
<iframe src="http://metabase.picklesnpies.com/public/ques
Embed this question in an application
By integrating with your application server code, you can provide a secure stats question limited to a specific user, customer, organization, etc.

Figure 10.3 – The Sharing modal

Sharing a dashboard works almost the same, and might be better for this particular use case. Imagine the marketing team wants to add a little more branding and information to the saved question. They can use the Markdown feature, which we learned about in *Chapter 8*, *Building Dashboards, Pulses, and Collections*, to add more context to this question. They can also add new questions to the dashboard to give more information, as in *Figure 10.4*.

To make a dashboard publicly available, start by opening the dashboard. Find the **Share** icon in the upper right-hand corner. The same **Sharing** modal will pop up as in *Figure 10.3*, when we shared a saved question:

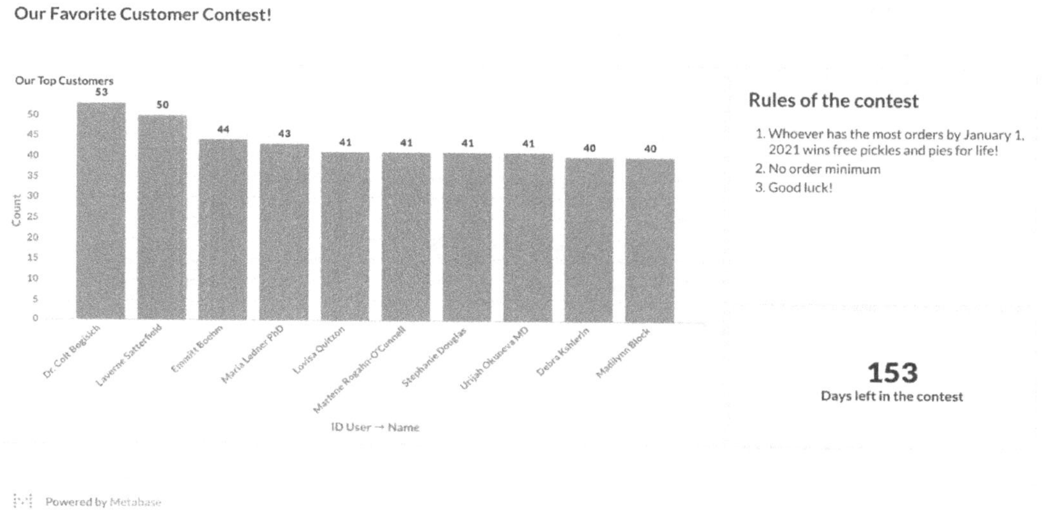

Figure 10.4 – An example of a publicly shared dashboard

Now that we've learned how to share questions and dashboards publicly, let's take it to the next level. Imagine the marketing team wants to put this dashboard on the Pickles and Pies website (which does not exist, but we're using our imagination). They want it to live at `www.contest.picklesnpies.com`, which they believe makes the contest look more official. It turns out it's very simple to do this in Metabase; let's learn how.

Embedding questions and dashboards on external websites

Embedding a question or dashboard on a website, such as `www.contest.picklesnpies.com`, is almost as easy as creating a public link. To get started, open up the Admin Panel:

1. Under the **Settings** menu, on the left side in the Admin Panel, find the **Embedding in other Applications** option.
2. Review the embedding license (`www.metabase.com/license/embedding/`).
3. Click the **Enable** button.

Now, when any **Admin** user clicks to share a question or dashboard, they will see a **Public** embed option. Instead of a link, the public embed is an **iframe** element, which is used to embed external HTML in an HTML document.

To embed the question or dashboard, copy the iframe element and insert it into the HTML of the page you wish to embed it onto. *Figure 10.5* shows an example of our **Total Orders** question, which I added to a new dashboard called **Shared Dashboard**, and then embedded on my personal website:

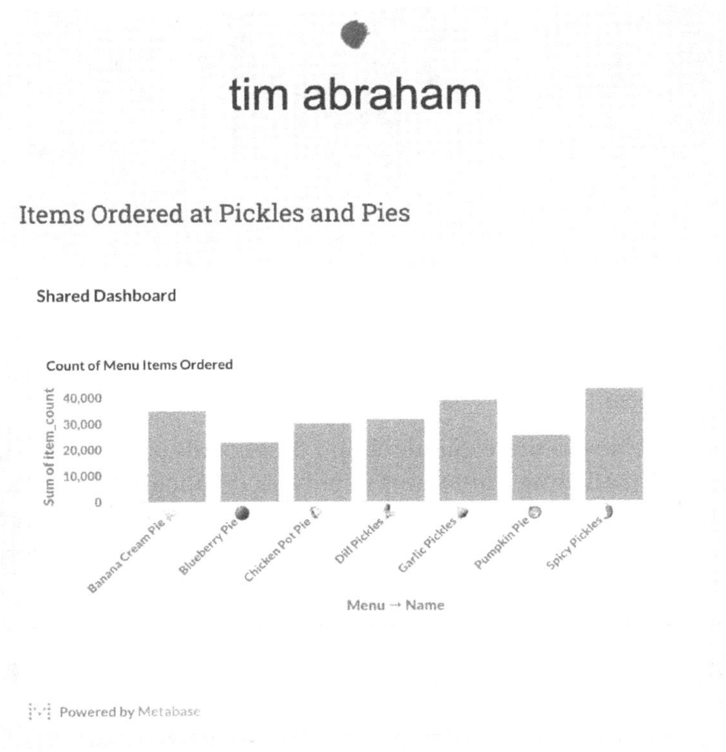

Figure 10.5 – Embedding a dashboard on my external website

Note that both public links and embeds retain Metabase's branding with a **Powered by Metabase** footer.

As you can see, public URLs and embeds are a powerful way of extending selective parts of your data in Metabase outside of your environment.

Now, let's learn about another cool feature: **x-rays**. We actually saw this very briefly when we first connected our `pies` database to Metabase, all the way back in *Chapter 4, Connecting to Databases*.

X-raying your data

X-rays are Metabase's way of guessing what's important about your data and creating a dashboard of questions for you. They take advantage of the fact that most questions involve either counting rows or summing a numeric column, grouping by a date column, and potentially grouping by another low cardinality column. The actual feature is more complex than that, involving some machine learning behind the scenes, but that's generally how they work.

While I don't believe that x-rays are an adequate replacement for a curious data scientist, I do think they're useful when used by a curious data scientist. Because x-rays are simple to create and fast to materialize, they make for a good base layer of simple questions that you can use or build upon to make more complex questions. Let's see an example.

Creating an x-ray

To get started, click **Browse Data | Pies**. Note that as you hover over each table in the `pies` database, an icon of a lightning bolt appears. Clicking the lightning bolt icon will create an x-ray of your table. Let's try it with the **Users** table.

Doing so will return an x-ray titled **Here's an overview of the people in your Users table**. It's pretty cool that Metabase is able to understand that the subjects in this table are people!

The x-ray has questions around total users, new users in the last 30 days, user growth, users per month, location of users by US state, and the distribution of users by credit card type and city. If you think about it, many of these were questions we created on our own over the last few chapters. That's a big reason why I think x-rays are useful: they'll often be able to give you a set of valuable but simple questions so that you don't need to build them yourself.

Not only does the x-ray return a set of interesting questions, but it also includes filters for some of the more relevant variables, such as **Date**, **State**, and **Credit Card Provider**. So what you're actually getting is more like an automatically generated dashboard. In fact, that's exactly what it is. If you click **Save** on this x-ray, it will be saved to a special **collection** called **Automatically Generated Dashboards**. Let's try it out:

1. On the x-ray, click the **Save this** button in the upper right-hand corner.
2. A notification will pop up in the lower right reading **Your dashboard was saved. See it**.
3. Now, in the **Our Analytics** collection, you will see a subcollection called **Automatically Generated Dashboards**. Click it. You'll see the dashboard that the x-ray created, along with all the individual saved questions created by the x-ray, as in *Figure 10.6*:

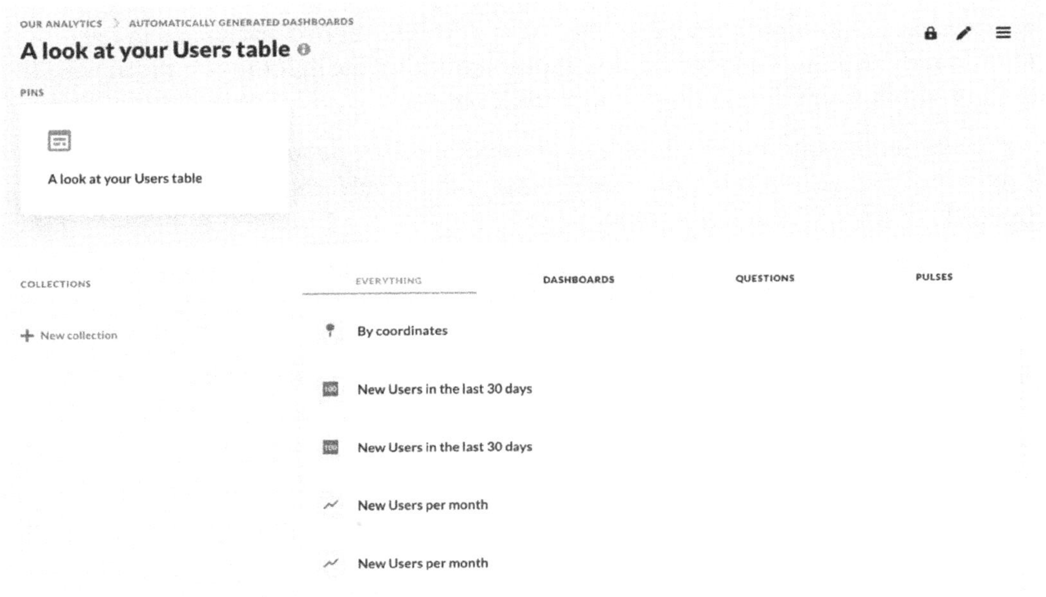

Figure 10.6 – Our x-ray of the Users table saved into a collection

As I wrote earlier, I don't think x-rays are going to uncover all the valuable insights in your data automatically, but the fact that we were able to get a dozen premade saved questions about our users with one click is pretty cool. Even if some of the questions from an x-ray aren't valuable for your specific use case, there's a fair chance that they are at least a step in the right direction. Maybe just modifying a single filter, or changing a **Group by** is all you need to make it relevant.

There are other ways to use x-rays in Metabase beyond x-raying full tables. Next, we'll learn how we can use this feature with individual questions.

X-raying individual questions

It turns out that you can x-ray more than just tables; you can also x-ray individual questions. While x-rays of tables produce a broad set of questions using all the information in a table, an x-ray of an individual question is great for drilling down into filtered states. Let's try one out:

1. Start by opening up the **Orders per Week** question.
2. Hovering over the line plot, click on any point that looks interesting to you – perhaps the first point, representing orders in the first week of 2019.
3. A menu will pop up next to the point, as in *Figure 10.7*. Click the **X-ray** option:

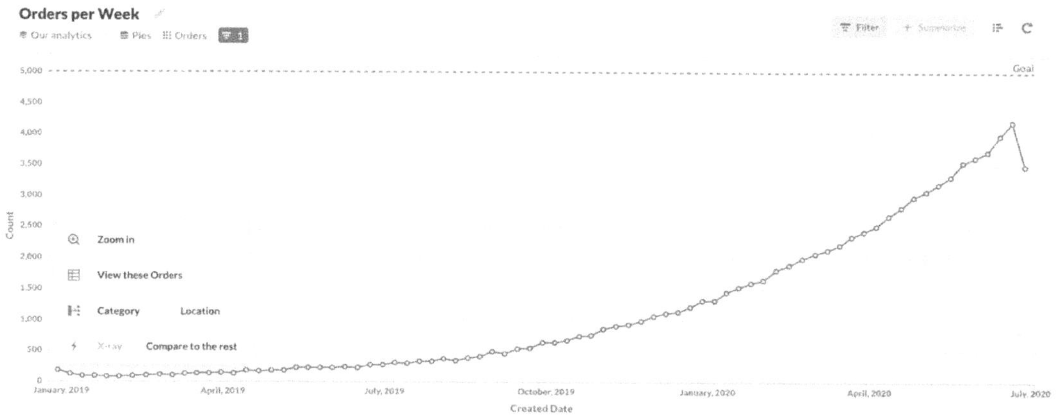

Figure 10.7 – X-raying an individual data point on a saved question

The **X-ray** option returns a set of over a dozen questions about orders in this specific week, including orders by day of the week, hourly orders, the distribution of orders by cost, credit card, and delivery type. Especially impressive are the questions that show information about the demographics of the users placing the orders, since it shows x-rays are able to intelligently join the **Orders** table to the **Users** table.

You are presented with more x-ray options on the right, as in *Figure 10.8*. Here, you can see a set of **related** questions. These are questions that Metabase has determined are similar to questions in the X-ray:

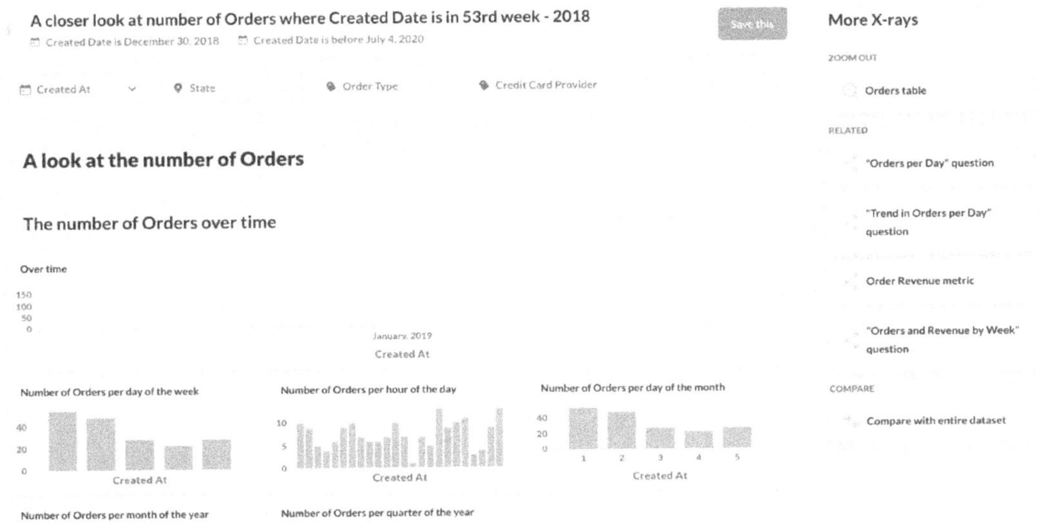

Figure 10.8 – An x-ray with more x-ray options on the right

Also on the right of the x-ray is the **ZOOM OUT** and **Compare with the entire dataset** options. Let's learn about both, starting with **ZOOM OUT**.

Zooming out and in on an x-ray

From the x-ray in *Figure 10.8*, click to zoom out on the **Orders** table to see an x-ray of that table. This is another useful way to use x-rays. In addition to zooming out, we can also zoom in. In the **More X-rays** section, we can now zoom in on many of the columns and metrics in our **Orders** table, or even run x-rays of tables that have foreign key relationships, such as the **Reviews** and **Users** table.

Just like with other x-rays we've seen, zooming in and out is a great way to generate a lot of good questions and potentially discovering new insights into your data.

Now, let's learn about the **Compare** feature.

Using the Compare to the Rest feature

To see how Metabase's **Compare** feature works, we'll start by x-raying the **Reviews** table:

1. Click **Browse Data | Pies**.
2. Click the lightning bolt icon in the **Reviews** table to x-ray it.
3. In the **More X-rays** section, scroll down to find and click the **Compare with Reviews of Pickle Products Segment** option. This was the segment we made back in *Chapter 5, Building Your Data Model.*

This will return a two-column x-ray, as in *Figure 10.9*. The column on the left contains questions about the **Reviews** table, whereas the column on the right contains the same questions but filtered by **Reviews of Pickle Products Segment**:

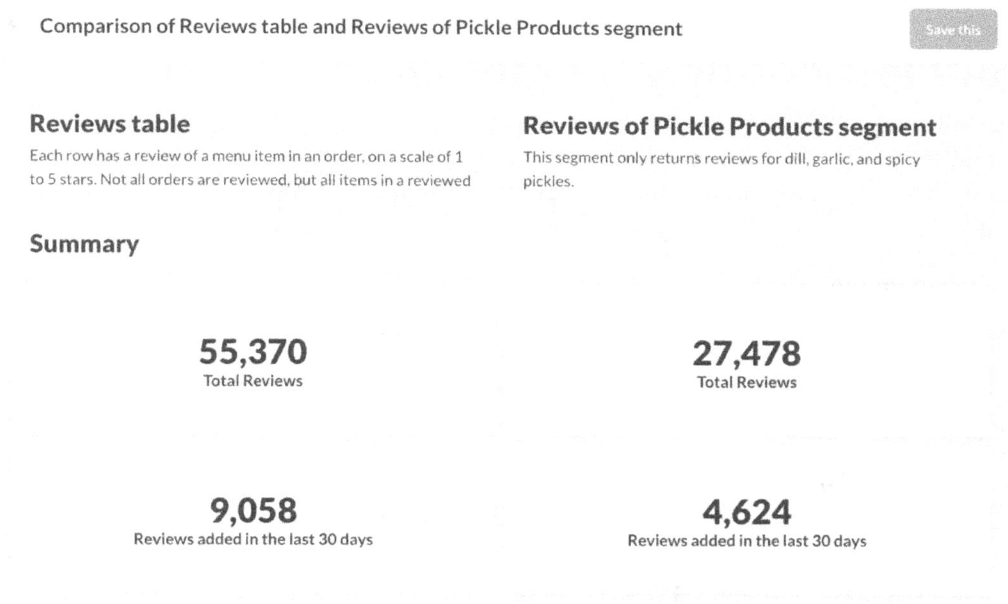
Comparison of Reviews table and Reviews of Pickle Products segment
Save this
Reviews table
Each row has a review of a menu item in an order, on a scale of 1 to 5 stars. Not all orders are reviewed, but all items in a reviewed
Reviews of Pickle Products segment
This segment only returns reviews for dill, garlic, and spicy pickles.
Summary
55,370
Total Reviews
27,478
Total Reviews
9,058
Reviews added in the last 30 days
4,624
Reviews added in the last 30 days

Figure 10.9 – Using the Compare feature on our Reviews of Pickles segment

This is a great way to see how one segment of your data compares to the table overall. This is a common routine in analytics, so it's nice to have it automated for immediate insights. With this comparison, we're able to quickly see that pickle products make up about 50% of all reviews, despite being less than 50% of the **Menu** items. Further investigation would show us that the reason for this is that they're ordered more often – primarily by the growing segment of users from out of state. One hypothesis as to why is that since pickles are non-perishable, they might transport better as delivery items.

As I wrote at the beginning of the chapter, caching, embedding, and x-rays are advanced features. Now that we know about them, I think we can elevate ourselves to power user status. Congratulations! However, no matter your mastery, there will always be more to learn. This is especially true with Metabase since the project is always actively being developed. You should expect it to always be evolving and improving. There will also, naturally, be times where you get stuck, encounter a bug, or simply don't understand something. In the next section, we'll address this.

You'll learn how to debug issues with your Metabase instance. Then you'll learn how you can tap into the active Metabase online community for even more help. Finally, you'll learn how you can give back to the project by contributing your own features. Even if your technical skills aren't up to par to contribute to an open source software project, you can still play an active role in the developer community by being active on GitHub.
Let's dive in.

Troubleshooting your Metabase instance

In Metabase, as with any software product, issues can arise that prevent you from accomplishing what you set out to do. Fortunately, help is available. Your Metabase instance has a dedicated center for all things help related in the **Admin Panel**. Let's navigate there:

1. Open up the **Admin Panel**.
2. Click **Troubleshooting**, in the purple bar at the top of the page.

This will take you to the **Troubleshooting** section of the Admin Panel. You'll start on the **Help** page, which has links to resources for various help-related tasks:

- **Metabase Documentation**: This is Metabase's own technical documentation. The Metabase team keeps this well maintained with each version release. We've referenced this technical documentation several times throughout the book, so you should be aware of this resource.
- **Post on the Metabase support forum**: Clicking this takes you to Metabase's Discourse page, which is a forum hosted on Metabase's website and maintained by the Metabase team as well as the broader Metabase community.
- **File a bug report**: If you think you've discovered a bug, you can click this and file it on GitHub. We've used GitHub several times over the course of the book, and you probably know at this point that the Metabase project lives on GitHub.

Now, let's explore the other pages within the **Troubleshooting** section. The menu, as seen in *Figure 10.10*, shows the other pages that are part of the **Troubleshooting** section:

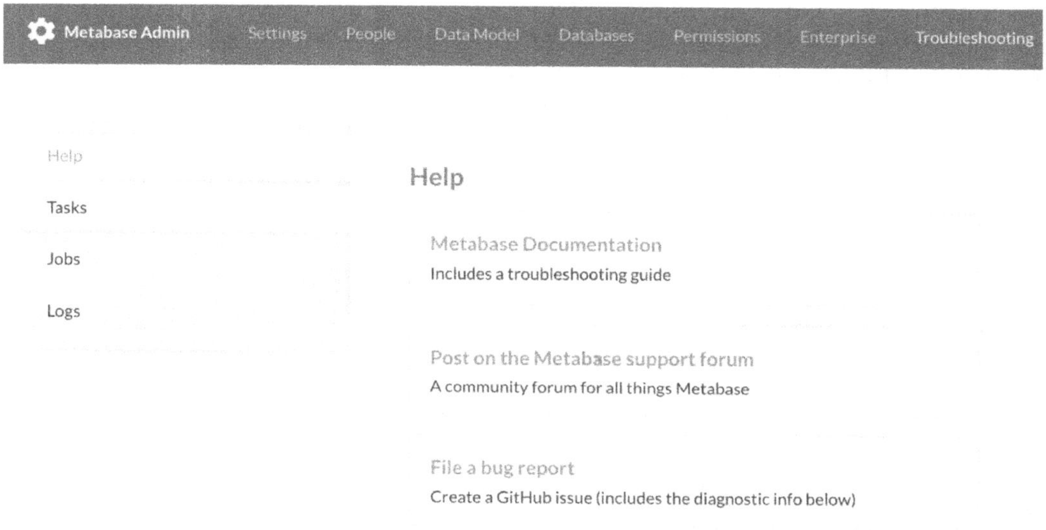

Figure 10.10 – The Troubleshooting section of Metabase

Let's briefly learn about each of these pages.

Tasks

The **Tasks** page shows you the tasks that Metabase has run in the background. Examples of tasks are sending pulses and scanning or syncing tables. For example, if you were to click **Admin** | **Databases** | **Pies** | **Re-scan field values now**, Metabase would kick off a `field values scanning` task. By clicking the **View** link in the details column, you can see additional information about the task.

Jobs

The **Jobs** page logs all the scheduled jobs that Metabase runs. Examples of scheduled jobs include things such as scheduling pulses and checking to see whether you're on the most up-to-date version of Metabase. By clicking **View triggers**, you can view more information about each scheduled job.

Logs

In *Chapter 2*, *Hosting Metabase on AWS*, we learned how to configure our Metabase environment such that it would store log files in Amazon S3. You can also see about a day's worth of logs here. Metabase's logs tend to be both verbose and cute. By verbose, I mean that they log a lot of what is going on in the background. And by cute, I am referring to the emojis they add in their log files, as in *Figure 10.11*:

```
[a87143b3-c797-4dc4-9b1b-9e2215680a22] 2020-09-02T12:00:00-07:00 INFO metabase.sync.analyze classify-tables Analyzed
[**************************************............]  77% Table 29 'public.reviews'
[a87143b3-c797-4dc4-9b1b-9e2215680a22] 2020-09-02T12:00:00-07:00 INFO metabase.sync.analyze classify-tables Analyzed
[**********************************************....]  92% Table 27 'public.users'
```

Figure 10.11 – Metabase's logging output as they scan the pies database

Occasionally, I'll encounter something wrong with my Metabase instance, such as it getting stuck performing some task or not accepting a parameter. When that happens, I can often debug what is going on by checking the logs.

Of these three sections, the **Logs** section is by far the most helpful and should be the first place you go when something goes awry. Often, the log file output will have a clear error message that will help you debug your issue. When that's not the case, the three options we saw on the **Help** page are your next best bets. Now, we'll learn about each of them.

Troubleshooting using Metabase's documentation

The first link on the **Help** page takes you to Metabase's official documentation. In that documentation, you can find their troubleshooting guide (`https://www.metabase.com/docs/latest/troubleshooting-guide/index.html`). This guide is like a choose your own adventure for common issues Metabase users tend to have. Since these are the most common issues, there's a good chance that the problem you're having is addressed here.

If you are unable to find an answer to your issue here, your next best option is to visit Metabase's support forum on Discourse.

Getting help on Discourse

Metabase uses Discourse (`https://www.discourse.org/`), an open source platform for discussing software, for discussions, help forums, and reporting issues.

Metabase's Discourse is hosted on a subdomain at `https://discourse.metabase.com/`. You don't need a Discourse account to search and read in Discourse, but if you want to post anything, you'll need to sign up.

At the time of writing, according to `https://discourse.metabase.com/about`, there have been over 28,000 posts on Metabase's discourse by over 4,000 users, so this is a heavily maintained and active site.

Discourse is constantly being monitored by the Metabase development team, as well as other members of the Metabase community. These are people who are passionate about Metabase and want to make it even more useful. In the past, when I have asked questions on Metabase's Discourse, I was able to get a response in less than a day.

Other Discourse use cases

In addition to being a support forum, Discourse is a great place to discuss Metabase. It doesn't all have to be about bugs and errors. You might find conversations about scheduling meetups in a city near you so that you can meet other Metabase users. Other conversations are about where to find great open source datasets. You might even find posts from people looking to hire someone to help set up their Metabase instance.

Discourse, in general, is just a friendly and casual place to get help with Metabase and interact with the community. Similar to Discourse, but more technically geared, is GitHub. In the next section, we'll learn what GitHub is used for.

Creating issues and filling bugs on GitHub

The entire Metabase project is maintained on GitHub at `https://github.com/metabase`. The main repository is `https://github.com/metabase/metabase`. Here is where all the code that runs your Metabase instance lives, as well as the all the *changes* to the code base since the project was first hosted on GitHub.

Development of Metabase on GitHub is done through **issues** and **pull requests**. You can think of **issues** as feature requests or bug reports, and **pull requests** as solutions to those feature requests or bug reports. Let's see an example.

An example of a GitHub issue and pull request

On November 9, 2017, an issue was opened on GitHub around having free-text markdown boxes in dashboards (*Figure 10.12*). We know, from *Chapter 8, Building Dashboards, Pulses, and Collections*, that this feature now exists. However, at the time that the issue was created, it didn't. The issue was what brought the need for the feature to the attention of the team.

You can find the issue and all the discussion around it at `https://github.com/metabase/metabase/issues/6360`. Metabase prioritizes issues based on the number of thumbs up they get, and as of the time of writing, this one has 29 thumbs up from other GitHub users. This issue in particular was proposed by GitHub user `mazameli`. This is the username for Maz Ameli, a product designer and member of the core Metabase development team, so his issue included a thorough proposal for what the feature should look like. Issues don't always have to be so fully fleshed out:

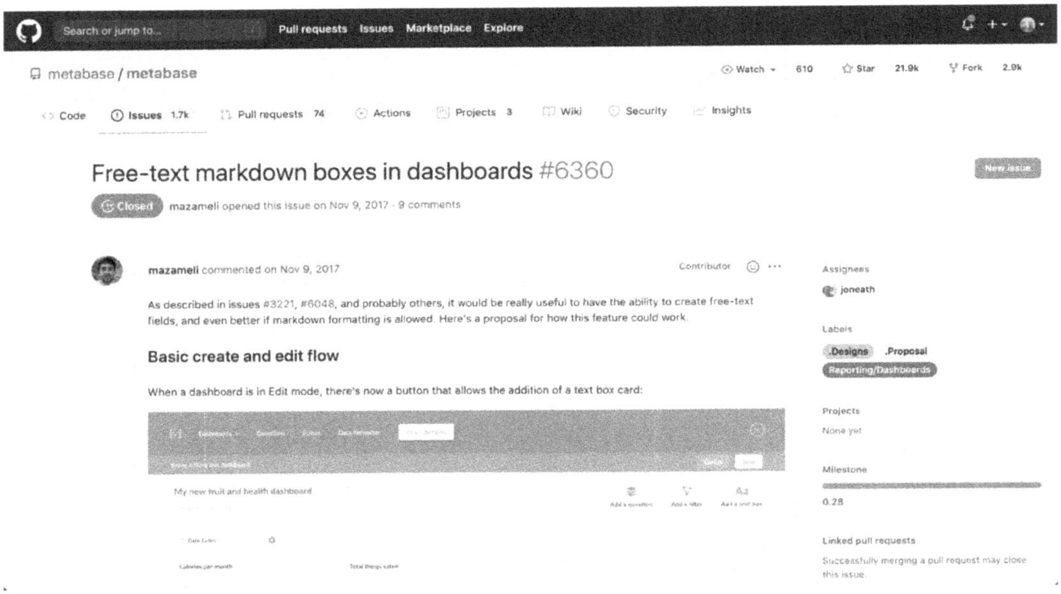

Figure 10.12 – An issue in GitHub to add Markdown to dashboards

If you scroll down toward the end of the issue on GitHub, you can see a comment by user `camsaul` (Cam Saul is an engineer who has worked on Metabase since the very beginning), reading **Implemented by #6436**, with a link to the **pull request** implementing the feature discussed in the issue. The date of this comment, as can be seen in *Figure 10.13*, is November 20, 2017. That's just 11 days after the issue was first created:

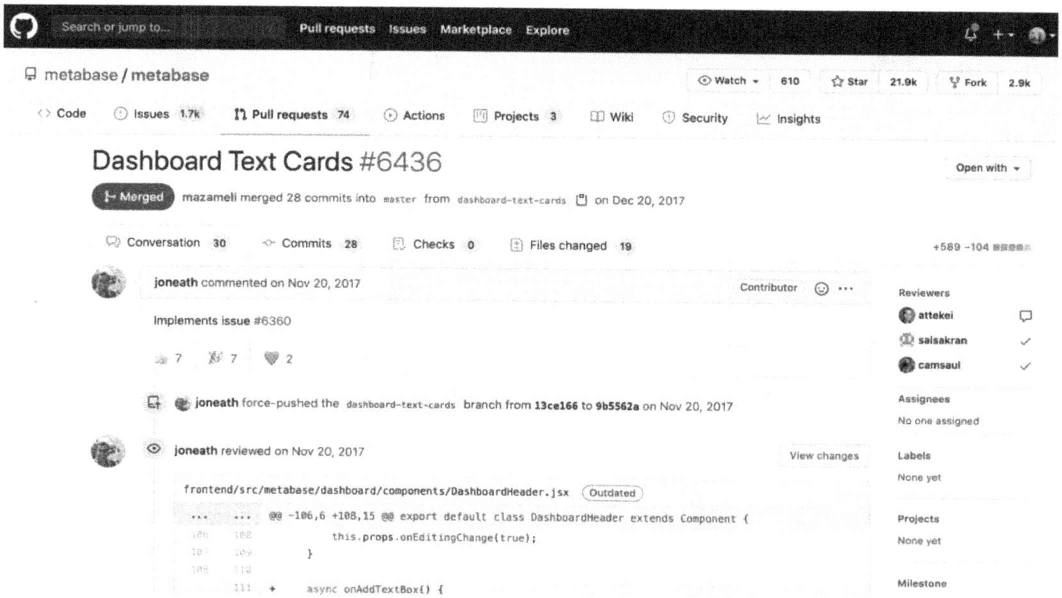

Figure 10.13 – A pull request implementing the Markdown in dashboards feature

In the pull request, you can see the conversation around the technical implementation of the feature, as well as the actual code changes. Scrolling toward the bottom of the pull request, you can see that on December 20, 2017, or 1 month after the pull request was created, the changes were approved and merged, and the issue was closed. Once a pull request is merged, the changes in it become part of the project's main branch. In other words, it becomes part of the official code of Metabase.

One thing that is really great about this pattern of creating issues on GitHub, having the community vote on them, and creating pull requests to discuss, code, and merge the implementation, is that it's entirely open for everyone to see and participate with. If you had an opinion about what the implementation of Markdown on dashboards should look like, you could participate in this discussion and have your ideas heard. If you knew enough about Metabase's code base, you could even build the feature! Today, most of the contributions to Metabase have been made by the dozen or so core members of the Metabase development team, but there is an increasingly long tail of contributors who are just people interested in the project. You can see all the contributors and the number of code commits at `https://github.com/metabase/metabase/graphs/contributors`.

When to open an issue on GitHub

If you have a feature that you think would be an amazing addition to Metabase, you can open your own issue on GitHub and have the community discuss and vote on it. Before opening one, though, it's always best to search past issues to see whether one already exists. For example, let's say you think a good feature is one where you can upload a CSV and use Metabase to create visualizations based on the data. Before creating the issue, let's look and see whether there are any open (or closed) issues related to this topic:

1. Go to Metabase's **Issues** tab at `https://github.com/metabase/metabase/issues`.
2. In the search box, you should see `is:issue is:open` prepopulated. This is added to filter the search results so that they only look at open issues. To this search box, add `upload csv`.

As of the time of writing, there is one open issue matching this search query: **Feature Request** -> **Uploading csv**. The link to this issue is `https://github.com/metabase/metabase/issues/6094`. Creating a new issue for the same request won't be very helpful; rather, it just creates more noise. So, rather than creating a duplicate issue, the best way to amplify your desire for this feature is to give the issue a thumbs up.

Contributing to Metabase on GitHub

All the way back in the first chapter, *Chapter 1*, *Overview of Metabase*, I mentioned that Metabase is primarily written in Clojure. If you are a good Clojure programmer, I'm confident that the Metabase team would love to get to know you and see whether you'd like to contribute to the project. In addition to Clojure, a lot of Metabase is written in JavaScript. JavaScript is a very popular programming language, often used on the frontend of products, but increasingly used everywhere. You can see the breakdown of languages that make up Metabase's code base on GitHub and in *Figure 10.14*:

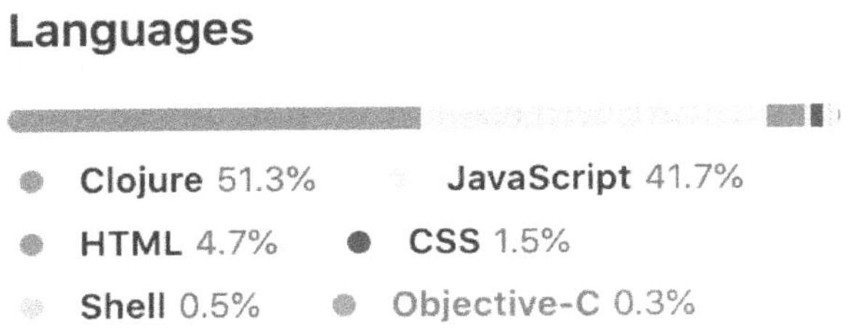

Figure 10.14 – The breakdown of languages that make up Metabase

If you decide you'd like to be a contributor to this awesome project, kudos to you! Before creating a branch and developing a major feature on your own, I recommend you engage with the community, both on Discourse and GitHub, and gauge the overall interest, need, technical feasibility, and fit with the project roadmap before starting to code. Metabase keeps their project roadmap on GitHub at `https://github.com/metabase/metabase/projects/1`, so everyone can see their future plans.

Perhaps one day your contributions will make Metabase even better at democratizing, demystifying, and simplifying data analytics.

Summary

In this final chapter, we learned about the advanced features of caching, embedding, and x-rays. These features can really help you get more out of Metabase. With the right cache settings, you can dramatically increase the speed and performance of your Metabase instance for all your users. With embedding, you can display questions and dashboards on external websites, opening up the power of Metabase to the public. With x-rays, you can also generate many insightful and useful questions with a single click of a button.

We then learned where to go for help. Sometimes, you can troubleshoot your issues by simply scanning log files in your own Metabase instance. Other times, you can find what you need in Metabase's technical documentation, their Discourse support forum, or in their GitHub. We learned more about how the project is maintained on GitHub, and how you can get involved with its development and shape the future of Metabase.

Other Books You May Enjoy

If you enjoyed this book, you may be interested in these other books by Packt:

Apache Superset Quick Start Guide
Shashank Shekhar
ISBN: 978-1-78899-224-4

- Get to grips with the fundamentals of data exploration using Superset
- Set up a working instance of Superset on cloud services like Google Compute Engine
- Integrate Superset with SQL databases
- Build dashboards with Superset
- Calculate statistics in Superset for numerical, categorical, or text data
- Understand visualization techniques, filtering, and grouping by aggregation
- Manage user roles and permissions in Superset
- Work with SQL Lab

Redash v5 Quick Start Guide

Alexander Leibzon, Yael Leibzon

ISBN: 978-1-78899-616-7

- Install Redash and troubleshoot installation errors
- Manage user roles and permissions
- Fetch data from various data sources
- Visualize and present data with Redash
- Create active alerts based on your data
- Understand Redash administration and customization
- Export, share and recount stories with Redash visualizations
- Interact programmatically with Redash through the Redash API

Leave a review - let other readers know what you think

Please share your thoughts on this book with others by leaving a review on the site that you bought it from. If you purchased the book from Amazon, please leave us an honest review on this book's Amazon page. This is vital so that other potential readers can see and use your unbiased opinion to make purchasing decisions, we can understand what our customers think about our products, and our authors can see your feedback on the title that they have worked with Packt to create. It will only take a few minutes of your time, but is valuable to other potential customers, our authors, and Packt. Thank you!

Index

Symbols

A

B

C

D

E

F

G

H

I

J

L

M

N

O

P

Q

R

S

T

U

V

W

X

www.ingramcontent.com/pod-product-compliance
Lightning Source LLC
Chambersburg PA
CBHW082116070326
40690CB00049B/3169
* 9 7 8 1 8 0 0 2 0 2 3 1 3 *